In memory of
Charlotte Holland Wanamaker,
1915–1997

SAM WANAMAKER
A Global Performer
by Diana Devlin

OBERON BOOKS

LONDON

First published in 2019 by Oberon Books Ltd
521 Caledonian Road, London N7 9RH
Tel: +44 (0) 20 7607 3637 / Fax: +44 (0) 20 7607 3629
e-mail: info@oberonbooks.com
www.oberonbooks.com

HB ISBN: 9781786827098
E ISBN: 9781786826275

Cover design by James Illman

Front cover image: Bison Archives Photographs
Back cover image: Chicago Public Library, Special Collections, GTA, PHF, Photographs, 54/11.
Author image: Simon Way

Printed and bound by CPI Group (UK) Ltd, Croydon, CR0 4YY.
eBook conversion by Lapiz Digital Services, India.

Contents

Foreword

Early in January 1972, a letter was delivered to my pigeon-hole at Goldsmiths College in south-east London, where I was a Lecturer in Drama. It was from an organization I had never heard of: The Globe Playhouse Trust. It read as follows:

31st December 1971

Dear Miss Devlin,

Dr. E. Martin Browne[1] has suggested that you might be interested in doing some voluntary work in association with the activities of our Trust. In particular, he felt that you might be very interested in the fact that we are arranging a six week summer study course in Shakespeare and the Elizabethan theatre for graduate students from all over the world. The number will be limited to fifty, and there will be a distinguished array of lecturers, many of whom you see listed on the right.

Should you be willing to work with us, I'd be delighted if you could telephone me at the above number, and we could arrange a meeting at your convenience.

Yours sincerely
Sam Wanamaker
Executive Director[2]

I have not kept the letter, but its author unearthed the carbon copy fourteen years later. 'Only you, Sam,' I said, when he produced it, 'would have been thinking about the Globe on New Year's Eve.'

I knew who he was. In 1956, as a stage-struck teenager, I had seen Sam Wanamaker playing the lead in *The Rainmaker,* a comedy about a conman, who promises to bring rain to a drought-ridden cattle ranch. Intrigued by the letter, I rang the number, and arranged to meet Mr Wanamaker in the George Inn, Southwark. An impressive, black-haired figure greeted me, with a firm handshake and an unmistakeable American timbre in his strong voice. Over lunch, he explained his ambitious project: to build a new

1

Globe theatre, close to its original site, and to regenerate the whole area. He drove me round the cobbled Bankside streets in his Jaguar car, pointing out, in particular, the beautiful rose window visible in the ruins of Winchester Palace.

I helped run Sam's Summer School, and after that I never went away. When he turned the education arm of his organization into a limited company, I joined the Board. When a new company was formed to run a Museum and Arts Centre in the building Sam owned near the original Globe, I joined that Board too.

When I could spare the time from professional work, I helped run promotional events, although, as the years went by, I did begin to wonder why I was putting so much effort into a project that might never happen. Once, in the 1980s, I wrote to Sam explaining that my teaching schedule was too heavy for me to organize a concert for him. I received a cable:

YOUR REALISTIC LETTER DEEPLY DISTURBING AM USED TO BEING LET DOWN BUT NEGATIVE ATTITUDES LIE IN NOT ONLY DROPPING BALL BUT IN NOT HELPING TO FIND SOMEONE TO PICK IT UP WILL NOTHING NOW HAPPEN UNLESS I DO IT MYSELF.

I reorganized my schedule and arranged the concert. Afterwards, we had a frank conversation, and he wrote:

Dear Diana

Our tete-a-tete at Dinner last night was a good release for both of us. You know how much I love and respect you and appreciate your dedication to the project – however awkward your feelings!

(I can't wait to get out too!)

Love Sam[3]

That was the sort of exchange that made me continue. On another occasion, when the little Museum which was the public face of the project, was closed, unstaffed and dark, Sam called on the phone:

There's some American visitors coming into town who might give us some money – can you go and talk to them?

I ushered them into a small chilly vestibule. We stood under a naked light bulb, while I expounded on the magnificent future that lay ahead when the Globe was built. 'On your imaginations let us work', I urged them, recalling the charismatic figure I had watched so many years ago, conjuring up rain where there was none.

I knew that Sam's life and career was richer and more varied than was suggested by his devotion to the Globe project over the last twenty-five years of his life. But until I started exploring further, I did not realize how much richer. Or how many projects were teeming in his head that never came off. One hundred years after his birth is a suitable occasion to celebrate a man whose ideas were sometimes ahead of his time. He could be his own worst enemy, easily offended, often offending. His successes were made possible by his vision, energy, determination and talent, by the support of many friends and colleagues, and by his wife Charlotte, whose faith in what he could achieve never wavered. Some of what he 'envisioned' has now come about. What has not, may still work on our imaginations.

1

'An American Chicago Born'
Saul Bellow

Samuel Watenmaker, later to be known as 'Sam Wanamaker', was born in Chicago, in June 1919, the younger son of Russian Jews from Ukraine. Theirs was a classic emigration story of the early twentieth century.

His father, Manes Wattenmacher, then fifteen years old, came to Chicago in 1910. He had travelled from Nikolaev (now Mykolaiv), a shipbuilding town in Crimea. It was a major Jewish centre about fifty miles from Odessa, within the Pale of Settlement, the western region of Russia where Jews were allowed to live. The family had moved there from Bessarabia, the year before he was born. The first anti-Semitic 'pogrom' (Hebrew for 'storms in the south') had taken place in 1821 in Odessa, and the worst was also there, in 1905, when 2500 Jews were reported to have been killed. The Wattenmacher family were among many who took on the lengthy, fraught task of emigration, paying their way step by step, starting on a journey full of physical, emotional and bureaucratic challenges.

The first to go was Manes' sister, following her husband to Canada. His older brother Nathan was the next, in 1907. The family business was tailoring, and he soon found work in Chicago as a capmaker. He saved up money to send for his parents and siblings to make their way to him, first his brother Abraham, then, Manes, with his parents, and two sisters. They went from Nikolaev overland, packing a few belongings onto a wagon which took them to the railway station, where they embarked on a nine-hour journey to Kiev, on to Austria and then to Antwerp, where they boarded a Liverpool-built passenger ship, SS Mount Temple. The crossing was wretched, as they huddled in insalubrious quarters in steerage. (Yet they were fortunate, since, seven months later, the Mount Temple struck rocks outside Halifax, and was hit by a huge tidal wave, all the passengers having to be taken off and lodged on an island until they could be rescued.) When they disembarked at Port St John, in New Brunswick, their health was checked and the whole family was hospitalized. Finally, once they were declared fit, they took the Grand Trunk Rail Road from Montreal, and arrived in Chicago, to be greeted by the two brothers already there. By this time, Nathan was married and his wife gave birth two weeks after they arrived. But at exactly the same time, Manes' mother, Gittel, died of heart disease, a sad start to his American life, as he began living in a city for the first time, and in a foreign country.

Manes joined his brothers in the Jewish quarter on the West Side. Chicago was the second city in the USA, after New York, and the third biggest Jewish city in the world, after New York and Warsaw. First incorporated in 1833 with a population of 350, it had developed rapidly, with a population of 4000 by 1840. In 1848, the opening of the Illinois and Michigan Canal created a shipping route from the Great Lakes through Chicago to the Mississippi River and the Gulf of Mexico. Soon after that came the railroads, making it the transportation hub of the Midwest. The first European immigrants were the Irish, after the potato famine, and then Germans – Lutherans, Catholics and Jews. Next came Poles, and Polish Jews, and then, from the 1880s, Serbs, Czechs and Russians. The centre of an agricultural area, the city was nicknamed 'Porkopolis', because of its meat trade. After the introduction of refrigeration, thousands of thousands of hogs and cattle were shipped to Chicago for slaughter, preserved in salt and transported to eastern cities. The smell from the yards spread for miles around. In 1871 a great fire had destroyed much of the city. In rebuilding it, the developers put up the first skyscrapers, in the Loop, the central business section. Innovative architects and landscape designers arrived, creating parks and modern buildings. In 1893, the World's Columbian Exposition, created to mark 400 years since Christopher Columbus's arrival, had shown off the city at its best, with its mixture of classical buildings, amusements and technological marvels. But the splendour of the Exposition was in sharp contrast to the conditions in which many of the inhabitants lived. By 1905, 80% of the population of Chicago were immigrants or children of immigrants. Of the Russians, the overwhelming majority were Jewish, fleeing the Czarist régime, like Manes and his family. There were sharp economic divisions. Dominic A Pacyga, biographer of the city, wrote:

> Since its foundation, the city had been a magnet for moneyed investors on the one hand, and men and women willing to do grueling labor on the other.[1]

The Wattenmachers simplified their surname (which had already been changed from its Cyrillic version) to 'Watenmaker', and Manes became 'Morris'. He soon found work, joining Hart, Schaffner and Marx, a garment factory, where his job was making pockets for vests (waistcoats).

The business was run by German Jews, members of an immigrant group that had settled in the city long before the Russian Jews arrived, and were in a position to exploit them. Morris quickly became a member of the United Garment Workers Union. In September 1910, within months of his arrival, a strike broke out, when sixteen women protested at a cut in piece rate and a biased bonus system. By the end of the first week, 2000 women had joined. When the union and the Chicago Federation of Labor sanctioned the action, over forty thousand joined the strike, including Morris and his brothers. There was much violence, and five men lost their lives. Morris was out for the full twenty-two weeks of the strike, but as union support was beginning to drift away, the workers were forced to reach a deal. There were some improvements in conditions, and the strike paved the way for the foundation, three years later, of a stronger union, the Amalgamated Clothing Workers of America (ACWA) in which Morris soon became an officer, in the same branch as the woman who had started the strike. He had quickly become politicized. In 1911 he joined the Young Person's Socialist League, and worked for the presidential candidacy of Eugene Debs, founder of the Socialist Party of America, who actually gained 6% of the popular vote in 1912.

In January 1914, Morris's father died. Now an orphan, he still had his brothers and sisters and their families. When the war broke out, the immigrant communities were divided by their loyalty to their European roots, while the Americans were isolationist. Morris began courting another Russian Jewish immigrant, who was also working in the garment industry, Molly Bobele. She was three years younger, and came from Zhitomir (now Zhytomyr), in northern Ukraine, though the family was originally from Poland. She had emigrated to Chicago in 1913, when she was fourteen, with an uncle and aunt, leaving her sister and parents behind. Their town had suffered a pogrom in 1905, but the family had survived. Morris and Molly were married in March 1916.

In 1917, as Germany became more aggressive, the American government, under Woodrow Wilson, broke off diplomatic relations, and finally declared war that April. In June, Morris was required to complete a draft card. Under the influence of Eugene Debs, he declared himself a Conscientious Objector, but in fact escaped the draft because he had a young son, William, born that January. So he continued at Hart, Schaffner and Marx, and in June 1919, Morris and Molly's second son was born, Samuel Watenmaker.

The Jewish writer, Israel Zangwill, who coined the term 'melting pot' to describe the absorption of immigrants into America, wrote:

7

> While there is always a difference between the old and the new generations, the difference between the Jewish immigrant and his American child is that of ten generations.[2]

Certainly, the youth of the two brothers bore little resemblance to that of their parents. The 'lingua franca' was English. Morris and Molly learnt to speak it, but always with a heavy accent; they also learnt to read and write. The boys learnt some English even before they went to school, while at home the family spoke Yiddish. They were poor, but not destitute, living in a flat with two bedrooms and a kitchen; there was always food on the table, and occasional ice-creams and cakes. Morris's staunch support of the ACWA meant that there were weeks when he was on strike. At those times, bread and potatoes were their principal foods. The Jewish community was close-knit, sharing the annual festivals, congregating in the temple, sometimes mulling around the busy Maxwell Street market, sometimes meeting at the Jewish People's Institute, which ran a wide range of educational, social and recreational programmes.

When it was time to start school, William and Samuel, 'Bill' and 'Sam' to their friends and family, mixed with immigrants from other parts of Europe. Children from every immigrant group sat in the same classrooms; education was an important part of the process of assimilation and Americanization. But there, the boys first encountered anti-Semitism, which was rife in Chicago, as it had been in Russia. Catholic children, whether Irish, German, Austrian, Polish or Czech, were taught to hate the Jews. The playground was the worst. There they were met with yells of 'Kike!' and 'Christkiller!', and were often pelted with stones. Samuel, though younger, was stronger than his brother, and often got involved in physical fights to protect him. When, later in life, he looked back at those early battles, he felt that they formed a significant part of his character, giving him the conviction that he must stand up for himself. 'Constant aggression and fighting shapes you.'[3]

There were compensating treats. Sometimes, on Saturday afternoon, the boys were given ten cents to see a movie at the Biograph cinema in their neighbourhood. Sometimes their father took them to see Yiddish actors and comedians at the Glickman's Palace Theater near the Maxwell Street market, or at the Jewish People's Institute, where the Yiddische Dramatische Gesellschaft presented classical and contemporary plays. (One local actor, Muni Weisenfreund, later became famous as the Hollywood star, Paul Muni.) Once, the famous New York Yiddish actor, Jacob Ben Ami, came to Chicago, giving Samuel his first taste of great acting. The boys' sense of their cultural background was fed by plays like *The Dybbuk* and the work of Sholem Aleichem. Morris was also active in the Nicolaever Verein, which he helped to found in the 1920s, the local society for immigrants from his native town. Some of the Yiddish comedians were people he had known there.

During the 1920s, while still being a staunch union member, Morris began supplementing his income with a retail business, opening a haberdashery store in the neighbourhood. Prohibition had come in 1920, leading to the rise of bootleggers and gangsters. One family tale relates that members of Al Capone's gang used to hide their guns in Morris's shop after a raid.

In 1926, the family was augmented when Molly sent money for her parents to emigrate. Morris's politics would have led him to look on the Bolshevik Revolution with approval. But the Soviet régime had been a disaster for his in-laws, who lost all that they owned, and escaped to Poland. There, they obtained immigration visas, made their way to Southampton, embarked on SS Romerio to New York in November, and eventually arrived in Chicago, penniless and broken in spirit.

Samuel was ten years old when the Wall Street crash happened, followed by the Great Depression, which directly affected the family. Their uncle Abraham moved to Los Angeles, where his wife had family. Morris lost his job at the factory but struggled on in Chicago. He gave up haberdashery, but made a tiny income selling old magazines and books. There were charitable organizations to which people could turn, but it was a period of dreadful hardship. 'Starvation was a fact,' Samuel remembered, 'and particularly among the immigrant groups ... The early thirties to me and to my family were filled with the despair of unemployment, the fear of starvation, and the humiliation of poverty.'[4] His brother remembered seeing veterans on the street corners selling apples for 5c, long breadlines and a sense of desperation and despair everywhere.

Yet, when they entered high school, these years were fruitful for the boys. Public education in Chicago was well established. Educationalists saw it as a way of absorbing immigrants into American life, while for immigrant parents it was a way of advancement for their children. By 1909, the children of immigrants made up 67% of the pupils. The educationalist John Dewey, who believed in teaching 'the whole child', had taught at the University of Chicago for ten years. Partly through his influence, the Education Committee of the City Council introduced progressive ideas into the curriculum. The school that William and Samuel attended had been founded in 1888 as the Northwest Division High School. In 1917, it was renamed Tuley High School, in honour of Murray F Tuley, an eminent Illinois judge. In 1919, a major expansion was completed, with new classrooms, a swimming pool, shop rooms and one of the largest assembly halls in the city, seating 1500. It stood in the midst of an area of high illiteracy, and the majority of the students were from immigrant parents, including a large Jewish population. As well as traditional subjects, the students could make music, theatre and art, and participate in a variety of sports. Samuel took up wrestling and athletics. Many of the students were self-motivated and bent on improving themselves beyond what was offered by the school curriculum. They organized their own academy, offering lectures by fellow-students in the sciences, literature, anthropology and other subjects, in a church they were allowed to use. One such student was the future writer, Saul Bellow, who was in the same year as William. William described his time at the school as one of the most exciting and elevating experiences of his life. He entered Tuley High School in 1929, Samuel in 1931. Their education opened their minds and fostered their ambitions.

While the School offered opportunities for advancement, there were other kinds of education to be acquired in the city. During his time at Tuley, William got himself a job in a local drugstore. He loved the strange chemical smells, the bizarre colours of the drugs – not to mention candies and ice-creams – the strange ointments and the smart white jacket he was allowed to wear. He was also impressed at the power and knowledge of the doctors, 'the sage, the keeper of those deep, dark secrets of life and death'.[5] When he was offered the chance to clean the doctors' offices for an additional 50c a week, he enlisted Samuel's help, wrangling an additional 50c for him too, and they dragged pails and mops upstairs and scoured the doctors' floor.

Gradually, William became aware that the drugstore was being used as a venue for bootlegging, with smart gentlemen driving up every few weeks in their Packard sedan, dressed in dark double-breasted suits, black fedoras, silk shirts, rings on their fingers, huge watches on their wrists. Cash was handed over, and then a case of whisky was carried out of the door. Soon William found himself involved in the game too, delivering hooch to various people about the city, and watching dollar bills passed to policemen, so that they would turn a blind eye. He only stopped when one day the gangsters had a disagreement with the drugstore owner, brutally attacked him, and thrust a dollar bill into William's hand: 'Listen, kid, you keep your god damn mouth shut, uh?'[6] He never went back to the drugstore, but continued to be fascinated by the doctors, who were as smartly dressed as the gangsters and drove equally large cars. It was the beginning of his determination to become a doctor.

The paths of the two boys now began to diverge. They complemented each other, William quieter and more cautious than his outgoing brother. Samuel was to be a lawyer. He was already doing well in the debating class at Tuley, developing an eloquence that would stand him in good stead as an attorney. But there were other influences that began to work on him. He was fourteen at the time of the World Fair in Chicago. The Fair was intended to ameliorate the effects of the Depression and would rival the Columbian Exposition of forty years earlier. It was the brainchild of Anton Cermak, a Czech-born immigrant, elected as the Democratic Mayor in 1931, beating the Republican incumbent, 'Big' Bill Thompson, who had been associated with Al Capone. Cermak's solution to the continuing economic depression was to prime the pump, a Keynesian strategy that would soon be adopted by Franklin D Roosevelt. In November 1932, Roosevelt was elected President for the first time. In February, Cermak went down to Miami to attend a reception for him. Roosevelt recognized him standing near the Presidential car and beckoned to him. Cermak approached, an assassin shot him in the lung, and he died a month later. A new Mayor was appointed, and the Fair went ahead.

The Fair was called 'A Century of Progress', but much of it was focused on the future, with a House of Tomorrow, futuristic architecture, a Rainbow City, spectacular events, music, modern art and architecture, a German airship, and the first Major League Baseball All-Star game. It is unlikely the Watenmaker family would have missed visiting, and Samuel was ever afterwards inspired by the idea of large-scale events that might raise the spirits of a community or an audience. But he remembered the following year more vividly, when the Fair was revived and expanded. Over fifty years later, he would tell an audience of students that he had two memorable experiences at the Century of Progress. One was of 'a legendary lady called Sally Rand, dancing in the nude while manipulating two huge white fans'.[7] The other was a model of the Globe playhouse. In contrast to the modern exhibits, a number of traditional 'villages' had been included that year. The playhouse was part of the English village designed by the British Board of Trade Overseas. Samuel watched a cut-down version of *The Taming of the Shrew* inside it, his first experience of Shakespeare, to add to his knowledge of Yiddish theatre.

There were more theatrical thrills to follow. More exciting than mopping the doctors' floor in the drugstore was the opportunity to usher at the Auditorium Theatre, the grand playhouse built in 1889, to rival the Metropolitan Opera House in New York. Willam and Samuel both heard, from the topmost circle there, the farewell performance of the great bass-baritone Boris Chaliapin. Then came Samuel's first opportunity to appear onstage, when the Ballets Russes de Monte Carlo presented *The Firebird* there, and William and he were hired as spear carriers. The main impression he retained of this experience was the tantalising proximity of the girls in the corps de ballet, who were 'beyond beauty – they were like the fairies and angels of myth and legend – these sixteen heavenly beauties made their leaping exits off the stage near where I was standing, and in a flash, with the help of their dressers, stripped off their tutus and bodices to change their costume.'[8] For a fifteen-year-old boy, it was a highly titivating experience.

Back at Tuley in the fall of 1934 for his senior year, William having now graduated, Samuel continued to shine in the debating class. He had not yet formulated any other ambition than to train as a lawyer, as Morris and Molly hoped, although he had taken part in some class plays. But one day, the drama teacher, a lively woman called Beulah Margolis, visited the debating class and was struck by his eloquence and strong presence. She cast him as the lead in her production of *The Man Who Married a Dumb Wife* by Hungarian writer, Ferenc Molnár. And unbeknownst to Samuel, she invited a talent scout to join the audience. On the strength of his performance Samuel was offered a full scholarship in the Fine Arts Department at Drake University, in Des Moines, Iowa. He would be studying Theatre Arts, alongside those studying Music and Art. The offer clarified Samuel's mind; he was enthused by what he had experienced of theatre, and eager to follow up the chance to study it. No doubt the full scholarship helped to win his parents' approval.

The following fall, he left home for the first time, aged sixteen, and took the train to Des Moines, 350 miles or so to the west. Though he must have had some apprehension at starting a new life, he was not intimidated, but eager to put behind him the squalor of the Chicago slums and explore a new environment. The scholarship did not cover his board and lodging, but he quickly found a job. From 10pm and 3am every night, he ran the elevator at a local hotel. While it was stimulating to be studying theatre, he soon found that his fellow students were looking longingly towards Chicago, which he had just left. From them, he learnt that if you really wanted to be an actor, the place to be was the Goodman School of Drama, attached to the Art Institute in his own city. That was enough for Samuel. He went back to Chicago in the middle of the term, blagged his way to the school's Director, and with the chutzpah that was an early character trait, persuaded that gentleman to give him a full scholarship.

He could not have made a better decision. He now began three years of 'intense and joyous training'.[9] His journey by streetcar through the city to the parkland site of the Art Institute took him away from the slum environment in which he had grown up, and gave him some independence from his parents. The Goodman School of Drama indeed offered the best opportunity in the whole of the Midwest for a budding actor. It had been founded by William and Erna Goodman, as a memorial to their son, Kenneth Sawyer Goodman. A Chicago-born playwright, educated at Princeton, Goodman had approached the Art Institute in 1915 with the idea of establishing a theatre that would combine professional training with the highest possible performance standards. But he died of influenza in 1918, at the age of thirty-five. His parents then took up the idea and gifted $250,000 to the Art Institute. The Goodman Memorial Theatre and School opened in 1925. Its first artistic director was Thomas Wood Stevens, a colleague of Kenneth Sawyer Goodman, who had established the first degree-awarding theatre program in America, at Carnegie Tech. Stevens ran the Goodman for five years. A year after he left, it ceased to be a professional theatre, and operated solely as the Goodman School of Drama.

The Director of the School was Maurice Gnesin, who had come from the Duluth Playhouse in Minnesota. He introduced children's theatre, and brought in a Russian actor, David Itkin, who had worked at the Jewish Habima theatre, when it was part of the Moscow Art Theatre, where the great director Konstantin Stanislavsky had devised his famous acting system. Itkin introduced improvisation, which he saw as the basis of acting, and he devised lessons that encouraged his students to behave with simple emotional logic. The students studied voice and speech with Mary Agnes Doyle, an Irish/American tutor, skilled in oral interpretation. Under her tutelage, Samuel lost the strong Chicago accent he had when speaking English and acquired clear American diction. In his second term, he played his first part, in the Children's Theatre season, and was given one line in David Itkin's main production of Strindberg's *The Father*, where his name was listed as 'Samuel Wanamaker'. William and he had taken the step of formally changing their surname. (Later, Morris and Molly also adopted the name.)

Towards the end of the academic year, Samuel learnt that the Globe playhouse that had impressed him so much two years earlier was being re-erected for the Great Lakes Exposition in Cleveland, Ohio, in celebration of that city's centenary. There would be performances of Shakespeare, directed by Thomas Wood Stevens and the English director Ben Iden Payne. They had mounted the excerpts that Samuel had seen in 1934 and both were keen to present Shakespeare in what they called a 'modified Elizabethan style'. No doubt Maurice Gnesin put in a good word, having himself been brought to the Goodman by Stevens.

Samuel auditioned and was hired. Once again, he set off from Chicago, to play small parts in the shortened versions. He was employed by Globe Theatre Productions, Ltd, to play in their 'Blackfriars Company', his first professional job. He was 'Second Citizen' in *Julius Caesar*, 'Biondello, servant to Lucentio' in *The Taming of the Shrew*, and 'Attendant' in *The Comedy of Errors*, directed by Thomas Wood Stevens. In *As You Like It*, directed by Ben Iden Payne, he played the more significant part of 'Corin', in *King Henry VIII* he played Gardiner, Bishop of Winchester, and in *A Midsummer Night's Dream* he was 'Philostrate'. The idea of performing in a reconstruction of the Globe appealed to him. Around this time he saw the film of *As You LIke It*, starring Laurence Olivier and Elisabeth Bergner, and his enthusiasm for Shakespeare grew. He may also have seen Orson Welles' famous production of *Julius Caesar*, which had toured to Chicago in 1935. (He did not, at this time, take a scholarly interest in the design of the Globe, which was based on a 1616 panorama of London by Claes Visscher, showing the playhouse as an octagonal structure, a supposition that later scholars would reject.)

During Samuel's second year at the Goodman, there was more Shakespeare. He watched one of the 3rd year students play Leontes in *The Winter's Tale*, in a costume provided by Globe Theatre Productions. His name was Mladen Sekulovich, son of a Serbian immigrant. Within a year or so, he would be playing on Broadway as 'Karl Malden', and would later make a successful film career. Samuel himself got to play a more significant Shakespeare part than at Cleveland, in a Children's Theatre production of *A Midsummer Night's Dream*. He played Bottom, an appropriate role, as his confidence and ambition grew: 'I have had a dream, past the wit of man to say what dream it was; ... it shall be called Bottom's dream, because it hath no bottom.'

In the same production, a small, pretty, vivacious girl called Charlotte Holland was playing Hermia. They had shared classes before, but not been in a production together. They began to date. She later told how, when he took her back to her Lakeside home, which was in a more prosperous part of town than his, he considered nicking a car, then recollected that he did not yet know how to drive. It was not love at first sight, but it was the beginning of their relationship.

For his second summer job, he was taken on by the Peninsula Players, a 'summer stock' company (as such seasonal companies were called). It was in an idyllic position in Door County, Wisconsin, at Green Bay on Lake Michigan. The company had been founded two years earlier by a brother and sister, Richard and Caroline Fisher. She was a photographic model, who had also done some acting in Hollywood, where she had met Rodion Rathbone, son of the English actor, Basil Rathbone. She and her brother, who wrote and directed, wanted to create a theatrical colony at their home on Fish Creek, an inlet of Green Bay. They had begun with a production of Noël Coward's *Hay Fever*, performed behind a motel, with Caroline in the lead and Richard directing, while 'Mama' Fisher cooked the meals and prepared the costumes, and 'Papa' Fisher, a civil engineer by trade, was the handyman. Financially, the season had been a disaster, 'But,' Caroline told the *Chicago Daily Tribune*, 'the Door County people were sweet to us. Most of them knew we'd pay when we could.'[10] Two years later, they bought a former boys' camp, and set about building a theatre there.

When Samuel arrived, 'Papa' Fisher was laying out the site, and he threw himself into the venture, hauling gravel, mixing concrete, laying the foundations and building the timber walls. Samuel enjoyed being in on the beginning of the venture, and the whole project had an impromptu feel to it, like Judy Garland/Mickey Rooney films: 'Why don't we do the show right here?' The company included both of Caroline's parents and her sister. The audience sat under the stars. Samuel's parts were far from romantic, including Sir Witful Witwould in *The Way of the World*, an opportunity to hone his diction, and Canon Chasuble in *The Importance of Being Earnest*, as well as a role in a play by Richard Fisher. 'Carol', as she was known, was Samuel's first experience of Hollywood glamour, and he fell for her in a big way, finding every moment in her presence sexually charged, but it was 'the love of a romantic, childish adolescent'. He knew she was going out with Rodion Rathbone (whom she married the following year), but he nevertheless cherished his memories of this 'beautiful' time: 'So many firsts, first car wreck [so he had some driving experience by this time], first passionate unrequited love affair, first star-filled nights, first Northern Lights.'[11]

Back at the Goodman for his final year of training, Samuel played opposite Charlotte in *The Adding Machine* by Elmer Rice, and they began to date more seriously. Her family background is complicated by the fact that her father was adopted. He was born in Minsk, of Russian Jewish parents, in 1884. His parents divorced, he was adopted by his stepfather, and acquired the name 'Arthur Holland'. According to his naturalization papers, he arrived in the United States in 1892 from Germany, first New York, and later Chicago. Charlotte's mother's family also came from Russia originally, and settled in Canada. Her mother, Anna Le Vine, or Levine, was born in Toronto in 1892, and had numerous siblings. There is no record of what brought her to Chicago, or how she met Arthur Holland. They were married in 1909, when she was 17, but giving her age as 19. Charlotte's brother was born in 1911. He was named Arnold, after Arthur's stepfather, but was always called 'Ernie'. Charlotte was born four years later. In the 1920 census, Arthur's mother tongue was listed as 'Jewish' ie Yiddish, while Anna's was listed as English. In adult life Charlotte described her mother as a Canadian Catholic. Whatever language the Holland family spoke at home, Charlotte certainly knew enough Yiddish to converse in that language, especially after her brother married into a Russian family.

Little is known of Charlotte's journey towards acting. She entered the Goodman School the same year as Samuel, when she was twenty years old. However eager she was, she would have needed to work and save money before she could afford to train. Her father had died of appendicitis, when she was eight years old. He had been a telegrapher in a bank. Her mother had worked in a confectionery shop, but gave that up to look after her two children.

Goodman students soon found that they could earn money by doing radio work. This was the 'golden age' of radio, the main source of dramatic entertainment at that time, offering plays, comedies, and the fifteen-minute daytime drama serials that soon became nicknamed 'soap operas', since they were often sponsored by soap manufacturers. Chicago was the centre for 'soaps', the first being *Painted Dreams*, by Irna Phillips, which began in 1930 on Chicago radio station WGN. They soon became popular, as sponsors realised that their audience of housewives had considerable buying power. Samuel and Charlotte were both offered work from time to time, he with WGN, she with the National Broadcasting Company (NBC). Charlotte was under 5ft tall, but made up for her lack of height through her energy and her warm, vibrant voice. After their joint appearance in *The Adding Machine,* she did not appear in any more productions at the School, being busy with radio work, while Samuel undertook a variety of roles there. He played the iconic part of Lord Dundreary in Tom Taylor's *Our American*

Cousin, Orestes in Euripides' *Electra,* Mr Crampton in Shaw's *You Never Can Tell* and Edgar in *King Lear.*

Meanwhile, the couple's relationship was deepening. During their final year at the Goodman, she needed emotional support. In the spring of 1937 her mother had been diagnosed with ovarian cancer. As Samuel set off for his idyllic summer, she had been dealing with her mother's illness. Anna Holland died in January 1938. She was buried in a Jewish cemetery, Shomer Hadas; she must have set aside her Catholic religion.

Charlotte and Sam – as he was now being listed, perhaps wanting a snappier name – both graduated from the Goodman in the summer of 1938, at which point he was invited to become an associate faculty member for the following year, at a nominal salary, while she continued to take parts on radio. The range of roles Sam had now undertaken gave him as good a grounding as an English actor would have got from playing in a regional repertory company. He was eager to begin his career. As European news began to cause concern, he hoped it would not interfere with his ambitions.

But Adolf Hitler's power grew. In May he had annexed Austria; in September the Munich Agreement was signed, allowing him to annex Sudetenland. In October, Americans were threatened much closer to home. Not German aggression, but invasion from outer space! when Orson Welles' Mercury Theatre of the Air broadcast a dramatization of H G Wells' *The War of the Worlds,* which many listeners, tuning in after the opening announcements, took to be real. The power of radio had never been more vividly demonstrated. But in November, came a night of genuine terror in Germany, with the Nazi outrages on Jews that came to be known as Kristallnacht. Still Sam, like most of his countrymen, hoped there would be no war.

He continued to act at the School, playing Lord Essex in Maxwell Anderson's *Elizabeth the Queen,* among other parts. He also began to direct, and found that he really enjoyed overseeing an entire production. Amongst other one-act plays, he directed the students in J M Barrie's *The Twelve Pound Look* and Eugene O'Neill's *The Long Voyage Home,* the fourth of the Sea Plays. He also played with the Chicago Civic Repertory Group, a non-profit theatre founded in 1934 with the aim of creating theatre along the lines of the Group Theatre, founded three years earlier in New York by Harold Clurman, Cheryl Crawford and Lee Strasberg to develop a distinctly American acting technique. In the spring of 1935, the Repertory Theatre had produced the Chicago premiere of *Waiting for Lefty,* the first-produced, one-act play by Clifford Odets, the dramatist most associated with the Group. Whether or not Sam had seen that production, he certainly began to take an interest in the work of the Group. The Repertory Theatre had its own theatre school, where Group Theatre members such as Morris Carnovsky and Robert Lewis lectured. However, the plays in which Sam appeared were lighter fare; they included a mystery drama, a comedy and a romance. In the summer of 1939, he sought out more opportunities to direct in summer stock, working in companies around Chicago. Radio work continued to provide both Sam and Charlotte with bread and butter.

It was already clear that they could make a living as actors, but their aspirations went further. In late-night discussions about the future, amongst their fellow-graduates from the Goodman, Sam was becoming eloquent about the contribution that theatre and drama could make to American life, and how they could all play a part in its development. They knew about the Federal Theatre Project, part of Roosevelt's Works Progress Administration, funding theatre and entertainment projects as part of the New Deal. It had come to an end just as they were leaving the Goodman, criticized by members of Congress for being too left-wing, but its ideals and principles lived on. Their own lives were enriched by the arts. The Goodman was attached to the Art Institute, where they had spent many hours. One of their close friends and fellow graduates was Ralph Alswang, already starting his career as a theatre designer. Music, too, was important, both classical and jazz, although Sam did not at that time develop a taste for opera. His first experience, a cumbersome production of *Die Walküre* by the Chicago City Opera Company had completely put him off.

Every ambitious actor had to make the decision whether to look towards New York and Broadway or towards Los Angeles and Hollywood to further their career. For idealists, there was a sense that Hollywood was an artistic cop-out. Certainly, Sam and Charlotte had set their sights on New York. More and more, they had the sense of a partnership; his grand visions, her firm belief that they could be fulfilled. Their growing love for each other would sustain the knocks that would inevitably come. Sam had developed confidence and ambition, but there was an underlying fear that he would not achieve what he hoped for, and Charlotte's faith then buoyed him up. The street life of his childhood had made him determined to fight his corner, no matter what. Charlotte made him aware of other qualities. He later claimed that she had taught him about compassion and morality.

In the event, it was Charlotte, not Sam, who was first given the chance to work in New York. In the autumn of 1939, she was cast in a new series.

Against the Storm was a cut above the usual soap opera. The writer was Sandra Michael, originally from Denmark. She had already written *Monticello Party LIne*, a typical day-to-day story revolving around two couples in Illinois who shared a telephone line. She wanted to write 'as if housewives were intelligent', and persuaded the head of Procter & Gamble to test a more demanding show. She began writing it on 3 September, the day Britain declared war on Germany. The storyline centred on a Professor at a fictional university in Connecticut, a setting which allowed her to include literature and poetry readings, and to cover themes such as war resistance and the danger of fascism.

Once it was established, Sandra Michael began another series, written in collaboration with her brother. *Lone Journey* was about a businessman who was dissatisfied with his life in Chicago, and retreated to the mountains of Montana, where he and his wife purchased a ranch. The storyline focused on their attempts to begin a new life. Sponsored by Lever Brothers, its theme tune was 'American the Beautiful', and as the writers objected to the term 'soap opera', it was billed as 'the distinguished American radio novel'.[12] Sam was cast in a continuing role, while Charlotte played a small part in an early episode.

Early in 1940, the broadcast of *Against the Storm* was moved to the NBC studio in New York and Charlotte was asked to go with it. For Sam, it was no doubt, privately, somewhat galling, that the chance came for Charlotte earlier than for him. He was involved in mounting a production at the Jewish People's Institute. He had chosen a play by Irwin Shaw (himself the son of Russian Jewish immigrants), *The Gentle People*. The Group Theatre had produced the play on Broadway the previous year, directed by one of its founders, Harold Clurman. The cast included a number of Group stalwarts: Elia Kazan, Lee J Cobb, and Martin Ritt, as well as the Goodman graduate, Karl Malden. It was subtitled 'A Brooklyn Fable', and concerned a couple of harmless fishermen on Coney Island who rise up against an oppressive gangster, played by Franchot Tone. It was as if Sam was trying to bring New York to Chicago, while Charlotte was doing the reverse, setting off alone on the Twentieth Century Limited, the famous express train service to New York.

A few months after Charlotte departed, Sam too was offered radio work in New York, continuing his role in *Lone Journey* and also playing in *Guiding Light*, a more mundane 'soap' by Irna Phillips, the doyenne of the genre. In May, he lured Charlotte back to Chicago, where, with no period of formal engagement, but confident of her acquiescence, he had organized their wedding, without telling her beforehand. He was not quite twenty-one, and had to get parental approval. She was twenty-five, but looked younger. It was a simple ceremony in front of a Rabbi. And then they set off together, not by train, but in a blue Pontiac car that Sam had acquired by that time, perhaps a Torpedo, 'the car in which the best of the past meets the best of the future'. A long cross-country journey, before there were interstate highways, took them through Indiana, Ohio and Pennsylvania, across the Appalachian Mountains and into New York, where they would surely make their fortunes.

2

New York! New York!

S am and Charlotte were amongst a number of Chicago radio actors who made the move to New York around 1940, all eager to further their careers.[1] They were soon regularly employed at the NBC Studios on Rockefeller Plaza. Actors met on the third floor there, to record a show and then repeat it some hours later, broadcasting to a different time zone. Cast lists show the names of several radio actors who would subsequently make their name in Hollywood or on Broadway; future film director Joseph Losey was an NBC director. Friends and colleagues from Chicago considered Charlotte more gifted and accomplished on radio than Sam, her voice able to capture a range of emotions, while Sam's was less flexible. But they knew that he already had potential as a director.

During the long waits between broadcasts, the topic of discussion was often the state of their industry. Sam and Charlotte had been members of the Chicago chapter of their union, the American Federation of Radio Actors (AFRA); its president, Virginia Payne, came to New York at the same time as they did. AFRA had been founded in 1937, first in New York, swiftly followed by branches in Los Angeles and Chicago; in 1938, members had negotiated the first collectively bargained agreement with NBC and its rival, CBS (Columbia Broadcasting Company), achieving a substantial national wage increase. Sam knew it was important to support his union, but he did not, like his father, become a union officer.

The newly-weds settled into a small apartment and quickly acquired a spaniel and a Scottie. Away from family, they enjoyed their independence and were eager to take in all that New York had to offer – concerts, art galleries, and of course, theatre. In their first year, Laurence Olivier's production of *Romeo and Juliet* was playing, with Vivien Leigh as Juliet to his Romeo. Other highlights were Katherine Hepburn in *The Philadelphia Story*, William Saroyan's *The Time of Your Life*, and *The Man Who Came To Dinner* by George S Kaufman and Moss Hart. John Barrymore was making his last Broadway appearance in *My Dear Children*, a weak farce that showed this veteran actor in decline. The following year, there was

Arsenic and Old Lace, starring Boris Karloff, and Noël Coward's *Blithe Spirit*, with Peggy Wood, Clifton Webb and Mildred Natwick. Robert Sherwood's *There Shall Be No Night*, about the Russian invasion of Finland, starred the distinguished theatrical couple, Alfred Lunt and Lynn Fontanne, and won the Pulitzer prize, while Lillian Hellman's anti-Fascist play *Watch On the Rhine* won the Drama Critics' Award. Maurice Evans, an English actor who had settled in America, starred in the title role of *King Richard II*, in a revival of a production in which he had had a great success a few years earlier.

Disappointingly, by the time Sam and Charlotte arrived in New York, the Group Theatre, of which they had heard so much, had formally disbanded, and the Group Theatre Studio, established by two of its members, Robert Lewis and Elia Kazan, no longer functioned. But at the end of 1941, Sam got his first Broadway role, and found himself working alongside Morris Carnovsky, a Group Theatre actor, and being directed by Elia Kazan himself. The play was *Café Crown*, by Hy Kraft, a comedy set in the Café Royale, a Second Avenue restaurant where many of the Jewish theatre crowd hung out. Not yet an experienced director, Kazan had just finished filming *Blues in the Night*, which would turn out to be his last acting role. For this production, he decided to 'stop trying to imitate Clurman's and Strasberg's flood of rhetoric'. He would cast the play 'colourfully, with vivid "ethnic" types [and] move them around in a way that would seem spontaneous and unstudied.'[2]

Sam explored the Lower East Side of Manhattan, where Jewish immigrants had settled, many of them working in garment sweatshops, like his parents. It was all too similar to the West Side in Chicago, full of crowded tenements, but enlivened by Yiddish theatre. Nearby were 'little Italy' and Chinatown, while the most down-and-out derelicts and alcoholics dragged out their lives in The Bowery, New York's 'skid row'. He got to know the Fulton fish market, where mafia types hung out, and looked across to Ellis Island, where immigrants were processed. Eager to know the city thoroughly, he explored Harlem in Upper Manhattan, where Jewish and Italian immigrants had first settled, now largely occupied by the black population. The squalor of such neighbourhoods was familiar to him. He rejoiced to have put it behind him, and felt a reforming urge to see some kind of urban regeneration, that would offer the inhabitants a better way of life.

On 7 December, 1941, before rehearsals began, the news came through that the Japanese had attacked Pearl Harbour. Within days, the US was at war with Japan, Germany and Italy. Robert Sherwood's play about Finland, *There Shall Be No Night*, which was touring, was withdrawn from production, since Finland had allied itself with Germany, against the Russian Front. Sam's friend Cliff Carpenter, having visited Austria in 1938, and seen 'Juden Verboten' signs wherever he went, decided to enlist straight away. Sam did not. He felt that he was on the brink of theatrical success; he knew that he might be drafted, and preferred to wait for that contingency, rather than lose this opportunity. His brother Bill, in contrast, had already joined the Naval Reserve, and was mobilized at once.

Café Crown opened on Broadway in January 1942. Brooks Atkinson, critic of the *New York Times,* called it 'a hospitable comedy … simple but warm-hearted'.[3] Its world was comfortably close to that of the company, since Sam, Carnovsky, Sam Jaffe (another actor in the cast), and the designer, Boris Aronson, were all sons of Russian Jewish immigrants. Sam played Lester Freed, a young man eager to go to Hollywood. Kazan considered it his first success as a director. Sam had launched his Broadway career, on a salary of $75 per week. The play ran until May at the Cort Theatre and was followed by a week in Windsor, a small town in New York State, and then, more excitingly, a week in Chicago, giving Sam a chance to make something of a hero's return. For the New York season he had contributed a lighthearted note for the programme: 'At the Goodman Theatre he played mostly old men in beards, for which he won a scholarship.' For the Chicago programme he added, more seriously, 'He was also director at the Jewish People's Institute here and has been on several important radio programmes here.'[4] Added to his sense of achievement, a week after the play closed there, Charlotte gave birth to their first daughter, Abby. As a father, he was now classed as 3-D by the Draft Board, with his call-up deferred.

Charlotte continued with radio work, and this may have been when Agnes Casimir entered their lives, a woman from Dominica, who, as 'Aggie', became their devoted housekeeper. Charlotte was in several episodes of a series called *Counterspy,* and she took over a leading part in *Lone Journey.* The series that had brought her to New York, *Against the Storm,* continued, and now included readings from such writers as Edna St Vincent Millay and Walt Whitman. John Masefield 'shortwaved' his participation from Britain, ostensibly lecturing for the Professor. Even President Roosevelt accepted a speaking part, but that was shelved after Pearl Harbour. That year the programme won the prestigious Peabody Award, given for outstanding achievement in radio broadcasting. Sandra Michael, the writer, wanted it extended to half an hour, but that proved too ambitious for the sponsors, who took the show off at the end of the 1942. However, Charlotte was soon working on a spin-off for CBS, *The Open Door*, in which the character of the Professor had metamorphized into Erik Hansen, Dean of Students at the fictional 'Vernon University', played by the same actor. Charlotte played Dr Hansen's secretary, introducing students and townspeople, to whom he dispensed advice and comfort. Like all commercial radio programmes of the time, it began with warm words from the sponsor: 'Welcome friends, you've come to The Open Door and the Makers of Royal Puddings and Royal Gelatin invite you to enter and meet Dr Hansen.'[5]

According to fellow-actor Cliff Carpenter, directors were in awe of Charlotte's talent: 'When she got a challenging role in radio, she could treat the director and cast to a riveting display of pyrotechnics and intensity; she was possessed of dedication and unceasing search for truth in character.'[6] Another friend who knew her work, Blanche Zohar, a young actress, praised her versatility and described a sense of mystery and romanticism she was able to convey.

Sam continued with radio work as well, where his ongoing role in *Guiding Light* was 'Ellis Smith', an enigmatic figure known as 'Nobody from Nowhere.' But he was soon involved in another Broadway production, this time in a major role. He was cast in *Counterattack*, by Janet and Philip Stevenson, a play about a Russian soldier, who, with his companion, holds off a group of German soldiers in the cellar of a bombed house. He had top billing with Morris Carnovsky and Barbara O'Neil and the play was directed by Anglo-American Margaret (Peggy) Webster. The play not only provided Sam with a leading part, but strongly influenced his political thinking. America was now in alliance with Russia, and pro-Russian themes had official approval: '… The Russians became heroic men and women fighting to defend our home and way of life. We were exhorted by the Government, from the President and his wife downwards, to help the gallant Russians in every way we could … the cinema was suddenly flooded with romantic and wonderful motion pictures by and about the Russians'.[7] Such films included *Mission to Moscow*, *North Star*, *Days of Glory* and *Song of Russia*. Even before he started researching the background to the play, Sam was 'ripe to become a Communist, merely as a gesture of friendship with our Soviet allies'.[8] His role in *Counterattack* was the young soldier:

> The character I played had lived and worked on a collective farm – and so I learnt about collective farms in Russia and what they had accomplished by working together and sharing machinery. I learned about this young Russian soldier's schooling, and what he was taught there: the basic principles of socialism, the

heroism of the people of the Communist revolution, the poverty and misery of the people in Russia before the revolution, the identification with the French Revolution and our own American Revolution ...[9]

He was paid $150 a week, double his wages in *Café Crown*, and the play ran from January to April 1943. In June, Joseph Losey and a couple of other NBC radio directors launched *Words at War*, a thirty-minute series in which Sam took part. Sponsored by Johnsons Wax, it was a lavishly produced, wide-ranging anthology on war, written by Erik Barnouw, taking stories such as H E Bates' *Fair Stood the Wind for France* and *Lost Island* by James Norman. According to *Variety* it was 'one of the most outstanding programs on radio', while in *Newsweek* it was 'one of the best contributions to serious radio in many a year.'[10] It would go on to win the Peabody Award the following year.

Like many of their friends, Charlotte and Sam began to attend lectures on Communism. He saw its objectives idealistically: 'to raise the standard of living of all the people all over the world; to do away with poverty and illiteracy; to create a social system in which the <u>few</u> could not own or control the <u>most</u>'.[11] He was influenced by his childhood and youth, his father's strong support of trades unionism, and the inequality he saw in Chicago and New York, more than by his knowledge of what his maternal grandparents had suffered under the Soviet régime:

> Because of my own early poverty, and the suffering I had witnessed of my parents and those around me during the terrible years of the Thirties, my natural sympathies were with ideas such as these.[12]

With his growing political awareness, Sam was drawn to explore how theatre could be used directly for social causes, as it had been under the Federal Theatre Project with its Living Newpapers. He joined Stage for Action, a social activist theatre movement founded in 1943. Its aim was to produce free or low-priced topical theatre, that would focus on 'realizable post-show actions'.[13] Eleanor Roosevelt supported the group, Sandra Michael was involved, and there he encountered Arthur Miller, Paul Robeson, Studs Terkel, whom he knew as a Chicago broadcaster, and other similarly motivated people.

Paul Robeson was already known for his protests against racial discrimination. He was in New York that year in the Theatre Guild's production of *Othello*, playing the title role for the second time (having played it in London in 1930), with Uta Hagen as Desdemona, and José Ferrer as Iago. The production was directed by Peggy Webster, who had just directed

Sam. With 288 performances, it broke the record for Shakespearean revivals of the play. Although Robeson was not a skilled stage actor, his rendering of the Moor nevertheless impressed Sam, since he seemed by his very presence to embody the character. At Robeson's request, the Theatre Guild agreed to remove Washington DC and Baltimore from the subsequent tour calendar, since both cities segregated their audience. Racial discrimination against the black population of America struck Sam and Charlotte as no different from anti-Semitism.

At the end of 1943, Sam directed Stage for Action's first script, a one-act play by Arthur Miller, who had already written for the Federal Theatre Project, but not yet had a Broadway success. *That They May Win* was about the need for child care centres for working women, and was cast in triplicate, so that it could be performed at different venues, and at different times. Sam described it as 'a mobile, quick fire theatre to bring issues of the war ... to the people in their meeting halls, schools and community centres'.[14] One audience member was quoted saying 'It shows the importance of doing something now. It makes you feel you *can* do something, *must* do something.'[15] The 'something' that Sam and Charlotte did was to join the American Communist Party (CPUSA), as did Cliff Carpenter and many friends and colleagues.

Joseph Losey was directing contemporary, didactic dramas on the radio, but at the end of 1943, he left for his first assignment in Hollywood, after which he was drafted into the army. Sam followed in his footsteps as an Associate Producer at NBC, but those with 3-D classification were now being called up, and he too received his papers and was mobilized in April 1944.

It was the first time that Sam and Charlotte had been separated since their marriage. They were living in an apartment in Riverdale at that time, a pleasant area in the Bronx, the northernmost of the New York boroughs. Sam was worried about how the separation would affect Charlotte, both emotionally and economically. He wrote to the radio producer of *Counterspy*, for whom she had already worked, explaining that she was 'a psychopathic [sic – perhaps he meant pathological?] introvert when it comes to approaching people for a job'. Something of an exaggeration, but it seems she *was* shy at putting herself forward. 'It would be wonderful,' he wrote, if you could use her on the 15th [of April] or thereabouts to get her mind off her problems!'[16]

At no point did Sam suffer great hardship or danger during his military service. He spent six months as a private in Camp Sibert, Alabama, in a

Special Services programme designed to offer recreation and entertainment to the troops. He described his role disparagingly as 'Luggage carrying.'[17] Then he was shipped off to the South Pacific for nine months. His most intense time was at Iwo Jima, in March 1945. The island was still smouldering after one of the fiercest and bloodiest battles in the Pacific, but Sam later described his part in the proceedings with black humour: 'I stumbled up the beach … with the second wave of the Marines, lugging tennis rackets, ping pong sets and catchers' mitts'[18] – all intended for later relaxation. He and his companions dug a fox-hole to shelter in. During a raging typhoon, he got into trouble for failing to secure a tent that was blowing away in the huge wind, and shouting at the sergeant. He was at Iwo Jima for less than a month, and was then sent to Hawaii, to join the Entertainments Section, which Major Evans, the actor Maurice Evans, had been running since 1942.

The last months of Sam's army service thus returned him to his profession. Maurice Evans had taken American citizenship in 1941, and had thus become eligible for the Draft. In Hawaii, he became aware that the sort of men being drafted in 1944 included 'married men, university graduates and cultured individuals',[19] and he had therefore boldly mounted a production of *Hamlet*, arranging the text to emphasize its military theme. As in all the shows he oversaw, the men's parts were played by the soldiers, while professional actresses were flown in from the West Coast to play the women's parts. This production was so successful that, when he was discharged, in June 1945, Evans revived his production, known as *GI Hamlet*, on Broadway. Sam too took the risk of directing a serious play, as well as lighter diversions for the men. A new playwright, Tennessee Williams, who, like Arthur Miller, had worked for the Federal Theatre Project, had written what he called a 'memory' play, *The Glass Menagerie,* in which a narrator character looks back on past scenes in his life. It had premiered in Chicago and received glowing reviews, after which it transferred to Broadway, won the New York Drama Critics Circle Award, and had a long and successful run. Sam staged it in Hawaii, and played Tom Wingfield, the narrator.

The time in Hawaii was a pleasant interlude. Having been a city dweller up to that time, Sam fell in love with its beauty. 'It is one place in the world that I have real nostalgia for', he wrote some years later, in reply to a postcard. 'If I hadn't been there myself I would not believe the colour photograph … but I know that in fact the colours in the picture are not anywhere near as glorious as they really are.'[20] His brother Bill had been at Cherbourg after D-Day, but by 1945 was serving as an officer on a hospital ship in the Pacific. He managed to radio 'Sergeant Wanamaker', as he was by that time, on Hawaii, and they succeeded in meeting. In their personal recollections of the last months of the war, neither mentioned the atomic bombs dropped on Hiroshima or Nagasaki that August. A new and horrific kind of warfare had been introduced, yet there was relief that it quickly brought about VJ Day.

Wartime letters between Sam and Charlotte have not survived, though she kept him in touch with home life and sent him photographs of Abby. But two letters to Oliver Crawford, an old mate from the Goodman School have. They show that Sam tried to make his time in Hawaii productive in terms of self-development. He learnt to play tennis, he studied some Russian. He wanted to study piano and learn to type properly. 'I've wanted to work on a play, to write a couple of radio scripts, but I have not time for any of that when I return home ... then the fight begins anew for job and security and not time for much else.'[21] Early marriage and then fatherhood meant that he had acquired responsibilities that a single man in his twenties would not have had. Yet the time away from New York had only increased his ambition; he wanted to be more than a jobbing actor and radio producer.

Early in 1946, Sam was demobbed in San Francisco, made his way back to New York and was reunited with Charlotte and Abby. His main concern was how to get back into theatre, after a two-year gap. Lady Luck was with him. Three days after leaving the West Coast, he walked into his agent's office, still in uniform, since he had put on weight and his civvy clothes no longer fitted him. He was sent immediately to see Don Appel, an actor and director who had just written his first play, was about to go into rehearsal, and had lost one of his actors. The play was *This Too Shall Pass*, and the part Sam was sent up for was as if tailor-made for him – that of Mac Sorrell, a young Jewish GI, returning from the Pacific.

The story was a protest against anti-Semitism. It concerned Mac's disruptive arrival in the home of a mid-Western couple, a doctor and his wife. He comes as a guest of his 'pal', the son of the house. All goes well until the daughter announces that she wants to marry him, at which point the Christian mother turns fiercely against him and turns him out of the house. Sam was given featured billing, as for *Counterattack*, and a salary of $300 a week on tour, and $400 on Broadway. When the play opened at the Belasco Theatre the critics applauded the plea for racial tolerance that the play strove for, but found it weak and melodramatic. (At the end of the play the son rushes out, and is run over and killed by his Jewish friend.) But Sam's performance was picked out by more than one critic: 'Of the actors employed to represent these highly simplified people, I could really admire only Sam Wanamaker, whose performance as the young Jew was pleasantly modest and natural' (Wolcott Gibbs in the *New Yorker*); 'Sam Wanamaker turns in an extremely fine and sensitive performance as Mac, giving the role much more credence than the author allows' (George Freedley in the *Morning Telegraph*).[22]

The play offered Sam his first love-scene. The actress playing the daughter was Jan Sterling, whom Sam found attractive. She was blonde and blue-eyed, in contrast to Charlotte. Born 'Jane Sterling Adriance', the daughter of wealthy parents who divorced, she had been privately educated in Paris and London, where she had enrolled in a drama school run by English actress, Fay Compton. Returning to America in the mid 1930s, Sterling began her acting career in her teens. In 1941, she married an English actor, Jack Merivale, whose career, like Sam's, was interrupted by the war. When Merivale returned, and was cast in a Broadway revival of Oscar Wilde's *Lady Windermere's Fan*, she told him, according to some accounts, that she had fallen in love with Sam Wanamaker. It seems that they did have a short affair, but Sam was also eager to return to his family.

Charlotte and he found an unusual apartment at 53 East 88th St. It had once been a carriage house, and consisted of two storeys above a garage. They lived on the first floor (English style), and rented the top floor to Mercedes McCambridge, an Irish actress friend from Illinois. (Like the Catholic children in Chicago, she had been taught to hate the Jews, but had long got over such prejudice.) When she moved out, to go to Hollywood, their friends Cliff and Mac Carpenter moved in with their daughter Deborah, who was the same age as Abby. It was a happy arrangement, as the two couples shared many views on politics and theatre.

1946 was a vintage year on Broadway. The Old Vic Company from London toured again, starring Laurence Olivier as Hotspur in *King Henry IV Part I*, and the title roles in *King Richard III* and *Oedipus Rex* (somewhat unusually teamed with *The Critic* by Richard Brinsley Sheridan), and also presenting the aforementioned production of *Lady Windermere's Fan*, designed by Cecil Beaton, and in which he also acted. There was another Wilde production, as John Gielgud starred in *The Importance of Being Earnest*. Many of the theatre-going public were pleased to have this influx of plays from Britain, its companies free to travel once again, but Sam at this time found much English acting 'artificial and mannered, with no emotion or real feeling.'[23] American theatre was represented by several hit musicals: *Brigadoon, Annie Get Your Gun, Oklahoma!* and *Carousel*. The young Marlon Brando played in a production of Bernard Shaw's *Candida*.

In September 1946, Sam went up for a part which he knew he was most unlikely to be cast in. Written by Maxwell Anderson, the play was called *Girl of Lorraine* and was about Joan of Arc; the Swedish film star Ingrid Bergman was to make her Broadway debut in it. Anderson had structured it as a play-within-a-play, set in a Broadway theatre. Sam's agent had suggested him for Jimmy Masters, the play's director, a *persona* for Anderson himself. He read the script, but thought that at twenty-seven, he was much too young for the role. Nevertheless he agreed to meet the director, Margo Jones. She also thought he was too young, but allowed him to read.

Over a three-week period, Jones had seen hundreds of actors; she was greatly impressed with Sam's talent, and wanted to work with him. She had co-directed the original production of *The Glass Menagerie*, and thought he must have been excellent as Tom Wingfield, the part he had played in Hawaii. (She later wrote to Enterprise Productions, an independent company established by Group Theatre actor, John Garfield, suggesting that the play should be filmed with Sam playing the part again, and herself directing, but nothing came of that idea.) She was determined to cast him as Jimmy Masters, who was also to play the Inquisitor at Joan's trial. But Maxwell Anderson said 'No'. She suggested that if Sam grew a moustache, he would look more mature, and she finally won the day. Bergman gave her approval sight unseen.

This was a major opportunity. Sam would be undertaking a role far from what he had played before, opposite Bergman, already a major star, famous for her performances in, amongst other films, *Casablanca* with Humphrey Bogart, and *Gaslight* with Charles Boyer. He knew something of Anderson's work, having acted in his verse play, *Elizabeth The Queen*, while he was at the Goodman. That play and *Mary of Scotland* had first made Anderson's name in the early 1930s, and both had been adapted for the screen. He was eager to meet Ingrid Bergman and begin rehearsals.

Anderson's play was very different from Bernard Shaw's *Saint Joan*, first performed twenty years earlier, partly because of its structure, being a play about Joan of Arc in rehearsal. 'I have wanted an audience to share the excitement of seeing a play come to life on a bare stage,' Anderson wrote for the programme.[24] Bergman was to be the actress, Mary Grey, who is playing 'Joan', and who has doubts about the way the 'playwright' (who never appears) is handling the story, especially the way that, to achieve God's purpose for France and for her, Joan has to collude with corrupt people such as the Dauphin.

There was much riding on the production for Bergman. She had wanted to play Joan from childhood onward, and was familiar with the account of her trial. (Her oldest daughter thought that she was drawn to the idea of 'a poor peasant girl who had a calling to be heroic'.[25] When Bergman first arrived in Hollywood in 1939, she had confided her ambition to studio producer David O. Selznick; he said that the French heroine was not a suitable subject while France and Britain were allied in the war against Hitler. But she got wind of the fact that Anderson was working on his own version of Joan's story. He began writing the play in 1942, completed the script late in 1944, and started protracted negotiations with Bergman: 'I know ... that you are making a considerable financial sacrifice in taking time from pictures to do a play in New York,' he wrote, 'and that you would not act in the play at all if you were not confident that you would play the same role in the picture.'[26] It was originally scheduled for production in the autumn of 1945, with Raymond Massey, a well-established, Canadian-born film and theatre actor, playing Jimmy Masters. But Bergman was not then available, as she was working with Alfred Hitchcock by that time, on *Spellbound* and then *Notorious*. Eventually, she signed with the Playwrights' Company (established by Anderson, with several other writers, to present their plays), committing herself to seven months on Broadway. By the spring of 1946, Raymond Massey's name was no longer in the frame, and Fredric March was being considered. He turned it down, as he was about to appear in Ruth Gordon's *Years Ago*, for which he won a Tony Award. Before Sam appeared to audition, Margo Jones had assumed she needed a well-established actor in his fifties, such as those two.

Anderson, too, was particularly anxious that the play should do well. He had not had a major success since *Key Largo* in 1939, and his last play, *Truckline Café*, had flopped earlier in the year. At first rejected by the Playwrights' Company, it was eventually produced by Harold Clurman and Elia Kazan, in association with the Playwrights' Company, but received such appalling reviews that it closed after thirteen performances.

Rehearsals began, and at first all went well. The company rehearsed in the lounge area of one Broadway theatre, and on the stage of another, on the set of a different play. Margo Jones was an experienced director. She had worked on the Federal Theatre Project, travelled to Russia to see the work of the Moscow Art Theatre, and worked in the Drama Department at the University of Texas, where she had directed one of Anderson's plays. After the success of *The Glass Menagerie*, she had directed *On Whitman Avenue*, the first play to tackle the problem of racial discrimination, being concerned with a black family who move into a white neighbourhood and are eventually forced out. She was happy with her new project, telling Bergman: 'somehow I feel that I was born to work on this with you and Max and Sam and all the others'.[27] Sam began by being in awe of Bergman, her beauty and her spirituality, but found her so un-starlike in her behaviour, that she rapidly put him at ease.

But there were tensions from the beginning. Margo Jones was already aware that Bergman wanted Anderson to rework the script into a story primarily about Joan, reducing the play-within-the-play concept which had been his original inspiration. She had very firm ideas about the character. (Later, she would tell Bernard Shaw that he did not understand Joan as she did.) She and her assistant, Ruth Roberts, persuaded Anderson to make changes about which he was uneasy. She intimidated Jones. Whenever she asked the director how a scene should be played, Jones told her she was 'perfect', when in fact Bergman really wanted someone to help her and be objective. Jones also had some difficulty with the character Sam was playing; Jimmy Masters' 'hard-nosed philosophy and aggressive personality' was unlike her own 'collaborative, gentler approach'.[28]

At the end of October (by which time the play had been retitled *Joan of Lorraine),* the company arrived in Washington DC for a three-week pre-Broadway try-out. They were to play in the Lisner Auditorium of George Washington University. But, just as when Paul Robeson was touring *Othello,* the theatre adhered to the city's Jim Crow policy, enforcing racial segregation; black theatregoers would be separately accommodated to see the production. When the company was asked to do a preview for war veterans, it was forbidden, because the audience would have been racially mixed. The theatre and the company were at loggerheads. Anderson was in favour of some sort of compromise, but Bergman, encouraged by Sam, showed her indignation. On the opening night the theatre was picketed by the Committee for Racial Democracy and by members of Equity, the actors' union. But when Bergman emerged from the stage door, there were others who spat on her and called her 'nigger lover'.

Audiences found the play confusing, with the actors' abrupt transitions from modern characters in rehearsal to historic figures in the Joan story. One critic found the play boring. The theatre was cavernous, and Bergman had problems projecting her voice. Rehearsals continued during the day, and she grew increasingly nervous as the Broadway opening approached. Used to strong, male directors who were sure of what they wanted, she found

Margo Jones's approach unhelpful. Sam told Margo Jones's biographer that she was 'the kind of director who allowed actors to blossom as they felt', while Anderson's son, who was stage-managing, saw that she was having problems working with the two stars, and observed that 'she didn't push actors around'.[29] Bergman began to rely more and more on Sam's guidance, which he was very willing to give. He was playing the part of a tough, decisive director; actor and character began to merge. When one week of try-outs remained, Anderson, on behalf of the Playwrights' Company, fired Jones and put Sam and his own son in charge. He may have consulted Bergman, though she later claimed to have been shocked at the decision. Sam was also shocked. He called Jones and later described the phone conversation:

'Look, I don't want to do this if you feel it would be disloyal to you.'

'What's the difference? … They've fired me. I think it's wonderful that you should do it.'

And he admitted 'For me, it was an incredible opportunity'.[30]

Margo Jones's name remained in the programme and on the theatre marquee. Her absence from New York was explained as a family emergency which had called her away, but the theatre grapevine quickly carried the news that she had been fired. When the play opened on Broadway in November, Brooks Atkinson wrote in the *New York Times* that 'Under Margo Jones's direction, the performance makes fascinating use of the form of the play', but Howard Barnes, in the *New York Herald Tribune*, wrote that 'the staging of the two acts has been adroit, whether accomplished by Margo Jones, or Sam Wanamaker, who took over for her.'[31] Bergman was still sometimes criticized for inaudibility, but audiences flocked to see her, and she won a Tony Award. Margo Jones returned to Texas, where she later made her mark, establishing the first resident regional company in the US, in a theatre-in-the-round in Dallas.

Joan of Lorraine ran successfully for the seven months Bergman had agreed. Sam continued to work with her every week, so that, he claimed, 'She got rave reviews from the critics after opening night – but she was twice as good when the show closed'.[32] Exactly how close they became is a matter of conjecture; she herself was in love with the photographer Robert Capa at the time.

Towards the end of the run they recorded *Still Life* together for Theatre Guild on the Air, Noël Coward's one-act play about the affair of a married couple, later filmed as *Brief Encounter*. The script by Eric Barnouw transferred the setting from an English provincial town to New York. The broadcast survives in an amateur recording; Sam gives a competent reading, but does not catch the poignancy of the situation as well as Bergman.

As Bergman's leading man, Sam had suddenly become a 'success story'. Shana Ager, an up-and-coming journalist, interviewed him in the carriage-house apartment, where she met four-year-old Abby, 'wearing a cartridge belt buckled around her corduroy overalls', who shot at her with a Roy Rogers gun. Sam introduced 'My wife Charlotte Holland, the best actress in radio. As soon as she gets a part, she'll be the best actress on Broadway'. He was conscious that his career was significantly outstripping hers, and that his relationship with Bergman was close. Flattered by the attention, he waxed lyrical about the number of offers he had had. In Hollywood, Cagney Productions, Enterprise Pictures, Paramount and Warner Brothers were all asking for him, even before giving him a screen test. There were several offers to direct on Broadway, and he had been invited to become a partner in a 'large Broadway producing organization'. He talked about his idea of directing: 'Max [Anderson] once used an apt word for it *orchestration* ... Putting a play together so that everything is in relation to one basic theme played.' He went on to explain how the character Jimmy Masters 'has to compromise with the inadequacies and corrupt commercialism of the theater; but he won't compromise his basic beliefs on how the play should be done.' On the prospect of working in films, he maintained 'I'm not going to allow myself to get into the machinery of Hollywood. That contaminates you. I don't want to get soggy with that corruption.'[33]

Nevertheless, it was Hollywood that tempted him. Many of the possibilities he described were no doubt still at the discussion stage. But one became a genuine offer from Harry Warner, of Warner Brothers. In July 1947, Sam and Charlotte set off for Los Angeles, where he was to star in his first film, opposite Lilli Palmer.

3

Good Times, Bad Times

The theme of Sam's first film chimed with his family history. *My Girl Tisa* was about a Jewish immigrant, Tisa Kepes, newly arrived in New York at the beginning of the century. She lives in a boarding-house, where, amongst other residents, she meets a bright young lawyer who, despite being attracted to her, is determined not to get married. Tisa works in a sweatshop, where she is bullied by the owner. She is trying to bring her father to America, but is cheated by a corrupt travel agent. The young lawyer tries ineffectually to help, while falling in love with her. A happy ending is brought about in the form of a 'deus ex machina', when President Theodore Roosevelt appears at an opportune moment and just happens to overhear the inspiring words about America spoken by the heroine: 'Anything a man can imagine is possible'.

Although the film did not explore its themes very deeply, it was a warm-hearted tale and had a strong cast. When Sam looked back on his first film role, as Mark Denek, the young lawyer, he was critical of his performance, claiming that he was 'no film actor' at the time, that he had paid no attention to camera angles, and that 'The results were less than flattering'.[1] Nevertheless, it showed him off as energetic and charming. His co-star, young, wide-eyed Lilli Palmer, was herself a Jewish refugee from Hitler's Germany. She had begun a film career in England, married Rex Harrison, and followed him to Hollywood, when he starred in *Anna and the King of Siam*. She had already made two films for Warner Brothers, before she was cast in *My Girl Tisa*. The part of Mrs Faludi, the landlady, was played by Stella Adler, doyenne of the Group Theatre, and the sweatshop owner, who, Scrooge-like, is reformed by the end of the film, was Akim Tamiroff, a skilful character actor who had already been twice nominated for an Oscar as Best Supporting Actor.

Sam, Charlotte and Abby now had family in Hollywood. His brother Bill had married another Tuley High School graduate during the war, and when his wife's family moved to Los Angeles, they settled there too, and he restarted his medical career. Morris had returned to Hart, Schaffner and

Marx to help make wartime uniforms, while still trading as a bookseller. When Molly's father died, in 1946, Sam persuaded his parents they should make the move too, with his grandmother, away from the grime and harsh winters of Chicago, to the Californian sunshine. Morris (spelling his name as 'Maurice' by this time) continued in the book trade but also worked for his union, transferring his support to the International Ladies' Garment Workers' Union (ILGWU), and becoming Chairman of his local group in Los Angeles. Molly and he bought a Spanish-style house in West Hollywood, while Bill and his wife Edith lived in Beverley Hills. Sam and Charlotte rented a house in Foothill Boulevard, part of the historic Route 66, running along the foothills of the San Gabriel and San Barnardino Mountains.

Soon after Sam and Charlotte arrived, at the end of July 1947, they attended an important opening night in Hollywood, the American premiere of Bertolt Brecht's play, *Galileo*. Sam was not impressed by what he considered 'this Brecht nonsense'. The idea of breaking the illusion that naturalistic theatre strove to create, of wanting the audience to judge, rather than to feel, seemed anathema to him. He did not yet see the connection between Brecht's theatre and the work of Stage for Action. The English actor Charles Laughton was playing Galileo, and the production was ostensibly directed by Sam's old colleague, Joe Losey, who had first met the writer when visiting Germany before the war. Brecht's first choice as director had been Orson Welles, who had pulled out. Brecht then considered Harold Clurman and Elia Kazan, but eventually settled on Losey. However, the production turned out to be a Brecht/Laughton collaboration, and Losey was kept very much on the sidelines. Brecht's behaviour was described as 'consistently objectionable and outrageous ... harsh, intolerant and, often, brutal and abusive. The words *scheiss* and *shit* were foremost in his vocabulary.'[2] Not a man whom Sam could envisage working with.

When the filming of *My Girl Tisa* was finished, Sam took his family back to New York. Although he was keen to make more films, he was determined not to get sucked into the Hollywood studio system, by which contracted artists had to accept what casting they were given, and could be loaned out to other companies, with very little choice in the matter. He wanted to explore the options on offer on Broadway, and especially, to direct as well as act.

But before anything materialized, public events began to occupy the attention of Sam and many of his friends and colleagues. In September

1947, the House Un-American Activities Committee (HUAC) (which had been formed in 1938), put forty-three members of the cinema industry on a witness list. They were to go before the Committee and give evidence on the suspected infiltration of Hollywood by Communists. That spring, Bernard Baruch (advisor to Woodrow Wilson, Franklin D Roosevelt and Harold S Truman) had said in a speech that the country was in the middle of a 'cold war', and journalist Walter Lippman had popularized the term in his book, *The Cold War,* describing the threat posed to the West by the Soviet Union. Pro-Russian sentiments which had been encouraged during the war, when anti-Communistic propaganda was largely silenced, were now evidence of dangerous opinions and must be crushed. Sam described the swift turnaround:

> The war over, with bewildering speed came Churchill's Iron Curtain speech; our great heroic war allies (Stalingrad, Sevastopol, the siege of Leningrad) having lost ten million people against our common foe, instantly became our arch-enemy, replacing Hitler, Mussolini and the Japanese.[3]

Of those asked to give evidence, nineteen refused. Eleven of them were summoned to Washington. Leading figures in Hollywood, including Humphrey Bogart, Lauren Bacall, Danny Kaye and many other stars, formed the Committee for the First Amendment, and flew to Washington to support the eleven and protest the HUAC hearings. The weekend between hearings, Sam attended a conference in New York on 'Cultural Freedom and Civil Liberties'. With actor Larry Parks and director Irving Pichel, Sam lightened the atmosphere with a sketch entitled 'Drums of Silence', parodying the 'supine posture' of the studio heads.[4] Then he flew to Washington. He is clearly visible in a photograph taken at the hearing on 30 October, sitting behind Bogart and Bacall, his friend Ralph Alswang standing on the sidelines. Ten of those summoned refused to testify, pleading their First Amendment rights to freedom of speech. The eleventh was Brecht, who left America the next day, and never returned. Humphrey Bogart was one of several who became disillusioned when he discovered that most of those summoned either were indeed, or had been, members of the Communist Party. He felt he had supported them under false pretences. Sam, as a signed-up Communist himself, was under no misapprehension. But Charlotte and he were among many who had let their party membership lapse. They had never wished to undermine the American government, but simply to bring about a fair, democratic society, without racial discrimination or gross inequality.

Events moved swiftly. Towards the end of the hearings, the president of the American Motion Pictures Producers (AMPP) declared that he would never 'employ any proven or admitted Communist because they are just a disruptive force and I don't want them around.'⁵ On 17 November, the Screen Actors Guild voted to make its officers swear a pledge asserting each was not a Communist. On 24 November, the House of Representatives approved citations against the 'Hollywood Ten', as they came be called. The following day, the president of AMPP issued the 'Waldorf Statement', at the end of a closed-door meeting by forty-eight industry executives, held at the Waldorf-Astoria in New York. It included the sentence: 'We will not knowingly employ a Communist or a member of any party or group which advocates the overthrow of the Government of the United States by force or illegal or unconstitutional methods.'⁶ The Hollywood 'blacklist' was now put into effect, although the studio heads never admitted its existence, or gave it as a reason not to employ a director, screenwriter, actor or technician.

Sam began working on a new theatre play closely connected with recent events. The author, Emmet Lavery, lived and worked in Hollywood and was President of the Screenwriters Guild; he had failed in his attempt to enter Congress as a Democrat, and decided to write a political play. *The Gentleman from Athens* was about a West Coast roughneck, who is catapulted into the US Congress, where he promotes the idea of world government. (The title referred to a town in Los Angeles County, but also carried connotations of Socrates). Lela Rogers, mother of Ginger Rogers, and well-known to be a Red-baiter, took part in an ABC radio discussion and described his play as a 'Communist tract', even though she had not read it. Lavery sued her and the ABC producer for slander and libel, and won, but most of the play's backers withdrew their support. Lavery himself was called before HUAC the day before the Hollywood Ten. As a lawyer, he thought that it was ill-advised to plead the First Amendment. He himself charmed the Committee with his 'frank' and 'refreshing' comments. He explained that he was not, and had never been a member of the Communist Party. 'I think the problems of all citizens and this Congress is how to make people aware of the love that they have for America.'⁷

The would-be producer of *The Gentleman of Athens*, Martin Gosch, set about finding new backing, and presenting it on Broadway. He invited Sam to direct. They hired Anthony Quinn for the lead, at that time an experienced film actor who had not yet acted on Broadway. Sam asked his friend Ralph Alswang to design. After leaving Chicago, Alswang had studied under Robert Edmond Jones, and had recently designed the scenery for a revival of *Lysistrata*. After an out-of-town try-out, the production opened at the Mansfield Theatre on Broadway in a particularly cold December. The theatre had fallen into relative disuse, and was about to be leased to CBS for their work in the fast-developing medium of television. Brooks Atkinson, writing in *The New York Times*, found the play formulaic and full of sentimentalities, though he felt the author's heart was in the right place: 'If Mrs Lela Rogers really did think it was subversive, she must have been overeating red herring'.[8] The production was a resounding flop, playing for only seven performances, but at least Sam had made his debut as a Broadway director, instead of simply playing the part of one.

While he was looking for his next employment, Charlotte and Sam began to attend classes at the newly formed Actors Studio. It was founded by Elia Kazan, Cheryl Crawford and Robert Lewis, all of whom had been active in the Group Theatre. Classes took place in the Actors Kitchen and Lounge on W48th Street, a centre that offered meals to needy actors. At last, they could continue to work on Stanislavsky's system, to which David Itkin had introduced them at the Goodman. At that time, work at the Studio was sometimes ridiculed for its emphasis on internal methods of preparation, including sensory recall, imagination and improvisation, but Sam found that these methods helped to strengthen the believability of his work. He particularly enjoyed classes with Bob Lewis, who took a balanced approach to actor-training, reminding his students that Stanislavsky encouraged external preparation as well – speech, gesture and movement. Bob Lewis himself was impressed with Sam's diligence; he often prepared *two* scenes for class, with different acting partners.

The work of erstwhile Group Theatre members was prominent that season. *The Big Knife*, Clifford Odets' cynical take on Hollywood, was playing. Kazan's production of Tennessee Williams' *A Streetcar Named Desire* went into rehearsal just as the Studio opened, and was even more successful than *A Glass Menagerie*. Marlon Brando, hardly known until then, shot to stardom with his performance as Stanley Kowalski, and he later gave much credit to Kazan, and to Stella Adler, with whom he had studied. Jessica Tandy won a Tony Award as Blanche DuBois, and Karl Malden, Sam and Charlotte's old colleague from the Goodman, played Mitch. Their friend Blanche Zohar enjoyed explaining that Williams had named both sisters in the play after her, 'Zohar' meaning 'star' or 'Stella'.

The Wanamaker family had remained on close terms with the Carpenters, but they had all had to leave the carriage-house, when the property was bought by a developer. The household, consisting of Sam, Charlotte, Abby,

Zoe, Aggie the housekeeper, and Gussie, a French poodle, moved into a maisonette at 105 East 53rd Street, between Park and Lexington Avenues. Bedrooms and bathrooms were on the top floor, dining room, sitting room and kitchen on the lower floor. Charlotte branched out into interior décor, painting Abby's room in light blue, and tracing two plumed horses facing each on the wall by her bed.

Sam and Cliff began to look for a country retreat outside the city. They found what they were looking for in Long Mountain, New Milford, Connecticut. Sam and Charlotte took the three-bedroom farmhouse and an acre surrounding it, Cliff and Mac converted the barn and took an acre surrounding it, while the two couples held the remaining twenty acres in common. They all enjoyed escaping from New York. Driving towards the property, along a bumpy dirt road, in an old green, soft-sprung station wagon, Sam took delight in speeding towards each rise, so that he and his passengers flew up in the air, heads touching the roof, amid gales of laughter and shouts of 'Thank you Mam'. A city girl, Charlotte was not too successful at growing vegetables, but she continued to develop her original approach to interior design, painting the living-room floor like a Jackson Pollock painting, with a navy-blue ground, covered in multi-coloured drips and spatters. It was a place to relax and unwind from city life. Once, during a storm, Abby remembered Sam stripping down to his underwear and taking a shower in the run-off from the roof, his roars of laughter competing with the thunder. The surrounding countryside was wild and unkempt. Candlewood, a large manmade lake, was close enough for the children to visit. The actor Fredric March and his wife lived nearby, as well as the widow of sports writer Ring Lardner. Arthur Miller was not far away, as well as 'several other left-leaning writers, lawyers and doctors,' as Cliff put it. 'Thus we enjoyed a neighbourhood *not* consisting of individuals who might look on us with skepticism and suspicion.'[9]

In the the autumn of 1948, Sam was invited to direct *Goodbye, My Fancy,* a comedy by Fay Kanin, who co-wrote screenplays with her husband Michael Kanin. The play was to be produced by Michael Kanin in association with Richard Aldrich and Richard Myers, both well-established Broadway producers. Sam had been wanting to work with Richard Aldrich for some time. When he had told a journalist, a year or so earlier, that he had been invited to become a partner in a 'large Broadway producing organization', he was thinking of discussions he had had with Aldrich, about setting up a repertory group that would plan for a whole season of classical plays, like the Old Vic Company in England, which Aldrich had been instrumental in bringing to New York. In 1945, Aldrich had established a new company, Theatre Incorporated, in order to mount a revival of *Pygmalion,* starring his wife, Gertrude Lawrence, as Eliza Doolittle, with Raymond Massey as Henry Higgins, directed by the English actor, Cedric Hardwicke. The Old Vic tour of 1946 had been a co-production with Theatre Incorporated, and Aldrich followed this with a production of *Playboy of the Western World,* directed by Guthrie McClintic, who worked in partnership with his wife, Katherine Cornell, a leading American actress. By the time Sam returned from Hollywood, Aldrich felt that Theatre Incorporated had outlived its usefulness. Early in 1948, he produced one more revival under its auspices, a co-production of *Volpone,* starring José Ferrer. He then went into partnership with Richard Myers, with whom he had worked before, to bring the Gate Theatre over from Dublin. Sam hoped to revive Aldrich's interest in the idea of an American repertory company, but meanwhile, directing *Goodbye, My Fancy,* was another step up in his Broadway career.

The star was to be Madeleine Carroll, whose acquaintance Sam had made during the run of *Joan of Lorraine.* She was an English actress who had acted in Hitchcock's *The 39 Steps* and then gone to Hollywood. During the war, she had given up her career when her sister was killed in the London Blitz, working for the Red Cross, and then in a hospital in Italy where she treated wounded American airmen. She resumed her acting career in 1947, and this play was her Broadway debut. Like *The Gentleman from Athens,* it had a political theme, but was skilfully written, and much more lighthearted.

Goodbye, My Fancy concerned a Congresswoman who returns to her *alma mater* to receive an honorary degree, where she re-encounters the professor she was in love with, when a student. A controversial film which she has made about the horrors of war is to be shown, but a reactionary trustee cancels the showing. The professor fails to stand up to him, and after a series of misunderstandings, she realizes that she has grown to love the *Life* photographer who has followed her to the college. Donald Oenslager designed. Sam played the photographer himself, as well as directing. Combining the roles of actor and director meant that he was actively involved in trying to bring out the best that the actors could achieve, though it made technical rehearsals complicated. This time he had a success on his hands. The play opened at the Morosco Theatre and transferred to the Fulton in February 1949.

Charlotte was pregnant again, but this was not a period of happiness. During her pregnancy, she was devastated to discover that Sam had restarted his affair with Jan Sterling, his co-star in *This Shall Not Pass.* It was the first big crisis in Sam's marriage. He had hoped it was possible to carry on the liaison without Charlotte knowing, since he had no wish to hurt her or to risk their relationship, which was essential to him. Although Charlotte continued to be in demand for radio drama, her career had not kept up with his; she had begun to focus more and more on supporting and encouraging Sam in new ventures. Once she had recovered from the shock, she summoned the determination to give him an ultimatum. He promised to end the affair, and fortunately for her, this coincided with a career opportunity for him that would take them both away, not just from New York, but from America altogether. Sterling moved to Los Angeles, where she started a successful Hollywood career and, the following year, became the fifth wife of the actor Paul Douglas.

Sam was cast in a film which was to be shot in England. One of the 'Hollywood Ten', the director Edward Dmytryk, had moved there while his appeal was being heard, and had already made one film there. Now he was to co-produce and direct a screen adaptation of *Christ in Concrete*, a 1939 novel by Pietro di Donato, son of an Italian immigrant, about his father's life as a construction worker during the Depression. It was a project of Rod E Geiger, producer of Italian director Roberto Rossellini's film *Paisa*. Geiger had hoped to get Rossellini over to Hollywood to make it, but Rossellini had not taken up the offer. Once Dmytryk was involved, no Hollywood studio would touch the project. Geiger persuaded J. Arthur Rank in England to take it on, with Dmytryk directing it there, despite its New York setting. The newly founded National Film Finance Corporation (NFFC), designed to encourage British film production, gave it their support, since the film would be made with a predominantly British crew.

Sam was offered the leading part of Geremio, a more exciting and demanding role than he had played in his first film. The story concerns Geremio's marriage to a young Italian woman who emigrates to marry him, sight unseen. Her only proviso is that they should have a house to live in. He makes a down payment on a house that allows them to spend their first married nights there, only telling her the truth at the end of the honeymoon. Over the years, he struggles to earn the money to buy the house. His marriage deteriorates. As the Depression deepens, he commits his gang to a building project that is financed too cheaply to be a safe work place. At the point when he recognizes his error, the building collapses, and he is buried in a deluge of wet concrete, the day of his death being Good Friday. The compensation his widow is owed allows her to buy the house.

Sam gave in his notice to the company of *Goodbye, My Fancy*, which continued its successful run. He set up a meeting with Pietro Di Donato, to learn the craft of bricklaying. But his eye was still on his aim of creating a repertory company. In February 1949, he gave an interview to George Freedley, critic on the *Morning Telegraph*, describing the 'Repertory Group' he had set up, which, he said, had merged with Theatre Incorporated. No such Group was actually established, and it was probably no more than a scheme dreamed up in late-night discussions with Aldrich, José Ferrer and any actor or director Sam had managed to buttonhole. It indicates the scale of his ambition by this time; his eloquence was seductive:

> Our idea is to use stars who can get a chance to play what they like among the classics. They'll also play a supporting role with another star and we'll engage people on a season's basis. Helen Hayes was simply delighted with the idea. She's all for it, and so are the Marches [Fredric and his wife Florence Eldridge]. We've approached Guthrie McClintic both for himself as a director, and his wife Katharine Cornell. We want every top person who is willing to work with us and free themselves from the restraint of the long run, or, what is much worse, the weariness of long idleness, when no suitable new script can be found.

He said that he wanted to involve the company at La Jolla Playhouse in California, which Gregory Peck, Dorothy McGuire and Mel Ferrer had founded in 1947. '... and we'll welcome any European star who'd like to try his wings in America and who can play in English. This will be a completely flexible theater and we want to grow as we progress.' He said that he had already approached some scene designers. That probably meant he had discussed his ideas with his friend, Ralph Alswang. His last words to Freedley showed that he was well aware of the financial risk involved in mounting a whole season of classical revivals. He had already begun to consider how to negotiate with IATS, the union for stage employees: '... we are going to pay a call on the stagehands and electricians and ask them to guide us in the least expensive way of producing plays economically on the technical side.' [10]

In March, Sam was a panel speaker at the Waldorf Astoria Peace Conference, organised by the National Council of the Arts, Sciences and Professions. It was a large gathering of literary and artistic men and women, including Arthur Miller, fresh from his own first Broadway success, *All My Sons*, together with Lillian Hellman, Clifford Odets, Aaron Copland and Paul Robeson. Dmitri Shostakovich came from the Soviet Union and had the unhappy experience of trying not to compromise his position when asked if he approved of *Pravda's* denunciation of Igor Stravinsky and other composers. The appeals lodged by the Hollywood Ten had not yet been heard by the Supreme Court, and most people attending the Conference were optimistic enough to believe that international co-operation was possible. But any organization or event smacking of 'peace' was now considered by HUAC, and by J Edgar Hoover, Director of the FBI, to be pro-Soviet, and therefore suspect, and it was in fact funded by the Cominform, the Soviet Union's Communist Infomation Bureau. FBI surveillance of Sam's activities may have started then.

In May, Charlotte gave birth to their second daughter, Zoë. She took a break from her radio work, and as soon as she, Abby and the baby were ready to travel, the whole family flew off to London, far away from politics, the extra-marital affair, and Broadway theatre.

Sam rented a house a short drive away from Denham Studios, Buckinghamshire, where *Christ in Concrete* was shot. They enjoyed their first English spring, drinking in the scent of wisteria that festooned the house, while seven-year-old Abby tried to tame the stubborn donkey in the field in front.

Dmytryk had assembled a strong team for the film. Sam and Charlotte made friends with Ben Barzman, who wrote the screenplay, and his wife Norma, both of whom had been members of the Communist-leaning fraternity in Hollywood. The construction crew had to create the streets and buildings of New York in the studio, including 'Little Italy'. The cast was international. Lea Padovani, an Italian film actress, played the leading part of Annunziata. She had just left Paris, after a blazing row with her lover, Orson Welles, for whom she had been playing Desdemona in his film of *Othello*. Bonar Colleano, a New Yorker who had lived in England since before the war, played one of the bricklaying gang. (Born Bonar Sullivan, he had taken his stage name from his Australian circus family.) Kathleen Ryan, a beautiful Irish actress, played the woman that Geremio turns to, in compensation for his unhappy marriage. Sid James, a Jewish actor originally from South Africa, who would make later make his name in British comedy, played Murdin, the unscrupulous building contractor.

When Sam was not filming, they explored England, enjoying the gentler pace of life it offered. London itself, though impressive, was a bleak city. There were many bomb sites; petrol and much foodstuff was still rationed; the buildings were drab; few houses had central heating. But clothing had just come off ration, and the new National Health Service was in its first year of operation. Sam was in sympathy with much that Attlee's Labour government was doing, including the establishment of the Arts Council of Great Britain, offering government-funded grants.

One expedition that Sam made in London became iconic in his life history – his search for the original Globe theatre. He recounted at least two versions of the story. In one, he crosses the river on foot, map in hand, expecting at any moment to see the shape of the playhouse rise up on the river bank; in another, he leaps into a cab and asks to be taken to Shakespeare's Globe, the taxi driver's brow furrows, he consults his map (what self-respecting London cabbie carried a map?), shakes his head and deposits Sam on the doorstep of the Anchor Inn on the riverside. The essential part of the story was his surprise and disappointment at finding no playhouse, only a commemorative black plaque erected by the Shakespeare Reading Society, on the wall of a brewery, in a drab street of Dickensian warehouses, a block away from the river.

As far as the living theatre, the surprise success of the 1949 West End season was Christopher Fry's verse play *The Lady's Not for Burning*, directed by John Gielgud, with the young Richard Burton and Claire Bloom. The Old Vic theatre in Waterloo had not yet re-opened since receiving a direct hit during the Blitz, but its Company was enjoying its last season at the New Theatre, under the direction of Sir Laurence Olivier, even though he and Sir Ralph Richardson had both been given notice by the Old Vic board, during their absence the previous year. Olivier was again playing Richard III, with Vivien Leigh as Lady Anne, and Sir Peter Teazle in *The School for Scandal*, with Vivien Leigh as Lady Teazle, and she was playing the lead in Jean Anouilh's *Antigone*. American drama in the West End was represented by *The Heiress*, adapted from Henry James' story, *Washington Square*, which had been a Broadway hit the previous year. John Gielgud had taken over the London production, which starred Peggy Ashcroft and Ralph Richardson. Sam was strengthened in his enthusiasm for the idea of a seasonal company. If he looked for plays of more social significance, there was the Unity Theatre, the left-wing company in which Paul Robeson had acted before the war, and which had presented the British premiere of Odets' *Waiting for Lefty*.

Olivier was in the throes of setting up his own production company, and planning the first London production of *A Streetcar Named Desire*, to star Vivien Leigh as Blanche DuBois. (The year before, John Gielgud had directed *The Glass Menagerie*, the first of Williams' plays to be produced in London, starring Helen Hayes.) Olivier approached Sam about playing Stanley Kowalski, but he turned down the idea, claiming that he could not compete with Marlon Brando, who had made such a stir playing the part on Broadway. Bonar Colleano was cast instead. He was eager to get back to New York, to pursue his idea of forming a company.

Charlotte and Sam were delighted with their first stay in England, and began to think that they would like their girls to be educated there. Once the filming of *Christ in Concrete* was over, they wanted to see more of Europe, and set off across the Channel with Abby, Zoë and a nanny, all of whom they deposited in a hotel in Cannes, while they went sightseeing in France and Italy. Sam felt at home in Europe straightaway, finding a sense of connection with his parents' homeland to the east. In October the family took ship in Genoa and sailed back to New York.

Soon after their return, Sam was drawn back into politics when he spoke at a rally organized by the National Council of the Arts, Sciences and Professions, to protest against the 'Foley Square Convictions' – twelve members of the CPUSA's National Committee, convicted under the Smith Act, the statute that imposed penalties on those who advocated violent overthrow of the government.

Back in New York, *Goodbye, My Fancy* was still running, but the producers, Richard Aldrich and Richard Myers, had another project for Sam, and there was no suggestion that he should rejoin the cast. They invited him to direct the English actor, Sir Cedric Hardwicke, in a revival of Bernard Shaw's *Caesar and Cleopatra*. He flew to Hollywood, to meet Sir Cedric, whose career spanned both sides of the Atlantic. He was immediately apprehensive, as it was obvious that that gentleman regarded the project entirely as his own, and knew exactly how it should be directed. Hardwicke had already played Caesar over twenty years earlier, as well as appearing in *Pygmalion*, *The Apple Cart*, *Candida*, *Too True To Be Good* and *Don Juan in Hell*. He had been in touch with Shaw, who had given permission for the revival, and had written 'But you must not produce [still the English term for 'direct'] as well as act. You can of course tell the producer all about the original stage business; but producing is the ruin of an actor; instead of thinking about his own part he watches the others all the time and ceases to be an actor.'[11]

The two Richards were offering Sam $3000, hard to turn down, and Sam discovered that Lilli Palmer, his co-star, was to play Cleopatra. Hardwicke had first thought of Vivien Leigh, as she had played the role in the 1945 film, but she was already filming *Streetcar* opposite Marlon Brando. Lilli Palmer had expressed an interest, had paid a call on Bernard Shaw, and captivated him. Sam signed the contract, and set about planning the production. The set and costumes were designed by Rolf Gerard, a British designer of German origin. He had designed *Romeo and Juliet* for the young Peter Brook, at the Shakespeare Memorial Theatre in Stratford-upon-Avon; it was his first American assignment, and he would soon be snapped up by Rudolf Byng to design for the Metropolitan Opera. The lighting designer was Jean Rosenthal, a pioneer in this field. Sam commissioned original music from Irma Jurist, a friend of his, and cast Cliff Carpenter in a minor role. He hoped to create an original and exciting re-interpretation of the play, first performed in 1899.

By the second day of rehearsal, Sam knew the collaboration was not going to work. He was interested in exploring the modern relevance of Shaw's play, and did not wish to hear about the 'original stage business'. When Sir Cedric first heard the incidental music, he took issue with it. His version of events did not refer to Sam by name:

> In its abstract dissonances, I detected here and there the strains of Elgar's *Land of Hope and Glory*, which forever typifies British imperialism of days gone by. I asked what, if anything, was its significance. "I want," replied the gentleman who had ordered the score, "to show the parallel between the decadence of Ptolemy's court and the present decadence of the British Empire."[12]

The crisis came when Sam walked into rehearsal one day, found Sir Cedric coaching Lilli Palmer and blew his top. He knew that he could not win in any altercation, and decided to quit. Later, he wrote to Richard Aldrich: '...faced with a choice of standing by Hardwick[e] or me, ... you as producers could only stand by Hardwick[e], since your whole production depended on his remaining with the play.'[13] Sir Cedric diplomatically told the press: 'He did splendid work and he is an extremely talented and inventive director.'[14] He later recorded 'I had to disregard my mentor's warnings ... and proceed to direct myself'.[15]

Sam salvaged his pride by moving on straightaway to direct the company that was preparing *Goodbye, My Fancy* for Chicago. *Caesar and Cleopatra* opened in December 1949, and ran until April 1950. Brooks Atkinson wrote an unfavourable review in the *New York Times,* but Howard Barnes in the *New York Herald Tribune* found it 'a splendid revival.'[16] It lost money, and Aldrich wrote later: 'We [Gertrude Lawrence and I] have always known how talented you were and we are convinced that if you'd been a little older and exerted a little more self-control, and completed the direction ... we would have had a real financial and artistic success on our hands.'[17]

Early in 1950, the Supreme Court rejected the appeals of the Hollywood Ten, including Edward Dmytryk. They began serving prison sentences of varying lengths. When *Christ in Concrete* was finally released, the American Legion threatened to boycott theatres which showed the film. Retitled *Salt of the Devil*, it was shown only in a few art cinemas. In Britain, retitled *Give Us This Day*, since the film censor had forbidden the word 'Christ' in a title, it created little stir; perhaps audiences in austerity Britain were looking for lighter entertainment. It is a compelling and atmospheric film, drawing attention to the poverty of the Depression, and the exploitation of immigrant workers. It has since received favourable comment as an example of 'film noir'. The final image of Sam's disappearing face, as Geremio is sucked down into the concrete is powerful. Sam counted it amongst his best performances.

As the year progressed, the situation regarding the 'blacklist' worsened. Fear of 'Reds' had been exacerbated by the creation of the People's Republic of China the previous autumn. Senator Joe McCarthy began his rise to prominence. June 1950 saw, besides the outbreak of the Korean War, the publication of *Red Channels: the Report of Communist Influence in Radio and Television*, which claimed to identify all those working in the media who had Communist leanings. It was the product of *Counterattack, The Newsletter of Facts to Combat Communism*, which singled out a number of terms such as 'academic freedom', 'civil rights', 'peace' and the H-bomb, subjects perfectly legitimate in themselves but which were considered to have been 'cleverly exploited in dramatic treatments which point up current Communist goals'. *Red Channels* listed 151 of what Eric Barnouw, the historian of American radio, called 'the most talented and admired people in the industry'.[18] Sam's name was on the list, as well as many with whom he was already associated, including: Stella Adler, Morris Carnovsky, Aaron Copland, Arthur Miller and Margaret Webster.

The 'citations' listed against Sam included the following:

- that he had sponsored a rally to defend the Communist writer Howard Fast, sentenced for contempt of Congress;
- that he had spoken at a Scientific and Cultural Conference for World Peace;
- that he had signed a statement to abolish HUAC;
- that he had spoken at a rally against the 'Foley Square convictions';
- that he had signed a petition to the Supreme Court, to review the conviction of Dalton Trumbo and John Howard Lawson;

When he looked back on this period, Sam said, 'I believed it was right to stand up for these people [the Hollywood Ten] because I believed in what they stood for … I felt it was my duty. Yes, I knew it might get me in a little hot water, but I didn't think it would be that serious. I never believed that what I had done was in any way inimical to the interests of the United States.'[19] Also listed against his name was that he had entertained Veterans of the Abraham Lincoln Brigade, which had fought for the Spanish Republican Army, that he had chaired a conference for the National Negro Congress, and, perhaps the clearest indication of the paranoia affecting the country, that he had supported 'People's Songs', an organization founded by folk singer Pete Seeger, and others, to 'create, promote and distribute songs of labor and the American people'.

It was now clear that work in Hollywood was out of the question, and work in radio, or in television, which he had not yet tried, might soon dry up, but Sam remained optimistic about the theatre, and was determined to continue his efforts to create a repertory company in New York. He had found a new partner for the venture in Terese Hayden, one of the founders of the Equity Library Theatre, which showcased unemployed Equity actors in classic and modern plays and musicals, performing mainly in New York public libraries. Sam knew her personally because she was in *Joan of Lorraine* for part of its run. She approached him about setting up a summer season in a Broadway theatre. Together, they founded the Festival Theatre, assisted by an 'angel', Harriet Ames, who also helped on the production side.

Sam's aspirations were huge, but his concrete plans were practical. Hayden and he approached the owner of the Fulton Theatre on West 46th Street, where *Goodbye, Fancy* had played, and persuaded him to charge a low rent during July and August, outside the main Broadway season. Sam also negotiated concessions from the theatre unions. They would mount four plays, each for two weeks, using a basic lighting plot for all four shows, so that the changeover was simple. 'We don't have to rehang the lights for each show. We just re-focus them.' He admitted that 'it has been a Herculean task in raising even a small amount of money … for there will be only a slight profit,'[20] although there was the prospect of transferring successful productions to another theatre, while the repertory continued. He hoped to mount all four plays on a total budget of $30,000. This would entail all the participants taking much smaller pay than they would normally receive. Sam had been paid $750 per week when he was playing in *Goodbye, My Fancy*, and $3000 for directing *Caesar and Cleopatra* (but had broken his contract). For the Festival Theatre, he would take $150 for directing a production. Charlotte, who was to play a small part in one of the plays, was offered $50 per week, only two-thirds of what Sam had been paid in his first Broadway show, eight years earlier. Much good will was needed to attract the quality of actor he hoped for. Howard Bay, who had designed for the Federal Theatre Project, would oversee all four set designs, and one costume designer was appointed, Paul du Pont, veteran of many Broadway productions, including *Porgy and Bess*. The scenery would all be built, painted and stored in the theatre. The top ticket price would be $3.60.

Their first offering was *Parisienne*, a translation by Ashley Dukes, an English writer, of a French comedy by Henri Becque, about a married woman who plays two lovers off against other. It had scandalized its first audiences in 1885. Sam directed, and it starred Faye Emerson, a successful film actress who had recently begun working in television, and had her own show on CBS. Her public profile was heightened by the fact she had recently married Elliott Roosevelt, son of the late President. The cast included Romney Brent, who had played the Dauphin in *Joan of Lorraine*. A critic in *The Billboard*, trade paper for entertainment industry, applauded the aims of the Festival Theatre as 'worthy', but since the premise of the play was no longer shocking to sophisticated New Yorkers, it was dismissed as a 'dull joke.' The set and costumes were elegant, it was 'impeccably acted out by a fine company' and Sam had directed 'a neat and mannered production.'[21] Such an assessment might have warranted three stars in a modern review, but since it was published *after* the two weeks of performances, it did not help the box office. Sam also directed the next play, Ibsen's *The Lady From the Sea*, with Luise Rainer in the lead, a German actress who was already a legend for having won two Oscars in the 1930s; she had then turned to the theatre, playing, among other roles, Shaw's St Joan in Washington DC in 1940. Again, the play did not please. Luise Rainer was 'eloquent and appealing' but 'The story unfolds slowly in endless talk, most of it to little purpose'.[22] Terese Hayden directed the third play, *Borned in Texas*, by Lynn Riggs, who had written *Green Grow the Lilacs*, on which *Oklahoma!* was based. It was a rewrite of a comedy he had written in 1930, and starred Anthony Quinn and Marsha Hunt, with Cliff Carpenter in the cast. The reviews were the worst of the three productions.

The fourth play was to be Strindberg's *Crimes and Crimes*, in which Sam would star, and Howard Bay would direct. But it never happened. At one point it was announced that Blanche Yurka would play opposite Sam, a film and theatre actress who had played several Ibsen roles in the 1920s; at another point it was the Swedish actress, Viveca Lindfors. Whatever casting problems underlay these conflicting announcements, the fact was that the company had run out of money. Box office receipts were too low to meet the costs. The great experiment had failed, and the Festival Theatre neither completed its first season nor mounted another. In a letter to the few investors, Hayden and Sam wrote:

> We did produce three plays for $3000. We cut production and ticket costs by a quarter of Broadway costs. Festival Theatre achieved its planned budget … with few exceptions.[23]

Sam had hoped his venture would be the start of a permanent company, such as European cities supported. The calibre of all the participants was high. He was right in his judgment that many stars were willing to join his enterprise and be paid very little, in order to play an interesting part for a short run. He had also shown his ability to direct period plays as well as new work. But the choice of plays was perhaps too wayward – none was a popular classic – and New York was not the city to try the experiment, least of all during the height of the summer. His former colleague, Margo Jones, was doing better, developing her theatre in Dallas. Only a few years later, producers would discover that they could mount plays more cheaply *off* Broadway, and, if successful, transfer to Broadway. Not for the last time in his career, Sam had put his scheme into effect too early to be successful. He needed to rethink his ambitions. Meanwhile, he offered to split the $700 deficit with Harriet Ames.

Red Channels soon meant that radio and television were closed to all those listed in it – although, before the publication had its full effect, Sam did take part in his first television play. He was now well able to earn a living in the theatre, both as actor and director. He played the pompous Major Sergius Saranoff in a revival of Shaw's *Arms and the Man* which ran at the Arena Theatre on Broadway from October 1950 to January 1951. It was directed by Richard Barr, who had also directed the production of *Volpone* that was the last venture of Richard Aldrich's Theatre Incorporated. The cast included Anne Jackson and Francis Lederer, both of whom had played for the Festival Theatre. It was the first time Sam had acted in a classical revival since drama school; his range was wider than his previous Broadway roles had suggested.

It was about this time that Sam made a new acquaintance. He was introduced to an Englishman, Jack Perry, who was visiting New York with his wife, Doris. Perry was from a Jewish family (his original name was 'Parisky'), who had emigrated from Poland to London, where he had been brought up in the East End. Like Sam's father, he had begun his career in the garment industry and now ran a successful company supplying womenswear to major retail outlets The two men took to each other immediately and began a long-lasting friendship, which soon included their wives.[24]

Richard Aldrich continued to offer him work. During the last weeks of *Arms and the Man*, Sam began directing another classic revival, Ferenc Molnár's *The Guardsman*. (It had a kind of connection with *Arms and the Man*. Shaw had been offended by the operetta, *The Chocolate Soldier*, based on his play, and so, when it was made into a film, MGM took the plot of *The Guardsman* instead, but used the same music.) Aldrich's idea for making this production commercially successful was to cast Jeannette MacDonald, who was famous for her Hollywood singing roles, in the leading part. She had left Hollywood and was widening her career to include opera. The script was adapted to make her part, originally an actress, into a singer, so that she could have some songs added. Her husband, Gene Raymond, played her fictional husband. It was a glamorous production, with Miss MacDonald's gowns by Cecil Beaton, and the nearest thing to a musical that Sam had yet attempted. It opened in Buffalo, and played to enthusiastic audiences in twenty-three cities. But poor reviews meant that Aldrich did not bring it into New York.

To keep his hand in with more serious work, Sam continued to work at the Actors Studio. Lee Strasberg had started teaching there, and was attracting actors who would later make their names in film and theatre: James Dean, Anne Bancroft, Julie Harris, Paul Newman. Strasberg did not yet have the 'guru' status he would acquire once he took charge of the Studio and became known as the 'father' of The Method. Neither Sam nor Charlotte enjoyed working with him. Actors whom Strasberg thought were wonderful struck them as poor. Sam found he had the effect of making him feel guilty: 'Whatever you did you felt was not right He destroyed the instinct in a lot of people, because in acting you have something that's yours, that you come with, and if you're always questioning that you destroy it'.[25] But he continued to believe in the need for thorough research and internal preparation in approaching a role, and to strive for spontaneity and truth 'in the moment'. Charlotte and he preferred working with Bob Lewis and Sanford Meisner, another Studio teacher. Both those two rejected Strasberg's emphasis on 'emotional memory', which required the actor to relive a personal memory that connected with their character's situation; if over-indulged, this technique drew the actor into himself to the exclusion of the other actors and the audience.

As well as taking on paid work, and continuing to study, Sam had a new project brewing. He had read Howard Fast's book, *My Glorious Brothers*, a fictional account of Judah Maccabee (Judas Maccabeus) and his brothers, who rebelled against the Hellenistic Empire that ruled Judah, eventually restoring Jewish worship in the temple at Jerusalem in 164 BCE. This was the basis of Hanukkah, or Chanukah, the Festival of Lights celebrated in the Jewish calendar every year. Fast had published his novel in 1948, at the time of the Israeli War of Independence, and the establishment of the State of Israel. Sam no longer celebrated Hanukkah, but thought that the story of the Maccabees would make a wonderful film, especially if Marlon Brando starred in it. He would get Ben Barzman to write the screenplay, Leonard Bernstein to write the music, and film it in Israel. Late in 1950, with the help of Otis Skinner Blodget, theatrical agent, son of the actress Cornelia Otis Skinner, he set up a company, Atlas Productions Inc, in partnership with Hannah Weinstein, a budding film producer. It was typical of Sam that, in his enthusiasm for *The Maccabees*, as it would be called, he did not sufficiently consider what part Howard Fast himself would play in the enterprise. In March 1951, Fast wrote with some surprise: 'I could not see the ethical correctness in your proposal that the film be made without my name, and failing that, without my material.'[26] He was not enthusiastic about the idea. He did not think the story would be 'of great political import today', nor did he think that 'any decent film could be distributed in America under present conditions.' He did agree that Europe was a different matter, and he was determined that Sam and he should not end up on bad terms: 'If you want to yell at me – do so. We'll get it all clear and in the open. And <u>remain friends</u>.'[27]

The 'present conditions' that Fast referred to were indeed deteriorating. That same month, *Hollywood Life* carried an article warning of a Red takeover, and listing Sam amongst a dozen show people who were 'Red Fellow Travelers and Red Sympathizers'. The list included Lena Horne, Judy Holliday, José Ferrer, Orson Welles and Charlie Chaplin. 'Wanamaker', it was stated, 'has acted as a speaker at **affairs praising** the Communist ideology ... He belongs to red fronts ...' and it cited his involvement with the Abraham Lincoln Brigade, 'a noted red front ...'.[28] Five days before the article appeared, the actor Larry Parks appeared before HUAC and gave the names of several people he knew to have been members of the Communist Party, including Morris Carnovsky, Lee J Cobb and Joe Bromberg, a founder member of the Group Theatre. In April, Edward Dmytryk appeared before the Committee, reneged on his former support of the Party, gave several names and was released early from prison. The actor Sterling Hayden also gave names – and deeply regretted it afterwards. José Ferrer denied ever being a Communist, but avoided giving any names. Now, there was not just the 'blacklist' to contend with, but the very real possibility of being subpoena-ed by HUAC, asked what became known as the $64,000 question 'Are you now or have you ever been a member of the Communist party?' and pressed to give names of Communist sympathizers.

It was time for Sam to consider his position. Hannah Weinstein and Ben Barzman had exiled themselves to Paris. Determined not to be cowed, Sam agreed to join Clifford Odets, Paul Robeson and others at an event at the Riverside Plaza to honour three of the Hollywood Ten, John Howard Lawson, Dalton Trumbo and Albert Maltz, who had completed their prison sentences. Then he flew to France, ostensibly to discuss *The Maccabees*, but also to investigate a possible future in Europe.

4

An American in Britain

In the spring of 1951, Sam spent several weeks with Ben and Norma Barzman in Paris. Judging by one of Charlotte's letters, his plans were still unclear. She wrote to him: 'Though I'd love to go to Europe for a while, I wouldn't hesitate about going to Israel.' She liked the idea of seeing 'this new land'.[1] She wrote that she was using the period of separation from Sam to gain a sense of her own independence, and that she wanted him to be free to make his own decisions. His time in Paris was a boost to his morale. He learnt that *Christ in Concrete* was listed in *Cahiers du Cinéma* as one of the best films of the year. He was interviewed for an article in *L'Écran Français*, where he was able to express his views freely, and was quoted as saying 'Un artiste n'est plus un artiste s'il ne peut s'exprimer librement', and perhaps under the influence of the Barzmans, he added 'C'est pourquoi j'ai quitté les États-Unis'.[2]

Sam flew into London on 14 May. He was 'conditionally landed for one month ... not to enter any employment, paid or unpaid,'[3] but he immediately began to investigate the possibility of work. He had been given an introduction to Cecil Tennent, a member of the London subsidiary of the agency run by Myron Selznick, brother of Hollywood producer David Selznick. Just as when he was demobbed in 1946, his luck was in, and he was offered a part in a British film, *Mr Denning Drives North*, starring John Mills. It was a crime thriller that Alexander Korda had bought for London Films, and one of the characters was an American lawyer. Sam accepted the part, and applied successfully to have the employment condition removed, and his residence extended to September. Charlotte booked a cabin on the *Queen Mary* and arrived with the children, and much luggage, on 21 June. They moved into Parkstone, Langley, the pleasant country house they had stayed in two years earlier, within easy reach of Shepperton Studios, where the film was being shot.

Sam joined a cast of British stalwarts. The director was Anthony Kimmins, who had returned to directing films after a naval career. The story of *Mr Denning Drives North* was somewhat farfetched. Mr Denning (John Mills) goes to see Mados (Herbert Lom, a Czech-born British actor), an unpleasant young man with a dubious background, to buy him off from marrying his daughter. In the ensuing altercation, Mr Denning kills him by mistake, and conceals the fact, for fear of involving his daughter in the situation. The rest of the film is concerned with his efforts to cover up the 'accidental murder', supported by his wife (Phyllis Calvert), after he admits the truth to her. Meanwhile, his daughter has hitched up with Chick Eddowes (Sam), a young lawyer who, when Mados's body is discovered, and the murder attributed to a gypsy, sets about proving the gypsy's innocence, and gets close to uncovering the truth. But the daughter, discovering the truth herself, manages to avert suspicion from her father, through a nifty exchange of the 'AA' badge on his car with the one on Chick's car. Many scenes consist of Mr Denning driving his Rolls Royce back and forth between home and the place where he dumped the body. The morality of the plot is doubtful, since the viewer is supposed to be pleased that Mr Denning's deed has escaped discovery. The performances are typical of Engish film acting at the time, very proper except for the outbursts of violence. There was not much opportunity for Sam's usual in-depth approach to his work, and he was ever afterwards ashamed of his performance; the children were fined sixpence if they mentioned it. Still, he had made his first entrance on the English scene.

By the time the filming was over, Sam was quite sure that he wanted to settle in England for the foreseeable future. He rented a flat in St John's Wood. Charlotte broke the news to Aggie that they would not be coming back to New York. Sam wrote to Cliff Carpenter to ask him to make arrangements to sublet the apartment on East 53rd Street, and to find tenants for the Connecticut farmhouse. Arrangements also had to be made for Gussie, the poodle. He arranged for his brother Bill to pick up his Buick and drive it all the way back to Los Angeles, and set about getting his Ford station wagon shipped over to England. The next step was to find some project through which he could make some impact on the British theatre, and extend his residence.

In July, he approached Clifford Odets, asking for the rights to his play *The Country Girl* for a London production. It had recently completed a successful run on Broadway, the role of the eponymous heroine gaining Uta Hagen a Tony Award. Odets was interested, and wrote back:

> Lots of producers want to do the play there [in London], but I'd think hard about you and your set-up if you'd give me the pertinent facts. Yourself as actor, Yes! what others in other parts? How long would you play? And yes, I'd like to direct. Send me all the dope.[4]

Sam did not have a 'set-up' at that point. He was bluffing, as all theatre producers are tempted to do, telling one party whom they want to involve, that another party has definitely agreed, while saying exactly the same to that other party.

When Sam approached Henry Sherek, a well-established theatre producer (usually called 'manager' in Britain at that time), he assured him that he had the rights to the play. Sherek knew Sam's work as actor and director, having seen *Joan of Lorraine*. They took the idea to Laurence Olivier, who still held the lease on the St James's Theatre, and was willing to have Sam and Sherek produce the play there. That was enough of a 'set-up' to satisfy Odets, who did not pursue the idea that he would himself direct. Sam was to co-produce, direct and play a main part.

In August, Sam booked two one-way tickets from London to New York, via Paris, but the sections from Paris to New York were never used. Some months later he wrote to PanAm asking for a refund, explaining that an emergency had forced him to change his plans and return to London. It is possible that Charlotte and he had planned to return to clear up their two households, and that while they were in Paris, he learnt that a subpoena to appear before HUAC had been delivered. In later years, Sam gave conflicting accounts of what happened. In one version, he said that a subpoena was delivered to his flat in London, where it had no force. That is what he told the son of Donald Ogden Stewart, a 'Hollywood exile' in London.[5] On other occasions he said that there was an attempt to deliver a subpoena on him in New York, but as he was not there, it could not be served.[6] Perhaps he was genuinely confused as to where it had been delivered. Charlotte later said that their New York housekeeper (Aggie) told them that someone from the FBI had called at the apartment. There were certainly FBI files on both of them; if they had returned to New York, it was very probable that they would not have been allowed to leave again. Meanwhile, MI5 had already opened a file on them.

Notwithstanding that file, the Home Office extended Sam's residence for a year. In October, the family had to move out of their flat, but Sam had been given an introduction to the artist, Felix Topolski, who invited the family to move into *his* flat, which was temporarily empty, on Harcourt Terrace, looking out over Regent's Park. That month, Sam obtained from the County of London a Certificate of Registration as a theatrical employer. In December, they heard that the actress Glynis Johns, who lived nearby, was about to star in a Broadway play, and needed a New York apartment to rent. She and the Wanamakers swopped flats. They moved into Abbey Lodge, a generously proportioned flat just a stone's throw from the Park, with its own garden at the back. Sam became officially part of Henry Sherek Ltd and began work on *The Country Girl*.

Just before rehearsals began, Charlotte and Sam were witness to one of the saddest events brought on by the 'blacklist', the death of actor Joe Bromberg. He had been subpoenaed six months earlier, had pleaded the Fifth Amendment (the right not to be incriminated without a formal prosecution), and had suffered great stress ever since. Sam suggested to Lee Sabinson (who had produced *Counterattack*) that he cast Joe in the London production of *The Biggest Thief in Town*, a play by Dalton Trumbo, one of the Hollywood Ten. Sabinson had already produced it on Broadway. On arrival, Joe stayed with the Wanamaker family for several weeks, then, two weeks after he left them, just as his wife set sail for London to be with him, he died of a heart attack. Sam wrote to Hannah Weinstein: 'I am seeing to it that as many people as possible are made aware of the tragic circumstances which preceded, and was in the main the cause of Joe's death.'[7]

When Sam walked into the first rehearsal of his first West End production, he was something of an unknown quantity for the assembled company. They knew he had been blacklisted, and that he was a successful Broadway actor and director who had starred in a couple of films, and had just finished working on a British film. The playwright, too, was unfamiliar to many. Clifford Odets' plays *Waiting for Lefty* and *Awake and Sing* had been performed by the left-wing Unity Theatre in the 1930s, but not in the West End.

The Country Girl is set in a Broadway theatre, and Sam was to play Bernie Dodd, who, like Jimmy Masters in *Joan of Lorraine*, is himself a Broadway director. The play concerns a once-successful elderly actor, Frank Elgin (loosely based on John Barrymore), whose career has been on hold since he took to the bottle. Against advice, Bernie Dodd wants to cast him in his next production. The action centres on Elgin's wife, Georgie, and the part she plays in her husband's attempted come-back. Sherek and Sam assembled a strong cast. The first actor considered for the role of Frank Elgin was Alec Guinness, but another actor who had been sent the script was Michael Redgrave. He liked it, and was eager to do a modern play after his current project (the film of *The Importance of Being Earnest*) was completed, but he was unsure if the script was strong enough. He asked Sam, whom he did not yet know, for a week to consider. A chance encounter with Alec Guinness, whom he knew had also been approached, unexpectedly motivated him to accept the role, not knowing that Guinness had already accepted, believing that Redgrave had refused it! Sherek and Sam, preferring Redgrave, managed to negotiate their way out of the situation. Guinness later joked to Redgrave 'I'm only wondering how much I can sue the producer for.'[8] The heroine was to be played by Googie Withers, who, having started her career in frothy comedies that her name seemed to invite, had successfully made the transition to more serious roles.

Redgrave met Sam for the first time, with Henry Sherek, on Boxing Day, 1951. The contrast between the two producers could not have been greater, Sherek, large and expansive, *bon viveur*, waving his cigar, totally at home in the London theatrical fraternity. Sam, the brash, Chicago-bred younger man, about to make his first stage appearance in England.

In rehearsal, the first request Sam made to his two main actors was that they should both write down the pre-history of their characters, a preparation important in his Stanislavsky-based approach. They had never done this before, and were flummoxed. At this time, few in the English theatre were familiar with Stanislavsky; his acting method had reached America through a number of Russian emigré actors, including Sam's own teacher, David Itkin. Of those who had worked with Stanislavsky, only Michael Chekhov had come to England, teaching for some years at Dartington College, before emigrating to America himself. Redgrave was interested in Stanislavsky's ideas, but had not explored them in practice; Googie Withers had little knowledge of him. They were both reluctant to explore the past of their characters at such an early stage, feeling that it would force them to commit themselves to a preconception.

The next innovation Sam introduced was improvisation, asking the actors to use their own words in creating the action of a scene. They both found this difficult, especially in the New York accents they were assuming. Redgrave soon accepted the idea, appreciating the freshness it gave. But as rehearsals progressed, he took issue with Sam's approach, especially his attempt to get him to identify strongly with Elgin. Sam suggested that this would make rehearsing and performing the role a cathartic experience. In Edinburgh, on the pre-London tour, when they were performing at night, while continuing to rehearse during the day (just as the characters do in the play), Redgrave wrote a note to Sam, pleading to be left alone to find his part for himself. 'Frank is a man whose values and impulses are negative and destructive. I understand them, and must – to some extent – <u>live</u> them on stage. But I have got far beyond the point where living such things – however well I understand them – provides a catharsis. I am not a destructive or negative person.' He went on to say that Sam was making him feel 'persecuted (by night), bullied by day.'[9]

The English actors were familiar with theatre directors who were powerful and authoritarian, such as Basil Dean, reputed to be a theatrical tyrant, but they were startled by Sam's direct, down-to-earth manner, which came across to them as abrasive. As well, the real situation was dangerously close to the dramatic situation. Like Frank Elgin, Redgrave had problems with alcohol. Sam discussed the situation with Charlotte. She believed Redgrave's homosexuality created a conflict in his marriage, just as alcohol did in the character's, and that Sam as director paralleled Sam as Bernie, representing the male drive. (In the play, Bernie becomes strongly attracted to Georgie.) In a note to Sam, Charlotte wrote: 'I think he (and probably Rachel) [Redgrave's wife] realize that the conflict in the play was an exact conflict in their lives ... the struggle between normalcy and perversion [sic].' At one point, she had encountered both Rachel and one of Redgrave's 'boys', together. Charlotte thought that Frank Elgin's line about drink, 'I need it, Georgie, I need it', signified Redgrave's sexual conflict, and that Sam/Bernie acted as his conscience. However, she ended her note with a more practical explanation for the difficulties: 'Let us not dismiss the fact that he [Redgrave] has had a gruelling year, and this has been a difficult five weeks.'[10] So Sam tried to be kinder. 'Dear Sam,' Redgrave wrote on one occasion, 'Your note last night gave me so much encouragement. Thank you. Yours Mike.'[11]

Away from the theatre, Sam enjoyed getting to know England and Scotland. Visiting Edinburgh, he was impressed by its great granite buildings and the beautiful Royal Lyceum Theatre where they were playing. He sat in the Caledonian Hotel and looked in vain for 'haggis' on the menu, so that he could try the famous Scottish dish for the first time. 'We don't serve haggis', the waiter told him, no doubt in an accent worthy of Miss Jean Brodie, 'It's not the kind of thing we serve in this hotel.'[12] But he promised to get one for Sam, and proudly served it to him the next day.

In Manchester, towards the end of the tour, Sam at last had some time to write to his brother and explain how the family was getting on in their new country, expressing himself with a touch of euphoria:

> England is a wonderful country, with wonderful people in it everywhere. They are submitting to their trials and tribulations economically with great fortitude, and they are much further advanced politically and intellectually than the stupid masses of American people, who are blinded and deafened with all the T.V. Radio and newspapers etc. that swirl around them. There is a warmth and a relaxation and a maturity about these people, no quality of which the general American masses reflect.

He wrote that Charlotte and the children were happy, 'although not without some degree of home-sickness and insecurity about the immediate future.'[13]

Also while in Manchester, Redgrave and Sam attended a performance in a basement theatre which excited them both. Despite the friction in rehearsal, they had much in common, including left-wing politics. The production they saw was *Uranium 235*, an extraordinary compound of drama, ballet, verse, mime, burlesque, revue, satire and song, dramatizing the issues raised by the discovery of nuclear power. The author was Ewan McColl, writer, folksinger and Communist; the company was Theatre Workshop, run by his then wife, Joan Littlewood. Both men returned to London determined to bring the production into town.

As there was an English operetta called *The Country Girl*, the title of the play had been changed to *Winter Journey*.[14] It opened at the St James's Theatre at the beginning of April 1952, and was received with huge acclaim. Harold Hobson described it as 'a magnificent evening's entertainment'. It was 'an outstanding success'. Alan Dent found 'all three [of the main performances] quite beyond praise', and referred to 'the play's expert and imaginative direction'. Philip Hope-Wallace wrote that Sam Wanamaker 'makes an impact like a sudden close-up on the screen, apparently not acting at all, or only acting himself, yet being continually a genius onstage (a rare thing)'. 'When he holds the tension of a silent scene, he holds it so securely that he seems, almost visibly, to hold it at will.' 'His arrival at the St James Theatre last night was an event for London.'[15]

Sam and Sherek had a box-office success on their hands. As the run continued, the theatre-going public became aware that something new was happening. In August, there was a spread in *Picture Post*: '*Winter Journey* is a play written by an American, Clifford Odets, and produced by an American. The result is a detonation of astounding force ... After four months, the emotional time-bomb ... still keeps capacity audiences on the edge of their seats.'[16] In October, there was an article suggesting that 'London needs a shot of theatrical benzedrine', and claiming that Sam was providing it:

> Sam Wanamaker proceeded to excite his audience with an intense and virile performance suggestive of a fire walker who had forgotten to put himself in a trance before stepping onto red-hot bricks.
>
> In doing so, he threw down the gauntlet at the suede-covered feet of those English actors whose recent unemotional breeze-in-a-teacup offerings have driven me and others to dumb distraction.[17]

Some in the acting fraternity also recognized a new force. Sam received a letter from actress Chattie Salaman, sister-in-law of Alec Guinness:

> *Winter Journey* was for me both contemporary, significant and had style – it made the dreary genteel naturalism of which we see so much in the English theatre seem rather pathetic – and what I have since heard of your interest in other people's work has encouraged me to risk writing to you.[18]

She invited him to visit the Old Vic School, the most innovative drama school of the time, run by the French director, Michel St Denis. The School was about to close and she wanted to talk to Sam about helping the young actors who would be left without a leader. The performance that Sam saw there impressed him. He wrote to St Denis: 'It is the only work I have seen in England which gives me any hope at all about schools and teaching in the theatre in this country.'[19] But he was not tempted to set up any kind of studio work, as Salaman hoped. In answering her, he wrote that people talked about needing someone to guide and lead them and then waited for him to take the cue:

> Unfortunately, being a foreigner and having many plans and activities which fully occupy me, and because I believe it would be psychologically wrong for me to do so if I could, I cannot accept the role of such a leader or Messiah.

He suggested that if she did get a group together, he might work with them, 'But it must be your group not mine.'[20]

As the run progressed, Sam worked to keep his performance fresh. When, on occasion, there was a round of applause at his exit, he 'tore his hair', knowing that he had not succeeded in keeping the audience 'in the moment'. He was pleased when someone in the gallery was overheard saying: 'It's as if he was doing it for the first time – just thinking about it now.'[21] During at least one performance, Sam broke the 'fourth wall' convention, startling the audience by making an entrance from the auditorium.

Despite the success of the production, Sam's relationship with the company did not flourish, and seemed to centre on his sensitivity to any perceived slur on his Jewishness. Patricia Marmont, an understudy in the company, claimed: 'Sam's Achilles' heel was anti-Semitisim'.[22] Seeing the play while it was still on tour, Sherek had told Sam he was overacting, throwing his arms about. 'Just like the Habima Players,'[23] referring to the Israeli company who had recently toured. But Sam took it as an anti-Semitic comment. His relationship with Googie Withers remained prickly throughout the run. There was none of the rapport he had established with his other leading ladies, Jan Sterling, Ingrid Bergman, Madeleine Carroll, Lilli Palmer. She described a phone conversation she had with Sam:

'You don't like me, do you?'

'Not much, no.'

'You don't like me because I'm a Jew and a Red.'

'No, it's because I don't like you.'[24]

In his memoir, *In The Mind's Eye*, Michael Redgrave made no mention of the crisis in Edinburgh, but did remember that Sam and he continued to improvise during their first scene, and that one night, after the show, three weeks into the run, Sam rang him in a fury:

'You called me a kike.'

'When?'

'Tonight. On stage.'

'No,' I said, 'I called you a tyke'.'[25]

Sam had mistaken a Yorkshire term, half insult, half admiration, for a slur on his Jewishness. The strain of working in a different culture had roused memories of being taunted as a Jew during his childhood.

From then on, backstage became something of a war zone, Sam communicating with his co-stars only by written notes. Redgrave referred to the estrangement, and the pain it caused him, in an undated note:

I have been torn between two explanations: that your extraordinarily arrogant and brusque behaviour springs from your anxiety ... – or that you heed the theory that a happy company is a self-satisfied company and therefore lazy and second class. It's a tenable theory, after all.[26]

His first explanation was the more accurate. In a letter to Cliff Carpenter, Sam expressed his sense of relief that the production was a success, and explained that he had been conscious of a prejudice against Americans, that people seemed to harbour objections 'to them coming over and taking our jobs, to the way in which I work, which is apparently totally different to the usual approaches and methods of English directors and actors, and to the brazen, apparently ego-centric idea that I could co-produce, direct and act – all in the same play'.[27] Underlying his aggressive behaviour was an awareness that he was regarded as an outsider, and a knowledge of the risk he was taking, daring to attempt a new career in a foreign country.

Both stars nevertheless acknowledged Sam's theatrical achievement. Redgrave wrote:

> Wanamaker was excellent in the play, and his direction was first class. I owed a good deal of my own performance to him ... Like all clashes of personality, it was agonising at the time and afterwards it is hard to imagine how it happened.[28]

Googie Withers afterwards described Sam as 'a monster', but she wrote him a gracious note at the end of the run and gave him credit at the time for what she had learnt from him:

> He traced [Georgie's] story back for me and reconstructed in detail incidents that are no more than touched upon in conversation during the action of the play ... When I saw the character's past so clearly, the play took on a strange reality for me. All the other characters became real people whom I felt I had known for years – long before the action of the play opened. I had never thought so deeply about any of my previous parts, but in future I shall certainly approach other plays in the same manner ... Maybe the back-stage settings of *Winter Journey* lend the play a certain glamour ... but it is really the accurate observation of the human race by Clifford Odets and the Stanislavsky touch in Sam Wanamaker's direction that leads the cast, even now, weeks after the first night, to explore and discover fresh excitement in their parts.[29]

During the summer, when the play was well into its run, Charlotte had her first opportunity to work outside America. She was invited to be vocal coach on an Anglo-German film about Martin Luther. It was a serious and scholarly portrait, funded by the Lutheran Church, directed by Irving Pichel, one of the original 'Hollywood Nineteen', who had not had to testify to HUAC, but had nevertheless been blacklisted. Charlotte set off for Wiesbaden, in West Germany, armed with Mary Agnes Doyle's *Art of Speech, Daily Dozen Diction Drills,* to work with Irish actor, Niall McGinnis, as Luther, and an international cast. Her job was to bring a consistency amongst a range of accents and pronunciations. She was reluctant to leave Sam and the girls, but the offered fee was $1000, plus travel and living expenses, and that was not to be sneezed at. Sam was having difficulty accessing money which he wanted to send to America to boost his account there, and had sunk much of what money he had in buying a lease on Abbey Lodge, as Glynis Johns no longer had any interest in retaining it. Sam's secretary, Miriam Brickman (later to become a successful casting director), took care of the girls, and Charlotte consoled herself by writing long screeds to Sam. She did not enjoy Germany, conscious that the Holocaust was only a few years back. In a letter to his parents, Sam wrote: 'A Jew going to Germany today has many psychological problems to face.'[30]

After a run of six months, Redgrave and Googie Withers did not renew their contracts. There was some talk of Lee J Cobb taking over from Redgrave. In the event, Canadian actor, Alexander Knox, took over, with Anglo-American actress Constance Cummings playing Georgie, for a post-West End tour. One critic, returning to review the new cast, thought that Sam's performance was even better. No accounts of his subsequent productions tell of quite such fierce backstage storms as he had had with the original cast. He had proved himself and could relish his achievement. 'I love it,' he said, 'It's nice, this success ... [It] has renewed my feeling about doing an American play with a mixed British and American cast. I've proved it can be done.'[31]

Charlotte and Sam began to feel settled in London. Abby attended a local primary school. 'Our two English lasses', Sam wrote home, 'are indeed thriving here, in a healthy, peaceful, intelligent and cultured atmosphere.'[32] They made particular friends with Swedish actress, Mai Zetterling and her partner, Herbert Lom, and with Lois and Teddy Sieff (of the Marks and Spencer family), and Lois's daughter Jennifer, who was the same age as Zoë. The Wanamakers were not the only 'exiles'. Donald Ogden Stewart and his journalist wife, Ella Hill, settled in Hampstead, and arranged Sunday afternoon 'at homes'. Carl Forman also moved to London and continued to write screenplays under a pseudonym. Joe Losey arrived, 'expecting to swell the ranks of the refugee contingent',[33] Sam wrote to Charlotte. But he returned to New York, to try his luck there for the time being. Hannah Weinstein also moved to London, and founded a film company, Sapphire Productions. (The project to film *The Maccabees* had been quietly dropped.) She was soon inviting blacklisted writers such as Ring Lardner Jr to write screenplays for her, under pseudonyms. Writer Hy Kraft arrived, and Cy Endfield, another blacklisted film director.

Friends still in America wrote in despair or black humour. Ollie Crawford described how the country had been confiscated by 'the McCarthys'. Elia Kazan had named several names to HUAC, and consequently been banned from the theatre where a show he had directed was playing. A friend recounted to Sam that the producer, Irene Selznick, announcing this, immediately threw up on the stage.[34] Sam wrote to Lillian Hellman after she refused to answer questions: 'Please accept my deepest respect and thanks for what you have done for America.'[35] Sam's English friend, Jack Perry, was banned from entry there, because he had started a company which traded with the People's Republic of China, and had sent supplies there which he had bought in America.

In England there were no laws threatening Communists. Sam and Charlotte were free to associate with theatre people who were members of the Communist Party of Great Britain, or firm supporters of the Labour Party. Clement Attlee had lost the election in the autumn of 1951, and the Conservatives were back in power, with Winston Churchill as Prime Minister. But the Welfare State was too firmly established for it to be dismantled. Sam helped to establish connections between American and British actors, and amongst his friends and colleagues, his left-wing views were well-known. Nevertheless he did not want to jeopardise his career by too open association with Communist enterprises. It was a delicate balancing act. At the time *Winter Journey* opened, he was invited to attend a party hosted by a Canadian Communist who was interested in creating a group of like-minded people in the film industry to work towards 'peace'. Sam replied with circumspection, wary of being associated with an official organization, insisting that he could only attend in a purely private capacity:

> ... You must understand that being an American in Britain one must tread with careful precision on matters involving peace which has now become a highly political and controversial subject. You may know of the recent activities of the Un-American Activities Committee in America and the work of our American State department in connection with the rescinding of passports belonging to people having been found connected with political and unfavourable groups abroad. Therefore, you see I must be extremely careful about protecting that position and not doing anything which will give cause, just or not, for any action of the above nature ...
>
> I hope you will understand this rather difficult position of mine and I hope to be able to attend the party, and of course, sincerely hope for the success of it and all it represents.
>
> Very sincerely, Sam Wanamaker[36]

He was thinking of such people as Paul Robeson, whose passport had been withdrawn in 1950. Sam's status was vulnerable, in that Charlotte and he, with the children, were on temporary visas in Britain. He had only recently been authorized to open a bank account in England, having lived on loans from his London agent whenever his ready funds ran out. If he lost his American passport, he would be virtually stateless. He would have trodden with even more 'careful precision' had he known that a photostat of this letter was held in MI5 files, provided to the Special Branch of the Metropolitan Police by a 'delicate source'.

It was important that Sam have another success to follow *Winter Journey*, to consolidate his professional position in England, and to allow him to extend his residency once again. While he put out feelers for a major project, he took on a limited assignment. Redgrave and he had contacted Oscar Lewenstein, who was running the Embassy, a small theatre in Swiss Cottage, and persuaded him to present *Uranimum 235*, the hour-long Theatre Workshop play that had so impressed them in Manchester. Like Sam, Lewenstein was of Russian Jewish descent. He had Communist sympathies, having run the left-wing Unity Theatre, where his productions had included American social plays, not only Clifford Odets' *Awake and Sing*, but also *The Gentle People*, the Irwin Shaw play Sam had directed at the Jewish People's Institute in Chicago and Hy Kraft's *Café Crown*, the play in which Sam had made his Broadway debut.

Sam was to direct the limited run. He had an immediate rapport with Joan Littlewood and Howard Goorney, her righthand man. She had seen *Winter Journey* and felt that Sam would be better working on her kind of play: '... you certainly are an actor – too good to waste your time on this stuff ... Your production is too true and logical for the writing ... Certainly it was interesting to catch a glimpse of American production methods à la Kazan.'[37] Unfortunately, a trivial dispute arose, about paying for some drapes, perhaps exacerbated for Sam by the fragility of his financial situation. He withdrew from the production, and Littlewood took over. The Oliviers and other stars attended; one performance was booked out by the British Peace Committee, the night before their national conference. The play transferred for a short run at the Comedy Theatre, in the West End. Afterwards, Howard Goorney wrote: 'It has been a source of sorrow to us all that our relations with you should have become so strained; it was the last thing that we wanted, not merely because of what you are doing, but also because friends are so few and far between – real friends that is.'[38] MI5 kept a review of the production in its file on 'Samuel Wanamaker'.

Soon after starting work on *Winter Journey*, Sam had changed his agent, partly to be represented by someone who worked in association with MCA, his American agency, partly because he felt Cecil Tennent was not enthusiastic enough about his work. Tennent replied that he too worked in association with MCA, and that he was simply being 'realistic about production problems'.[39] Sam was now with John Findlay, of Linnit and Dunfee, to whom he outlined his ambitions. He was expansive about his hopes and plans. He would like to present new, un-produced plays in the West End for possible production in New York as well; acquire properties for films in the way of novels, or original screenplays or treatments; present any plays MCA would like to have first produced in England – 'but I would fight to control the rights in America as well.'[40] He was also keen to direct films, but Findlay warned him: 'There are obvious snags, which you already realise, of your nationality, and the fact that you have not yet directed a picture.'[41]

One project into which Sam put much effort was *Anne of The Thousand Days*, Maxwell Anderson's play about King Henry VIII and Anne Boleyn. It had played on Broadway at the same time as *Goodbye, My Fancy*, starring Rex Harrison and Joyce Redman, an actress from the Old Vic Company. Directing a verse play about English history would show his versatility, and establish him more firmly in his new country. The subject of the monarchy would allow for some pageantry that would suit Coronation Year, despite the tragic end. He first enquired about the London rights in June 1952, and suggested that Leslie Hurry, who had recently designed Christopher Marlowe's *Tamburlaine* at the Old Vic, should design, and Ralph Vaughan Williams write the music. He buried himself in Tudor history and began to approach suitable actors. He started, surprisingly, with Alec Guinness, perhaps hoping to mollify him: 'I don't know whether the wound which you have received in regard to *Winter Journey* carries with it the memory of my hand on the knife ... it would be a matter of great regret to me if you believed that I have personally done, or intended to do you harm.'[42] Guinness wrote back succinctly: 'Frankly, I can think of no less suitable actor for Henry than myself.'[43]

More appropriately, Sam approached Trevor Howard's agent, Al Parker. He was an American film director who had settled in England, continued to direct, and also set up a theatrical agency. Sam wrote to Charlotte in Germany that Howard was keen; he also began to envisage a film version to follow, perhaps with the Oliviers. He approached Joan Greenwood to play Anne Boleyn. Anderson's literary agent cabled: OK GO AHEAD TREVOR GREENWOOD. BEST MANAGEMENT YOU CAN SECURE.[44] Sam tried Hugh Beaumont (always known as 'Binkie'), who ran the largest London management, H. M. Tennent, but he did not like the play. Still, he hoped they might be associated in the future.

In November 1952, Sam muddied the waters by allowing a theatre magazine to announce the casting only a day after he had met Al Parker to discuss terms. Trevor Howard was not pleased, as he had not yet agreed, and the announcement would suggest that he was not available if a film offer arose. Sam, with a pretence of innocence, wrote that he had wanted Howard to sign a 'general agreement' and then 'look at terms',[45] an entirely unlikely scenario. Al Parker suggested they do no further business. A colleague at the agency then told Sam that Parker had remarked: 'It is strange why actors, when they become Managers, are more difficult to deal with than Managers are.'[46] A week or so later, Parker expressed himself more outspokenly, after Sam had approached another of his clients directly and apparently made derogatory remarks about the agency: 'As one American to the other, why don't you take a tumble at yourself ... because you are pleased not to think well of our Company or me, doesn't bother me, and if it is true what others think of you, and important people, take my tip, change your ways, or you will find conditions will back up on you. I have no objection to you contacting our clients direct, but you will find they will refer you to me.'[47] Sam may have been secretly impressed at Parker's directness – within a few years, he himself was represented by him.

Negotiations continued. Sam also made contact with S. T. Bindoff, a Tudor historian, who read the play and sent him a full breakdown of historical inaccuracies: A) Minor Inaccuracies, B) Chronological Confusions C) Unhistorical treatment of major issues D) Miscellaneous points.[48] Max Anderson's literary agent promised, no doubt ruefully, to take the criticisms to the playwright in Hollywood. But by the beginning of 1953, it was becoming clear that the project would not fly. Sam had to admit that he had not found a co-manager and Trevor Howard was too expensive. 'Many have commented on the high cost of producing, the non-commerciality of historical plays and the play's lack of historicity.'[49]

In total contrast, Sam obtained the rights to a play that José Ferrer had directed and starred in on Broadway, winning him a Tony Award and the writer the Pulitzer Prize. *The Shrike*, by Joseph Kramm, was a melodramatic piece, about a man who is brought to the city hospital after an unsuccessful suicide attempt and is kept under supervision as a possible criminal lunatic. He has to choose between going into an asylum or going back to his shrike-wife. (A 'shrike' is a predatory bird, sometimes known as a 'butcher-bird.)

Sam produced it with Jack Hylton, another left-wing manager. Again, he directed and played the lead. Constance Cummings played the monstrous wife, having enjoyed working with Sam during the last weeks of *Winter Journey*. The play was not quite in the spirit of the times, just as the British population was gearing up for the Coronation of Queen Elizabeth, but it did consolidated Sam's reputation. Richard Findlater, writing in *The Observer*, was ambivalent about the play but certain about the performance:

An unpleasant play? Yes, indeed – one of the most unpleasant I've ever seen, but also one of the most powerful. And I have a suspicion that we needed to be reminded that such power and intensity are possible in the theatre, even if the direct attack of this kind of American drama seems an un-English activity to many of us.

The success of *The Shrike* largely depends on the astonishing virtuoso performance of Sam Wanamaker, as the man caught in a trap; we follow the victim through all the ambushes of his cross-examination by the doctors, into the nightmare fears of madness and the nauseated acceptance of his destiny.[50]

Sam had quickly established himself as a significant figure in the English theatre, on the basis of the two modern American Broadway plays he had brought to the West End, and more significantly, for introducing a new and exciting style of acting:

Unknown to English audiences, Sam Wanamaker opened at the St James's early last year and immediately became one of the most discussed character-actors of recent years.[51]

But, as with the Festival Theatre, he was eager to show that he had a wider range than he had so far shown. His next production tested that proposition.

5

Leave to Remain?

In his search for new projects, Sam had been reading, amongst other plays, those of the Irish playwright, Sean O'Casey, and had come across one that was hardly yet known, *Purple Dust*. 'It's a delightful play,' he wrote to Cliff Carpenter, 'well I won't say play, because it has no plot and no shape ... but it is a delightful sequence of burlesque routines'.[1] O'Casey had written a lighthearted critique of British imperialism, a theme that appealed to Sam. Two wealthy Englishmen come to Ireland, each with an Irish mistress, and set about restoring an ancient mansion house to what they consider to be its glorious Tudor splendour. The men's attempts are disastrous, their women run off with two of the natives and a flood rises around the house. At the end, the Irish foreman announces: 'Your Tudors have had their day, and they are gone; and th' little heap o' purple dust they left behind them will vanish away in the flow of the river.' In the final stage direction one of the Englishmen disappears down a passage '*as the green waters tumble into the house*'.[2]

O'Casey had completed the play in 1940, hoping for a production before publication, but as with many of his later plays, this hope was unrealized. When Sam started to investigate the background, he discovered that it had been performed by an amateur company in 1943, and then by the Old Vic Company at the Liverpool Playhouse, during a wartime tour in 1945. It had never been produced in America, though a Broadway producer was interested. He hoped to get in ahead of him, perhaps mount a production in Britain, and retain the rights if it transferred to New York. Probably through Oscar Lewenstein, who had produced O'Casey's *Juno and the Paycock* at the Embassy, Sam was put in touch with the playwright, who lived with his wife Eileen in Somerset. He took Charlotte and the girls to visit, and that resulted in a friendship between the two families which went much further than business discussions. Sam approached Daniel Angel, a producer already making his name in film production, but he refused to take it on – 'much too highbrow for me'.[3] Thane Park, chairman of the London Mask Theatre, a small company associated with J. B. Priestley's plays, agreed to partner Sam for a provincial tour.

In the spring of 1953, Sam gathered together a strong cast, including Miles Malleson and Walter Hudd, two well-known character actors, as the Englishmen, and two equally well-known Irish actresses, Eithne Dunn and Siobhan McKenna, as the mistresses. Rehearsals started. O'Casey wrote the lyrics for four new songs. Sam persuaded Malcolm Arnold to write the music, John Cranko to arrange dances, and the cartoonist Gerard Hoffnung to provide a playful front curtain. O'Casey was outraged when Sam proposed to call it 'A Musical Charade': 'If I had thought for a moment that the songs I wrote would have moved the play an inch towards the shape of a "charade" I would never have written them.'[4] Meek for once, Sam retained O'Casey's own description: 'A Wayward Comedy with Music'.

Purple Dust opened in Birmingham on 13 April, and then played in Liverpool and Glasgow, but the audiences were sparse. The director of the Glasgow Citizens Theatre wrote to Sam: 'I do hope you are having better houses in Edinburgh, though judging by the *Scotsman* notices, they still don't seem to understand what the play is about. I don't feel that I really expressed adequately my appreciation of the play and your wonderfully sensitive and inventive production.'[5] Sam consoled himself in Edinburgh by taking O'Casey to a 'ceilidh', where they enjoyed an evening of songs, bagpipes, poetry and whisky. The evening ended in fisticuffs over the authenticity, or not, of some of the Gaelic songs. His enjoyment of the event suggests a nostalgia for Yiddish evenings in his youth.

The production drew small houses in Edinburgh and Blackpool, the last stop on the tour. Try as he would, Sam could not convince anyone to finance a London run. 'Here I am broken-hearted,' O'Casey wrote to Sam, 'and you I'm sure feel the same damned way ... We did our best, and to do one's best is enough and as much as anyone can do. My love to Charlotte, to Abby and to Zoe.'[6] Sam continued to look for backers, but to no avail. Two young actors wrote to Sam regretting its postponement, and the misfortunes that seemed to dog O'Casey's plays. 'We have admired the work you have been doing in the British theatre in the last year, and hope that your further ventures may meet with success.'[7] Just as Chattie Salaman had written, they hoped he would work with younger actors, like themselves. Joan Littlewood commented: 'another example of the shocking lack of standards in the English theatre at the moment. If a new dramatic author of genius appeared on the scene he would not be noticed.'[8] In June, O'Casey wrote again: 'Never have I put so much energy into a play before, *before* writing it, writing it, and during rehearsals, and I don't relish the idea of putting a lot more into it. So I think better to cry quits.'[9]

Coronation Year was not an auspicious time to be critical of British traditions. Neither management nor audiences responded to this delightful satire on the relationship between England and Ireland. Gerard Hoffnung's front cloth may still exist somewhere,[10] but Malcolm Arnold's music and John Cranko's choreography, must be considered lost. In 1956, *Purple Dust* ran for fourteen months off-Broadway, a record for an O'Casey play. Sam could take credit for keeping the play alive. The collaboration with O'Casey was a particularly happy one, with no rows, although, unbeknownst to Sam, one member of the company who was considered a 'reliable source' later reported to Special Branch that Sam Wanamaker, Walter Hudd and Miles Malleson 'were prominent in initiating … discussions … with a distinct Communist bias … and were taking what appeared to be the Party line in the course of them.'[11]

The most immediate consequence for Sam was financial. The production made a total loss of £1543, and he had to sublet Abbey Lodge and move the family to rooms in a house in Elm Row, Hampstead. It would not be the last time that Sam's ventures had a serious effect on domestic life. Added to that, Charlotte discovered she was pregnant again. Sam was delighted, writing to his brother (whose wife was also pregnant), that he had always wanted a family of three children. It was imperative that he earn some money.

Without any immediate new project of his own, he went back into partnership with Henry Sherek and directed a play by Mary Hayley Bell (playwright wife of the actor John Mills), which toured through the autumn, and allowed him to get his residence extended, this time for just six months.

Meanwhile, he reverted to his earlier strategy, and looked for a recent American play that had not been done in London. Clifford Odets suggested that Sam might direct and play the lead in *The Big Knife*, which he had written as a disillusioned response to his years in Hollywood, and as a metaphor for political corruption. It tells the story of a movie star who has gradually compromised the standards he once lived by. His wife will leave him if he signs a new contract with the studio boss, but he does so. The play has a melodramatic plot which distracts from Odets' focus on the ruthlessness of the Hollywood studio system and its political implications: the year before, Charlie Castle, the star, has killed a child in a hit-and-run accident, with a young woman as passenger, his devoted publicist taking the rap and going to jail. When the woman passenger threatens to disclose the truth, the boss is ruthless in dealing with her, and Castle commits suicide, knowing he has sacrificed his conscience for success. Sam had seen the play in 1949, when Joe Bromberg had played the studio boss in what turned out to be his last Broadway appearance, and Lee Strasberg had directed.

The critic Brook Atkinson found it to be 'a soundly motivated melodrama' which did not bear the weight of Odets' indignation.[12] But its Hollywood setting, like the Broadway setting of *Winter Journey*, lent it some glamour.

Sam acquired the rights, and co-produced with Ralph Birch, an impresario from the north of England who was eager to be part of the London theatre scene. For the wife, Odets recommended Renée Asherson, who had played Stella to Vivien Leigh's Blanche DuBois, and was also known through her role as Katherine in the film of *Henry V.* Sam assembled a strong cast, several of whom he had already worked with. He cast the Australian actress, Diane Cilento, just beginning her London career, as the young woman whose tongue must be silenced. The play opened at the Duke of York's Theatre in January 1954. The critics shared Brooks Atkinson's reservations. Anthony Cookman, writing in *The Tatler and Bystander* commented on its obvious weakness: 'We cannot help noticing that remorse for the killing of a child while drunkenly driving a car, plays but a small part in his long-drawn-out agony.'[13] But T C Worsley, who reviewed for the *New Statesman*, admired both the play and Sam's performance:

> ... [T]he particular and striking merits of the play lie for me in the brilliance of its dialogue, which carries overtones far more subtle than usual in realistic speech; and in the revelation of a gifted and self-conscious personality using every trick and device to conceal from itself the knowledge that it is only pursuing its own self-destruction.
>
> It is a wonderful acting part, this of the actor-film star, and Mr Sam Wanamaker gave a superb virtuoso display in it. His extraordinarily imaginative and detailed understanding of the dilemma lived right from the very inside, communicated itself vividly in every gesture, inflexion, turn of the head. Behind and beyond the author's more obvious intentions, he conveyed to us the burden of self-awareness, pacing a cage that only the unaware could bear to live with.[14]

Milton Shulman, writing in the *Evening Standard*, had reservations, but compared it revealingly with what else was on offer in the London theatre: '... it is virile and exciting theatre – and such a relief from the insipid world of the vicarage-and-chintz that stimulates our own playwrights to nothing more disturbing than a discreet cough behind the back of the hand.'[15] Perhaps he was thinking of N. C. Hunter's *Waters of the Moon*, which Kenneth Tynan, up-and-coming theatre critic on *The Observer*, had described as 'opulently shallow.'[16] However, that play, opening in the same month as *Winter Journey*, had run for over two years, while *The Big Knife*, opening in January 1954, was closed by the spring. 'Aunt Edna', the typical audience member as defined by the playwright Terence Rattigan, liked her chintz.

One Saturday, early in 1954, Sam hurried from an evening performance to Queen Charlotte's Maternity Hospital, arriving in time to see his new daughter, who had been born an hour before. He announced the birth to friends:

TODAY'S bulletin

BORN: ONE FEMALE (as usual)

              SATURDAY NIGHT (she waited for me)

              ONE O'CLOCK IN THE MORNING (Sunday)

              WEIGHT:7 POUNDS 11 OUNCES (Big eh?)

              RESEMBLANCE: LIKE ME (unfortunately)

              MOTHER: IS RELIEVED (aren't we all)

              SHE IS ALSO FINE AND SENDS YOU ALL HER VERY

              SINCERE GREETINGS AND THANKS FOR THE

              INTEREST YOU HAVE SHOWN

              (me too)

              SHE'S AT QUEEN CHARLOTTE HOSPITAL

              P.S. The baby has no name. Any suggestions?[17]

She was named 'Jessica'. (Perhaps it was at this time that comic writers Frank Muir and Denis Norden coined the joke: 'Announcing the arrival of Mr and Mrs Sam Wanamaker Junior', which has to be spoken out loud to get it.) Sean O'Casey wrote to congratulate Charlotte: 'May the God of Abraham, Isaac and Jacob be good to the Wanamaker family, With love and all good wishes, Sean'.[18]

Spurred by the addition to his family, Sam began to develop ideas for a repertory season, such as he had hoped to create with the Festival Theatre in New York. This was not only because he wanted to make his mark through more than one-off productions, but also so that he could demonstrate continuous employment to the Home Office. His residence permit expired at the end of April. He applied to have it extended to April 1955, by which time he could legitimately apply for permanent residence in Britain, with no employment conditions, four years being the normal length of time qualifying an alien to make such application. He wanted that stability for his family. Abby and Zoë were both at school now. Since her trip to Germany, Charlotte had worked professionally once more the previous year, making a children's record, but now was officially listed as 'housewife' rather than 'actress' at the Aliens' Registration Office.

Sam did not envisage anything along the lines of the 'weekly rep' companies that performed in many of the provincial towns in Britain. These were more like the Peninsula Players he had worked with in his teens, but less idyllic. They employed the same actors for a whole season, demanding a hectic schedule of rehearsal and performance. (He had recently been asked to look at a script co-written by the future playwright, John Osborne, who was working in just such a company.) Sam wanted to mount a varied season of new plays and revivals, individually cast and well rehearsed. He boldly told the Home Office that he proposed 'to produce thirteen new plays at the Westminster Theatre',[19] since he and Ralph Birch were in discussion about taking over that theatre, outside the West End, for a season. He corresponded with Arthur Miller, to get the joint rights, with Oscar Lewenstein, to produce *The Crucible* for a limited run there. Unfortunately, Miller misunderstood what he meant by 'limited run', seeing it as some sort of try-out. Since the first production in New York had not had good reviews, he was wary of anything but a full, well-supported production. Sam wrote with his usual boldness:

> With regard to my directing it in this country, I feel, immodestly, that failing yourself I would be the best person in this country to do this play. Apart from my understanding of the vigour and strength of your style of writing, there is the matter of the very intimate and personal knowledge of the theme of the play, which I feel is, of course, essential to its clarity for a present day audience.[20]

Miller was not persuaded, and the Bristol Old Vic presented the British premiere of *The Crucible* later in 1954. Oscar Lewenstein did acquire the London rights, but he had plans for it to be produced by the English Stage Company, the new company he was busy setting up.

The officials at the Home Office who dealt with Sam's case were reasonably sympathetic. They had read a Special Branch report stating that he had been actively engaged in Communist Party front organizations in America:

> On the other side, it is clear that Wanamaker is a much bigger figure in the theatrical world than the majority of the Americans in this suspect category. He is a genuinely successful actor and producer ... He seems to have won a considerable reputation over here, and it is significant that Equity are supporting his continued stay as an entrepreneur taking over the Westminster Theatre.

But they did not extend his residence beyond six months, on the grounds that 'it is early yet to see how successful his plans are going to be.'[21] Charlotte needed to renew her American passport before she could be granted a similar extension. The MI5 file on Sam and Charlotte included a sterner statement from the Aliens' Registration Office at this time: in the event of an emergency he would be interned, and Charlotte's activities restricted.[22]

In the event, Sam worked with Ralph Birch only once more, directing *The Soldier and the Lady*, 'a Ruritanian satire' by Ian Stuart Black, that did not come into London. In the autumn, he applied to the Home Office once again. In the hope of getting a better result this time, he gathered supporting statements from a range of people. One was the writer Wolf Mankowitz, and another Roger MacDougall, a screenwriter. Both these were known to have Communist associations, but the other names were more likely to impress the officials: the actress Ann Todd, his friend Ted Sieff, managing director of Marks and Spencer, and somewhat surprisingly, Gilbert Harding, a journalist who, through the radio quiz *Twenty Questions*, and the popular television panel game *What's My Line?*, had recently been voted 'Personality of the Year.' Known for his irascibility, Sam and he had perhaps hit it off through being equally liable to fly off the handle. This time Sam was granted a one-year extension.

Oscar Lewenstein was keen to get Sam back to the Embassy Theatre, to direct a programme of three Yiddish stories by Sholem Aleichem (whose tales of 'Tevye the Dairyman' were to inspire the musical *Fiddler on the Roof*). Presented under the title *The World of Sholem Aleichem*, they had been an off-Broadway hit in 1953. Drawing on his childhood memories, Sam directed a cast of Jewish actors in a warm-hearted production.

T C Worsley admired the simple staging and the acting: 'Mr Wanamaker virtually disposes with scenery and the action moves with the rapidity of a film. This method calls for great flexibility and inventiveness in a producer, and an immediate hitting of the note by the actors. Both are there at the Embassy.' He found that 'Jewish acting has something of the vivid excitement and see-saw charm as does Celtic'.[23] A pity he had not had the chance to see *Purple Dust*.

In the spring of 1955, Sam acted in a feature film again, directed by Cy Endfield, a Hollywood exile. *The Secret* was a crime drama in which Sam played an American stranded in London without any money. A woman has been found dead on Brighton beach, and he knows that her daughter's teddy bear contains diamonds which she has smuggled into the country. He appropriates the bear and takes it to a racketeer, but the child melts his heart and the diamonds are stolen. The child was played by eleven-year-old Mandy Miller, who had first come to fame playing a deaf mute in *Mandy*. All ends well, and he falls for a local teacher, played by Mandy Miller's sister, Jan. The film was praised for its evocation of Brighton, but did not otherwise impress. Importantly for Sam, it filled his coffers and enabled the family to return to Abbey Lodge.

Encouraged by his return to film work, Sam spent some time developing a film project of his own with Wolf Mankowitz, about a gang of delinquent 'teddy boys', but it came to nothing. Instead, he took on another play, directing an adaptation of Émile Zola's *Thérèse Raquin*. Although he assembled a strong cast, including Eva Bartok, a Hungarian film actress, and Helen Haye, a well-respected English actress by then in her eighties, as well as himself, he did not succeed in melding them into an ensemble, and it was panned by Kenneth Tynan in *The Observer*. 'The point is,' Tynan summarized 'that the three stars seem to be acting in different capitals: London, New York and, arguably, Prague. A director of the new school, in short, has twisted the arm of an implausible old melodrama, leaving it twice as implausible as he found it, and twice as melodramatic.'[24] After that, Henry Sherek tried to persuade him to take the Henry Fonda/José Ferrer part in *The Caine Mutiny*. 'It's time you did another worthwhile play – no offence I hope.'[25]

But Oscar Lewenstein was tempting him with a more challenging project, asking him to direct Bertolt Brecht's *The Threepenny Opera* at the Royal Court Theatre in Sloane Square. At that time, Sam was still antipathetic towards Brecht, but he read it, went through some of Brecht's notes, and was intrigued, finally seeing the connection with Stage for Action, the idea of using theatre as a tool for social change. The Berliner Ensemble was playing in Paris that summer, so he went over there, saw *The Caucasian Chalk Circle*, took in the Chinese Opera at the same time, spoke briefly to Brecht, and decided to accept.

Lewenstein had originally intended *The Threepenny Opera* for the English Stage Company, which he had just established, but George Devine, the newly appointed artistic director, did not think it was suitable for his first season. The story of this company at the Royal Court has been told many times, always focusing on John Osborne's *Look Back in Anger* as the play which helped to change the course of the English theatre in the spring of 1956. But Sam's production of *The Threepenny Opera* three months earlier, the first professional Brecht production in London, was equally significant at the time. (The Unity Theatre, in its amateur days, had produced Brecht's early one-act play *Señora Carrar's Rifles.*) This gangster version of *The Beggar's Opera*, the eighteenth century satirical ballad opera by John Gay, had been performed in many parts of the world, but never in Britain.

The version for which Lewenstein owned the rights was by Marc Blitzstein. He was an American writer and composer, famous for the pro-union musical, *The Cradle Will Rock*, a Broadway sensation in 1937, directed by Orson Welles. Having studied in Berlin in the 1920s, Blitzstein had seen the original production of *The Threepenny Opera*. His version was produced off-Broadway at the Theatre de Lys in Greenwhich Village in 1954, with Lotte Lenya playing her original role of Jenny. She won a Tony Award, and the production ran for six years.

Lewenstein set about financing the production, and arranged that it would go into the Royal Court early in 1956, just before the English Stage Company began their first season. He tried to get backing from impresario Tom Arnold, who specialised in musicals, pantomimes and circuses, but he refused. However, his wife Helen, once known for her appearances in Christmas pantomime, decided *she* would back it instead. So Lewenstein, Wolf Mankowitz and Helen Arnold formed 'Peachum Productions Limited' and each invested £10,000. Sam's work on *Uranium 235* and the Jewish play sketches had convinced Lewenstein that he was the right man to direct it. The Home Office granted Sam yet another year's residence, at the end of which he would have been living in Britain for five years, well past the normal time to be eligible for indefinite leave to remain.

Sam watched the 1931 film and listened to records of the original production and the French. He began corresponding with Blitzstein, and set off with Charlotte on a trip to Berlin, with Lewenstein, to discuss the production with Brecht, and to see more of the Berliner Ensemble. The discussions with Brecht went well. Lewenstein and Sam had not known earlier that he was not altogether happy with Blitzstein's version, which was softer than the original. They agreed to put back some scenes and dialogue that he had cut. They met Caspar Neher, designer of the original production, who agreed to do their design, but differently. They met Lotte Lenya and she agreed to repeat her performance of Jenny. Lewenstein had feared that they would find Brecht humourless and rigid, and was pleasantly surprised at his openness, recognising that different times and different places required new approaches: 'We found that Brecht was the least dogmatic of men and he encouraged Sam and me to find the best way to produce *The Threepenny Opera* in London in 1956.'[26]

Sam and Charlotte managed to see five productions of the Berliner Ensemble, including *Mother Courage,* with Brecht's wife, Helene Weigel, in the title role. Ever after, Sam maintained that, however much her rehearsal method differed from a Stanislavsky approach, the resulting performance was 'indistinguishable from the style of a superb Stanislavsky-trained actress'. His talks with Brecht were a revelation, and importantly destroyed forever the residual guilt that he still carried from working with Lee Strasberg. 'He helped me throw away the books and get back to what turned me on as an actor, what it is that actors bring instinctively to their job.'[27] He gave a more graphic account when he next encountered Bob Lewis, his former acting teacher, who related that Brecht, 'in no time at all, and with a few fierce, caustic, scatalogical words, exorcised Wanamaker's guilt for ever.'[28] Brecht's final advice was: 'Remember – whatever you do, let the audience laugh and enjoy themselves. Don't let them take it too seriously.'[29]

On their return to London, Sam continued to correspond with both Blitzstein and Brecht. Blitzstein stressed the importance of 'bounce, style, high pace and a deft unsentimental approach ... I am against any realism for it, except where absolutely required. Mack's gang should be very funny; comedians, possibly acrobatic comedians ... The music should be left untouched; it is a masterpiece of economy and the exact cheesy beauty of sound needed.'[30] Sam assured him 'You've got people putting this thing on in London who understand and appreciate this work.'[31] Blitzstein was delighted that Sam had met Brecht and Neher and Lenya, but warned him Neher's German 'touch' was bound to be 'heavier, slower, more "headlined" and bludgeon-like than English or American audiences find attractive. (I suppose I mean effective.)'[32]

At the same time, Sam was getting different messages from Germany, as Brecht began to get cold feet:

Dear Sam

I am a little bit frightened when I hear you say that you are going to start rehearsals on Dec 28. It is my opinion that the designs of Neher, as beautiful as they are, are very difficult to execute without the model of which we have spoken. But this model cannot be made in a few days.

It is also impossible for me to judge the cast, just by giving me their names. I would have liked to know what they played before etc. But here the time now also too short.

I cannot quite forget that last summer, a similar rushed job, also urged on by Oscar Lewenstein, led to discredit the play Mother Courage and her

Children. So please, don't let yourself be rushed under no circumstances. It would be a pity.

Best wishes

Yours Bertolt B[33]

Brecht was referring to a disastrous production which Lewenstein had helped Joan Littlewood to mount, at a festival in Devon, in May 1955. She was underrehearsed and gave such a poor performance that Kenneth Tynan wrote: 'The result is a production in which discourtesy to a masterpiece borders on insult.'[34] Brecht's assistant, Carl Weber, confirmed his doubts:

> After the Barnstaple Courage which was not very good as Brecht heard, now he has the idea that no production of his plays should be done in England before the authentic "thing" had been presented there. (That has nothing to do with distrust in you, I can assure you, on the contrary, you were extremely successful with Brecht and he speaks very favourably about you.)[35]

The 'authentic "thing"' referred to the prospective visit of the Berliner Ensemble to London, the following May. Brecht and his collaborator, Elisabeth Hauptmann, both hoped Lewenstein and Sam could postpone until after that. But their plans were now set.

Lotte Lenya wrote regretting that she would not be able to do the London production. Instead, Sam intended to cast Miriam Karlin, 'a topflight actress', who had made a success in a Maxwell Anderson play, *The Bad Seed*, and had expressed a great desire to work with Sam, but she was unavailable. Instead, Maria Remusat was cast as Jenny, a French chanteuse, 'a dark-haired girl with a sultry voice and a deep brown voice'[36] whose repertoire included songs by Boris Vian, Charles Aznavour and Gilbert Bécaud, bringing that lighter 'touch' Blitzstein had recommended. Sam sent Blitzstein more details of his casting: Bill Owen, from the Unity Players, played Mack, 'dagger-like, sexy and dapper'; Ewan McColl was the Street Singer 'A real (if not only) authentic ballad singer in England. A leading actor in Theatre Workshop and an important writer in his own right (and in the Epic style too'. One of the other Unity players in the cast was the young Warren Mitchell, playing a member of the gang; Polly was Daphne Anderson 'A distinct and charming personality who knows and understands the content of what she sings'; Lucy was Georgia Brown 'A night club singer. Dark, sexy, very attractive with a superficial veneer and sophistication easily seen through.'[37] She had already started to make her name on television; this was her first stage appearance.

The production was set neither in the eighteenth-century London of *The Beggar's Opera,* nor the dark world of 1920s Berlin, but in London's Soho, on the threshold of the twentieth century. Neher sent his assistant, Ekkehart Grubler, to oversee the design, which had backdrops, side drops and lightweight curtains between the scenes; Sam had felt that English audiences were not ready for the open stage and half-curtain of Neher's original production, but he did introduce a forestage to the Royal Court, which remained a feature long after.

The play opened in Brighton, to what Lewenstein described as 'a typically hostile Brighton audience'[38] and came into London for a six-week run. Most of the notices were positive. Anthony Cardew (*Daily Herald*) was totally won over:

> So here it is at last – a musical that knocks the Americans into a cocked hat, and makes British composers sound like piano-tuners
>
> ... if you want to see a show with a violent, shocking difference, go to the the Royal Court.
>
> For Sam Wanamaker, the producer and the cast, last night was one of triumph.[39]

Milton Shulman (*Evening Standard*) also compared it favourably with recent musicals:

> The greenness of *Salad Days* and the naïvety of *Plain and Fancy* are symptoms of a depressing retreat into simpering wholesomeness.
>
> How refreshing it is then to be able to welcome *The Threepenny Opera* at the Royal Court, which is frankly dedicated to decadence ... Juggling lights, sets, props, asides with controlled and swift dexterity, Sam Wanamaker's production has blended this imaginative and catchy music, this mordant and stimulating atmosphere, this vivacious and enthusiastic cast into easily the most exciting musical in Town./ But I think you had better leave your aunt at home.

Cecil Wilson (*Daily Mail*) wrote that 'Sam Wanamaker's whole seething production with its mixture of wild fantasy and brutal realism reeks of the experimental '20's. Kenneth Tynan welcomed its arrival and found it 'loyally Brechtian'. Alan Dent (*News Chronicle*) found it 'funny, frightening and bizarre all at once.' Richard Findlater, writing in the left-wing *Tribune*, was less wholehearted. He started positively: 'It is good propaganda *and* good art: the theatre and Socialism are noticeably short of both commodities.' But he then went on to criticize the treatment:

By setting the scenes in Edwardian Soho, the adapters of *The Threepenny Opera* have coated the satire with period flavour and have weakened the impact of its savage satire.

However, he found that 'with the help of Sam Wanamaker's brilliant direction, [the characters'] essential world ... is brought to life with a harsh theatrical truth.' And he compared it favourably to the production and film of *The Beggar's Opera* 'smothered in prettification', because it restored John Gay's original purpose: 'to use the theatre as a political weapon.'

At least one critic hailed the event as a watershed, Bernard Levin writing that, after it 'the British theatre would never be the same'.[40] Lewenstein certainly believed that, writing in his memoir

> ... there is no doubt that *The Threepenny Opera*, together with the production at the Arts Theatre of *Waiting for Godot* in the previous August, more truly heralded the new dawn in the British theatre than *The Mulberry Tree*, the lack-lustre first production which followed *The Threepenny Opera* into the Royal Court.[41]

Sam had no thought of creating theatrical history, but he knew that he had gained a renewed awareness of what theatre could do:

> This was what was meant by the lusty and vital theatre of the Elizabethans, the spirited animation and acrobatics of the *commedia del arte*, the formal brilliance of the Chinese and Japanese theatres of joy and excitement, which floods back in my memory of visits to the circus and the music hall.[42]

Inspired by the sense of freedom Brecht had aroused in him, he wanted to act again, and had started on another project, even before *The Threepenny Opera* opened. It was another American play, a romantic comedy by N Richard (Dick) Nash, which he again co-produced, directed and starred in. *The Rainmaker* takes place 'in a western state on a summer day in a time of drought',[43] and tells the story of a charlatan, Bill Starbuck, who enters the lives of a farming family, promising to bring rain. Instead, he cons the awkward, shy daughter, Lizzie, into thinking she is beautiful and worthy to be loved. It had started as a one-act television play. Adapted for the theatre, it had a successful run on Broadway in 1954, where the designer was Ralph Alswang, Sam's friend and colleague.

Sam went into partnership with Jack Minster, an English actor/director who had recently started a production company with E. P. Clift, an experienced manager who had run Basil Dean's company. Sam renewed acquaintance with Ralph Alswang by correspondence, and acquired his design. 'I cannot tell you how wonderful it is to hear from you,' wrote

Alswang, 'we all here think about you and Charlotte.'[44] For the part of Lizzie, he cast Kate Reid, a Canadian actress near the start of her career, who had played the part at the Crest Theatre in Toronto. Wilfred Lawson, a well-known English character actor, would play Lizzie's father and he himself was to play Bill Starbuck, the 'rainmaker' of the title.

On the provincial tour preceding London, Wilfred Lawson's drinking problem became apparent, and Sam decided to recast before the London opening. 'When he was good, he was wonderful,' he wrote to Dick Nash, 'when he was bad, he destroyed the production. I felt we could not take that chance.'[45] However, a week before the London opening, Kate Reid fell ill, and the part of Lizzie had to be recast. Sam took a chance, and cabled Geraldine Page, who had played it in New York. His luck was in; she accepted. He made an emergency request to Hugh Jenkins, then Assistant General Secretary of Equity (later Labour MP and Arts Minister) and managed to get her a work permit. She flew in and was rushed to the theatre so fast she never learned the name of her hotel. But she soon felt at ease with Sam, as she too had trained at the Goodman, a few years after him. Meanwhile Sam himself was re-rehearsing *The Threepenny Opera* for its West End transfer. Jack Minster took over the direction of *The Rainmaker*, and the idea of recasting Wilfred Lawson was dropped.

The play opened at the St Martin's Theatre at the end of May. The emergency casting turned out to be a triumph. Miss Page took nine curtain calls; the crowd at the stage door included Trevor Howard and Bea Lillie. Her performance was: 'the most amusing and touching rendering of helpless spinsterish gaucherie since Dame Peggy Ashcroft was in *The Heiress*'; she was 'a wholly delightful comedienne with a remarkable variety of intonation and gesture which enables her to catch shades and nuances of feeling beyond the usual; one would never have guessed the transmutation could be so touching as Miss Page makes it.'[46] Even Kenneth Tynan was seduced by her:

> In outline, I admit, [the play] … sounds like a howling cliché, the old one about the mousy secretary who becomes the toast of the town as soon as she takes off her spectacles. But we are reckoning without Miss Page, who is a graduate of the Actors' Studio in New York. It is in her power to make a soiled cliché shine like a coin newly-minted; she pierces through the platitude to the truth.

He had words of praise for Sam as well: 'Sam Wanamaker, who has directed them flawlessly, plays the rainmaker with swaggering aplomb …' Cecil Wilson wrote: … [he] plays the swashbuckling rainmaker with his odd trumpeting voice and his odd touches of tenderness better than I have seen him play anything before.' The review in the *Daily Telegraph* read '… he has given no better performance since he made so vivid an impression in *Winter Journey* some years ago.' By October, Geraldine Page had to return to the US, to appear in a repertory of plays in Chicago, after her triumphant London début. The production closed soon after.

The run of *The Rainmaker* brought Sam to the end of his first five years in the English theatre. He had directed ten productions in all, and played the lead in five. He had brought elements of The Method into his rehearsals, though his own training in Stanislavsky's system preceded Lee Strasberg's work in the Actors Studio. He used improvisation to bring immediacy to each situation, and a rich knowledge, based on research, text and imagination, of the whole life of his character, leading up to each moment in the play. His achievement was all the greater considering that he had also directed these plays, eliciting the performances that he wanted from each of his cast, balancing the ensemble, and overseeing the technical aspects of the production. His work on Sean O'Casey and Bertolt Brecht showed that he was not limited to one genre or one approach. The critic T. C. Worsley best summed up the quality that he had introduced:

> Mr Sam Wanamaker has developed a recognisably idiosyncratic style of acting – a sort of poetic realism – which he not only practises himself, but somehow is able, too, to impose on his company. It may sound absurd, but it is most unusual in the London commercial theatre to see a company all acting in one style.[47]

As producer, director and actor, he was playing a significant part in widening the horizons of the English theatre. His former New York business partner, Terese Hayden, later commented 'Sam was very good for London and London was good to him'.[48]

The family now felt at home in London. Charlotte, having given up her career, put all her effort into supporting Sam and the girls, through a mixture of enthusiasm and wise insights. She provided a warm, hospitable home, where they entertained many friends and enjoyed art, music and conversation. Writer and broadcaster Peter Noble recalled a dinner party at Abbey Lodge in 1955, when the other guests included: Cy Endfield and his English about-to-be wife Mo, Eva Bartok, Gerard and Annetta Hoffnung, Wolf and Ann Mankowitz, as well as another blacklisted film producer (Bob Roberts), a Canadian writer (Ted Allen) and an actor who had been in *The Big Knife* (George Coulouris). They spent part of the evening improvising a TV panel game, *Find the Link,* on which Noble was to appear. 'It was an inspiration on

Sam's part to suggest this informal "rehearsal".[49] Perhaps this was also the evening when Sam tore Hoffnung's shirt off his back, while demonstrating how he had tried to pin down the tent, during the typhoon on Iwo Jimo.

The Sieffs remained close friends, as well as the whole Perry family, consisting of Jack and Doris, and five children. Blanche Zohar lived nearby, now married to American producer Mark Marvin. Mai Zetterling, on a visit to Paris with her then partner Herbert Lom, had confided to the Barzmans that of all the women she had ever met, she had most respect for Charlotte. Knowing that Charlotte often lacked confidence, Ben Barzman made sure to let her know this: 'I feel we are not fully aware of our own influence on people.'[50]

The family remained secular, only occasionally observing Jewish festivals and traditions. But Sam and Charlotte slipped into Yiddish if they wanted to have a private conversation. Abby had taken the 11-plus and was now at Parliament Hill Grammar School while Zoë attended King Alfred's, a progressive school in Hampstead. At weekends and holidays, Sam enjoyed leading the girls on outings, making sure to arrive at art galleries towards the end of the day, when the crowds had dispersed, taking them to the Robert Mayer Children's Concerts at Central Hall, Westminster ('no adult admitted except in charge of a child'), and, somewhat to their embarrassment, boldly pushing through gates or doors marked 'Private, No Entry' with the excuse 'Oh, I'm an American, I didn't understand,' if he was challenged.

A 'reliable source' had recently reported to Special Branch that Sam had spoken 'in disparaging terms of the treatment meted out to "true American democrats"' and had said that British tolerance towards Communism was 'in the true spirit of modern democracy.'[51] But the Wanamakers were still 'aliens'; they did not have indefinite leave to remain in Britain. Unexpectedly, in August 1956, the American Embassy asked Sam to surrender his passport. Their situation was suddenly precarious.

6

A Loyal American Citizen
1956–57

On 4 September, 1956, Sam presented himself at the American Embassy, where Mr Richard D. Geppert, the Vice-Consul, informed him of 'certain allegations' against him. When he asked for the allegations to be confirmed in writing, the Vice-Consul said that he was not 'authorized to set them down in writing'. Sam refused to surrender his passport, left the Embassy, and wrote confirming his request that the allegations be made in writing, thus gaining some time. It was another six weeks before he received the confirmation he had asked for, in a letter advising him that his travel abroad was 'not in the best interests of the United States'.[1]

The allegations were that Charlotte and he had been members of the Communist party from 1944 to 1947, that he was affiliated to a number of organizations cited by the Attorney-General, including the Joint Anti-Fascist Refugee Committee, the National Council of American Soviet Friendship and the National Negro Congress, and that he had been associated with organizations cited by HUAC, including the American Peace Crusade, 'Masses and Mainstream' (a Marxist publication) and the National Council of the Arts, Sciences and Professions, the organization which had sponsored the controversial Waldorf-Astoria Peace Conference at which Sam had spoken in 1949. Naturally enough, Sam's first question, which he again put in writing, was why these allegations were being made now, since none of them referred to any recent circumstances.

Although the influence of Joe McCarthy would soon begin to wane, the 'blacklist' in the American entertainment world was still very much in operation. Notes amongst Sam's personal papers record that he had been named, a month earlier, in testimonies by James F. O'Neil, who published the magazine of the American Legion, the veterans' organization, and who encouraged the identification of so-called 'subversives', and by Vincent W. Hartnett, part author of *Red Channels*, who had founded AWARE Inc, a new anti-Communist organization. AFTRA, the union to which Sam had belonged, had been taken over by officers in support of AWARE. When

John Henry Faulks, a radio host, tried to wrest back control of the union, he was named as a Communist in the AWARE bulletin. He was in the process of suing for compensation for his lost employment opportunities, bringing the whole question of 'blacklisting' out into the open.

The Vice-Consul in London offered no further explanation but invited Sam to respond to the allegations in a sworn affidavit. Sam replied that he would not submit such a document without legal advice. He found a lawyer, set about preparing his affidavit and got on with his career.

During the summer, Gerard Hoffnung had persuaded Sam to take on a most unusual engagement. By that time, Hoffnung had published three of his six books of musical cartoons, *The Maestro, The Hoffnung Symphony Orchestra* and *The Hoffnung Music Festival*. In the spring of 1956 he had taken part in an 'April Fool's' concert in Liverpool, and that gave him the idea that there should be a Hoffnung Music Festival at the Royal Festival Hall, presenting 'An extravagant evening of Symphonic Caricature'. Sam agreed to produce, which meant co-ordinating the various ludicrous items on the programme, and the hundreds of people involved. The concert began with *A Grand, Grand Overture*, composed by Malcolm Arnold, scored for orchestra, including Hoffnung on a giant tuba, together with three vacuum cleaners, a floor polisher, and rifles; it was dedicated to US President Hoover. Other items included a revised version of Haydn's *Surprise Symphony*, making it 'rather more surprising', *Concerto Popolare* featuring a battle between a soloist, playing the Grieg Piano Concerto, and an orchestra playing Tchaikovsky's Piano Concerto No 1. Sir William Walton conducted (with a fly-swatter) a one-note excerpt from his cantata *Belshazzar's Feast*: the word "Slain!" shouted by the chorus. Dennis Brain, an eminent horn-player, exchanged his instrument for a hosepipe in an arrangement of Leopold Mozart's *Sinfonia Pastorella for Alphorn and Strings*.[2]

At the first orchestra rehearsal, Sam felt some apprehension, fearful that it would all end in 'a terrifying shambles of amateur hijinks,' but he need not have worried. Malcolm Arnold took up his baton, said 'Let's have a bash', and gave the down beat:

> The impact of sound fairly lifted us all out of our seats ... At the end of the piece, with Malcolm supplying the noises of vacuum cleaners and rifles in the appropriate places, the orchestra dissolved into a convulsion of helpless laughter. I knew then that the Hoffnung Festival Concert was well on the way to being a unique and wonderful experience – whatever happened.[3]

All 3000 seats in the hall were sold within two hours of the box office opening. At the beginning, Ernest Bean, the manager of the Festival Hall, made a brief announcement:

> Ladies and Gentlemen: owing to circumstances beyond the control of the London County Council and the management of this hall, tonight's concert will take place exactly as advertised.

The BBC broadcast the concert on television, and EMI issued a recording in time for Christmas. It was, as Hoffnung's wife described it, 'a massive jamboree' and a huge success.

Earlier in the year, Marc Blitzstein had put Sam in touch with his mother-in-law, Lina Abarbinelli, a German-American opera singer turned Broadway producer and casting director, who was visiting London. They got on well, and afterwards exchanged some correspondence. Sam told her of his ambition to develop a company, and laid emphasis on the American repertoire, which, as he had written to Arthur Miller, he felt particularly qualified to direct. 'You are so right,' she wrote, 'about the list of fine American plays that have never been touched in England which would stand a good chance if properly presented.'[4]

She wanted him to meet a friend and colleague of hers, Anna Deere Wiman, a rich thirty-seven-year-old American theatre producer who had settled in London, and might be a useful ally. She was the wealthy daughter of Dwight Deere Wiman, a well-known theatre impresario in New York, who had made his money manufacturing farm implements. She had begun her career as a dancer, and turned to producing after an accident put an end to her dancing career. It was not difficult for Sam to arrange a meeting, as Miss Wiman was a business partner of Jack Minster, Sam's co-producer on *The Rainmaker*. She had backed some successful West End comedies that Minster produced. Abarbinelli was pleased to hear when the meeting had taken place: '[Anna's] enthusiasm has to be stimulated by people who, like you, are presenting something out of deep conviction and integrity – not like the usual high power salesman of some theatrical ventures. So please follow up your meeting.'[5]

Anna Deere Wiman was not the only rich American producer in London. For his next immediate project, Sam found three more who were willing to put money into an American play in London: the Danzigers, two brothers from New York, who had settled in England, and Nicholas Duke Biddle, son of a rich American philanthropist. Together with Jack Hylton, who had co-produced *The Shrike*, they agreed to produce *A Hatful of Rain*, by a little-known American playwright, Michael V. Gazzo, with Sam acting and directing. It had been a great success on Broadway the previous year. Set in New York, it offered Sam another opportunity to justify his claim that he was the right man to interpret American life for a British audience.

The play concerns Johnnie Pope, a young hero returned from the Korean War, living in the lower East Side in New York, with his pregnant wife and his brother Polo. His injuries have led to an addiction to morphine, which is known to his brother, but not to his wife or to his father, who has come to pick up money promised him by Polo. But Polo has secretly used the money to fund Johnnie's drug habit. For the plum role of Johnnie, Sam cast Bonar Colleano, with whom he had worked on the film of *Christ in Concrete*, for the wife, Sally Ann Howes, daughter of a well-known comedian, Bobby Howes. She had started her career as a child actor, gone on to be a starlet contracted to the Rank Organisation, and then worked in musical theatre. This was her first opportunity in straight theatre. Sam himself played Polo.

In his notes for the production, Sam defined the drug addict hero as the victim of society, represented in the play as the city: 'The size, speed, shape, sound, the materiality of modern society as expressed in its highest form – New York – is the enemy.' He aimed to evoke the nightmare world of addiction, drawing on his familiarity with Manhattan. He designed a rich sound tapestry: street hawker, fire and ambulance, police siren, baby or child, quarrels of tenants, radio blaring, car horns, street pneumatic drill, knocking of pipes, hissing of steam piles. The lighting plot included flashing neon, train lights and a street lamp. There was background music of slow jazz, including numbers by Duke Ellington, Ella Fitzgerald and less familiar artistes.[6] He prepared over twenty situations for the actors to improvise, and identified the themes he wanted to bring out, summed up in one main theme: 'Society is a jungle. Only in full understanding and love can man survive.'[7]

After a provincial tour, the play came into the Princes Theatre (now the Shaftesbury) at the beginning of March. The first night was attended by the usual sprinkling of celebrities, including the film actor Van Johnson, the French actress Martine Carol and the English actor Laurence Harvey. But the occasion turned out to be unexpectedly sad. Bonar Colleano's father James (famous as a high wire artist), sitting in the stalls, was taken ill, carried out, and died in hospital, the news being kept from the actor until the end of the performance. The usual celebratory party was cancelled, and the atmosphere backstage was hushed and sombre.

The critics were not perhaps ready for a play about such a grim subject. W. A. Darlington (*Daily Telegraph*) found the writing ponderous and full of self pity, and thought Sam's production was much too slow, missing the point that this was an evocation of the 'jungle' in which Johnnie Pope lived. The Princes Theatre was too big to draw the audience into the claustrophobic atmosphere Sam wanted to convey. Milton Shulman (*Evening Standard*) damned with praise: 'Mr Bonar Colleano and Mr Sam Wanamaker ... are expert at this sweat and nerves school of acting. They give the play far more than it deserves.'[8]

The programme for this production showed up the incongruity between this dark play, showing something of the underbelly of society, and the theatre-going habits of the English; audiences at a matinée were still invited to order afternoon tea to be served to them during the interval. Actors in the scene that followed an interval often had to contend with the rattle of empty cups, saucers, milk jugs, sugar basins, teapots and spoons, as trays were passed along the row to the usherette. One member of the audience complained of the thick haze of cigarette smoke in the auditorium, impeding her vision – although that might have helped create the appropriate atmosphere.

While working on the play, Sam had also been preparing his affidavit. Before he presented it, the Home Office at last granted him indefinite leave to remain in Britain, with no restrictions, nearly two years later than the usual length of residence required. Charlotte, Abby, Zoë and he were now resident aliens, while still being American citizens. Jessica, born in Britain, had permanent rights by birth. One hurdle down, the next still to be cleared. In April, Sam's legal advisor read the latest draft of his affidavit. 'I think we ought to leave out any reference to blacklisting,' she wrote, 'and deal only with the allegations which the Passport Division itself has raised against you. That after all is the basis on which (God forbid) you will have to litigate.'[9]

At this time, Sam was pursuing a new subject for a film. He had heard that there was a script, as yet unproduced, about Danny Mendoza, an eighteenth-century prize fighter, English boxing champion during the 1790s. Born in England of Portuguese-Jewish descent, Mendoza fought his first fight in 1780, at the age of sixteen. He was working for a tea-dealer, whose side he took when a porter overcharged him. He challenged the porter, who was much larger than him, and thrashed him in a forty-five-minute fight. Soon after that, he made history by boxing in the first match for which spectators were charged an entrance fee. He became famous for devising a new defensive strategy of side-stepping – ducking and blocking to avoid punches. And through his success, he helped to transform the English stereotype of a Jew from a weak, defenceless person to someone deserving of respect. Mendoza was the great-great-grandfather of the comic actor Peter Sellers. Perhaps it was through Sellers that Sam first heard of him; the story must have appealed greatly, at a time when he could not himself use physical force or agility in fighting his corner.

At the end of April, Sam submitted his affidavit to the Embassy. It was an eloquent and considered statement. He looked back and assessed what he had achieved in his life so far, albeit framed as an appeal to retain his passport. He began by stating that he had not been a member of the Communist Party since 1947, and that he had not at any time knowingly been a member of, or actively associated with a subversive organization. He protested that he was, and had always been, a loyal citizen of the United States and had never been associated with, or sympathetic to any activities detrimental to his country. He stated that these assertions and denials were equally true for his wife. He then went through each of the organizations cited, minimising his involvement with them, and risked some irony, by adding a number of other organizations which he had supported, including 'The Damon Runyon Cancer Fund' and 'Mrs Wm Hearst's Milk Fund'.[10]

He then gave an account of his life and career including: his upbringing in Chicago during the Depression; his education and training; his arrival in New York with Charlotte, to work as an actor; the research he had undertaken in preparation for playing the part of a Russian soldier in *Counterattack*, exploring the ideals behind Communism, and the national praise for all things Russian, once the Soviet Union was fighting against Hitler; his support for the Communist Party; his war record; his later disillusionment with the Communist Party, leading him to give up his membership before leaving for Hollywood in June 1947; his professional success in America. He admitted, even though it was not listed amongst the allegations, that he had joined the stars who flew to Washington in October 1947 to attend the hearings of the Hollywood Ten.

Only when it came to describing his first trip to England, in 1949, did he give his account a slant that served the purpose of the document. Omitting all mention of the blacklist, he claimed that, when he returned, to make a film in England in 1951, he had not intended to remain. But after the success of *Winter Journey*, and the prospect of his next production, *The Shrike*, 'I decided (with my wife),' he wrote, 'that we would make our home in London for the next few years.' The reason he gave was entirely professional. 'I felt there was no one in the theatre in England who could correctly and honestly interpret American plays for the British people, in the methods and style for which these plays were written.'[11] He cited an article by Brooks Atkinson, leading critic of the *New York Times*, about the difficulty in bridging the divide between English and American actors and plays. He went on to explain how he was expanding his work into management, and how mounting a production was less costly in England than on Broadway.

He left his strongest point until near the end, no doubt deliberately:

> I have had the pleasure and honor of receiving the former American Ambassador ... and his wife whenever I have appeared in the theatre – and have been invited and attended several receptions at the residence of the Ambassador in Regent's Park, London.

(He mistakenly named the Ambassador as 'Robert Aldrich', who had directed the film of *The Big Knife*, when he meant '<u>Winthrop W.</u> Aldrich', Ambassador from 1953 to 1957.)

> Mr Aldrich, has publicly stated that my work has been of real value and significance in the work of the Embassy to create greater understanding between the American and British peoples.

He went on to emphasise the importance of this quasi-ambassadorial role:

> ... only by the propagation of American books, plays and films in European countries can the mind and the way of life of America be widely known. I believe that everything possible should be done to encourage sympathy between the United States and Europe in these difficult times.[12]

He ended with the request that the State Department's decision to withdraw his passport be reversed, and that Charlotte and he be 'severally at liberty' to have their passports renewed 'as and when our circumstances so require'.[13]

By the time Sam submitted the affidavit, Winthrop Aldrich had left London; perhaps he did put in a good word in Washington. On 29 May, Sam received confirmation from the Vice-Consul that 'the Department of State has reviewed your file and has authorised the granting of passport facilities.'[14] At last, his status was settled. He was free to live in Britain and to travel where and when he wanted. The only fly in the ointment was the bill of £525 he received from the lawyer who had been advising him, amounting to several months' earnings in the theatre. When he protested that he could not afford to pay, and asked her to lower it, she wrote back: 'I shall neither reduce my bill (which is low) nor sue you for payment. You just pay what, if anything, you like.'[15] A satisfactory outcome.

Sam immediately sent a copy of his affidavit to the London office of Columbian Pictures, hoping to interest them in the Mendoza idea, but he heard no more. Instead, he was in negotiation with Mickey Delmar, an English film producer, to 'direct and star or co-star where US participation or story may require it.'[16] No specific projects were named, and Delmar does not appear to have produced more than one film. But by July, Sam had quite different plans, which he was pursuing with Anna Deere Wiman.

On the pre-London tour of *A Hatful of Rain*, early in the year, the management had been unable to book the Royal Court in Liverpool, the city's number one touring venue, because the Christmas pantomime was still playing. Instead, they had booked to play at the 'Pigalle Theatre Club'. This was housed in a theatre which had opened in 1888 as The Shakespeare, presenting *As You Like It*, and had later presented variety shows. Sam was struck by the beauty of the Victorian building, which had been restored and re-decorated, and he then heard that the club was going into voluntary liquidation. He contacted Anna and persuaded her to join him on a trip to Liverpool to look at the theatre. She too was charmed, and they began to make plans to take it over. Sam wrote to Mickey Delmar: 'Much as I regret taking myself out of the film scene at present, this project in Liverpool does, and can mean so much more in the long run than anything I may do on a temporary basis.'[17]

It was just what he had been looking for, the opportunity to run a theatre himself, outside the West End, but meeting West End standards. He knew that Liverpool was a lively city. It had a university, an impressive library, the Walker Art Gallery, St George's Hall with its concert hall and organ, the Royal Liverpool Philharmonic Orchestra, housed in an art deco concert hall, a number of jazz bands and skiffle groups, and several theatres, including the Liverpool Playhouse, a repertory theatre, the Empire, a large house suitable for musicals and concerts, the Royal Court and the Pavilion, in Toxteth, which combined variety and cinema. The shipping industry was still thriving. That summer of 1957, the city celebrated 750 years since King John had granted it a town charter. Its politics suited Sam's sympathies, as it had a strong trades union tradition, and a Corporation run by the Labour Party. He was confident he could attract receptive audiences to quality productions in an elegant and comfortable theatre, despite the growing popularity of television.

Sam and Anna Wiman formed a company, W W Productions, with themselves as directors, together with Miss Wiman's accountant, John Ralph Briggs. Sam was 'Artistic Director', an unusual term at this time, she was listed as 'Management'. They acquired a short lease for the building. Most of the money came from Anna, while Sam was to lead the artistic policy, as well as acting in the company and directing. During the summer and early autumn, plans for the new company went ahead, and the project gained generous press coverage. The *Liverpool Echo* ran a competition to name the new theatre. Suggestions included: the 'Globe', the 'Wanamaker', and more frivolously, the 'Royal Sam' or the 'Wanaspeare'. The majority of entrants chose the 'New Shakespeare'. 'It links the greatest name in the British theatre with the memories evoked by the old name of the theatre,' announced Sam, 'We plan to make it famous throughout the theatrical world.'[18] An interior designer was brought in to alter the building to their requirements and add some elegant Victorian touches.

It was to be far more than a producing theatre. One lesson Sam had learnt from the summer he had run the Festival Theatre in New York was the wastefulness of running a building that was empty for much of the day. He remembered how the Goodman in Chicago had been attached to the Art Institute, and that the theatre had mounted plays for children as well as adults. Anna and he planned what was in fact the first 'arts centre' in England. It would be open for twelve hours a day, seven days a week. Central to the organization was the New Shakespeare Theatre Club, whose members could wine and dine there. They appointed Lovat Fraser, who had previously managed Olivier's company, as General Manager. The restaurant was to be under the personal supervision of Major Donald Neville-Willing, who had run the Café de Paris, London, and there would be a lounge serving Smorgasbord.

Sam invited Esme Church, director of the Northern Children's Theatre in Bradford, to bring some of her productions to the New Shakespeare. There was to be a Film Society, presenting international films, as well as children's films, jazz programmes, and art exhibitions in the theatre basement. The idea of such a centre, open day and evening, offering a range of entertainment, was completely new. (Eighteen months later, the actor Bernard Miles would open the Mermaid Theatre in Puddle Dock, London, welcoming visitors throughout the day, offering food and drink, and running the Molecule Club for children.) 'We aim to make this a Community Theatre', Sam wrote for the opening programme, '… a centre where everyone, young and old, rich and poor, can find something that will be of interest, whether it be drama, comedy, serious music, jazz, art, films or fashion.'[19]

There was a particular advantage in having a theatre club. At this time, all plays for public performance had to be approved by the Lord Chamberlain.

He would either apply a blue pencil to any passage considered unsuitable, or forbid public performance altogether. The way to get round this censorship was to mount *private* performances, open only to members. Sam knew the New Watergate Theatre Club in London, a few yards from the Westminster Theatre. In 1956, this Club had moved to the Comedy Theatre (now the Harold Pinter). There, somewhat to Sam's chagrin, the director Peter Brook had staged the world premiere of the full-length version of Arthur Miller's *A View from the Bridge*, banned by the Lord Chamberlain because of its incestuous theme. The company had also staged Robert Anderson's *Tea and Sympathy*, banned for its homosexual content. Sam now planned to stage both these plays for members of the New Shakespeare Theatre Club, beginning with *A View from the Bridge* as his opening production.

He set about finding an actor to play the lead, but this turned out to be more difficult than he had anticipated. Of English actors, he tried Anthony Quayle, who had played it in London, Jack Hawkins, Trevor Howard and Harry Andrews. Turning to American actors, he tried Kirk Douglas, Van Heflin, Ernest Borgnine, Anthony Quinn, Lee J. Cobb and Broderick Crawford. Perhaps the newness of the venture discouraged them. Also, there was a need to clarify what he had in mind. He wrote to Kay Brown at MCA, the biggest theatrical agency in New York:

> ... the Liverpool theatre project is not a repertory company, as each play will be individually cast and rehearsed in London, and in many cases we will be expecting to bring the plays directly to London whether they are revivals or new productions. It may put some people off if they thought this was a minor repertory or stock company.[20]

By October, news of the project had reached the Security Service. Sam's confirmed status as a permanent resident with an American passport had not brought MI5's interest to an end. A 'reliable source' informed them that Donald Ogden Stewart Jr, son of the blacklisted screenwriter, was helping Sam set up the theatre, and a Special Branch report concluded:

> There is little doubt that this Theatre and Club is intended to be used as a vehicle for disseminating extreme Left wing political propaganda under the guise of culture and progressive education, and if successful, will be a great asset to the Communist Party.[21]

The Chief Constable in Liverpool was asked to investigate what was going on at the New Shakespeare. Ironically, Cliff Carpenter was writing optimistically to Sam at just the same time, saying that the political climate in American was beginning to change: 'The politicians and the public have different preoccupations. There is a general sense that whipping a dead horse any longer is not only dull but ludicrous'.[22]

Sam had now successfully cast *A View from the Bridge*, with Marc Lawrence, a blacklisted film actor living in London, to play the longshoreman Eddie Carbone, and Catherine Feller as Beatrice, his niece. She was a talented eighteen-year-old, with whom Sam had acted in a television play the year before. Sam directed, and played Alfieri, the lawyer who acts as a narrator.

On the 31 October, the theatre, and the play, had a Gala opening. Anna Deere Wiman, wearing a 'knuckleduster' diamond ring and a mink stole, crashed a bottle of champagne against the walls. 'Mrs Wanamaker, a petite blonde with an elfin haircut, had a cocktail dress in champagne faille.'[23] Critics from the national press attended, and gave the new venture an enthusiastic send-off. 'The sophistication and glitter of London's West End came to a side street in Liverpool' (*Daily Mail*); 'For sheer visual beauty inside and out, this theatre has no peer in Britain' (Kenneth Tynan, *The Observer*); 'Certainly the venture I commended five months ago is off to a grand start' (Michael Walsh, *Daily Express*).

The production was also praised: '... Sam Wanamaker brings out the blunt tragedy in all its relentlessness (*Manchester Guardian*); 'Wanamaker's ingenious production gives a new and added edge to the play' (*Daily Express*). Patrick Gibbs (*Daily Telegraph*) felt that the production improved upon Peter Brook's in London, and Kenneth Pearson (*Sunday Times*) endorsed that: 'The production ... was generally agreed to be superior to the recent one in London.'[24]

Sam was particularly pleased with the last two comments. He wrote to Arthur Miller:

> I was disappointed that I had not been approached first to do the play in London in the first place, and felt that you had made a mistake in putting it into the hands of an English director and actors. I have the greatest respect for Peter Brook and Tony Quayle, but they had absolutely no concept of the characters or the texture of the play.
>
> The same thing happened to the production of *The Crucible* in this country and I feel, therefore, in the light of what has been said by several critics and other serious-minded people, that your plays must be given to me, or to other people who understand them, when they are presented in this country.[25]

Miller replied diplomatically:

> The reception in Liverpool of your production has made me very happy, just as its success in London did. I do not agree that Peter Brook and Tony Quayle had absolutely no concept of the characters, but it is not unpleasant to argue about a success. I suspect that your production was more American, as it should be, but that does not necessarily mean that the other was defective.[26]

Underlying the new venture lay a question as to how the partnership between Sam and Anna would fare. They had argued over the signage outside the theatre: Anna wanted Marc Lawrence's name above the title; Sam did not. Anna was quoted in a gossip column, saying, 'Oh dear, I am so tired of these plays about perverts. Oh for some comedy in this grey, grey world. But Sam won't hear of it.'[27] Sam himself wrote to a friend in New York:

> Anna is as usual creating new difficulties and throwing her weight around. I am afraid I have had to throw my own weight right back at her. Unless she is made to understand once and for all that she is not the boss of this venture because she has put up a lot of money – and the sooner this is straightened out the better – we cannot settle down and have a really wonderful theatre.[28]

But the success of the opening, and their genuine wish to create that 'really wonderful theatre' helped them forget their differences.

The first exhibition was mounted in the art gallery under the stage, with pictures lent by Mrs Donald Ogden Stewart from her personal collection; the first children's play was presented, announced by a town-crier, whom Sam had procured after great difficulty. Such a person was rarer than he had expected. The next production was, as Anna had lamented, another play about 'perverts'. But the third production would be more light-hearted and open to the general public.

Robert Anderson's *Tea and Sympathy* had been a success on Broadway, with Deborah Kerr playing Laura Reynolds, the sympathetic wife of a housemaster at a boys' boarding-school in New England, where one of the pupils is alleged to be sexually involved with another master, when in fact the boy is in love with her. She had already repeated her performance in the film, while Sam's former co-star, Ingrid Bergman, had played the part in Paris, and Scottish actress Elizabeth Sellars had starred in the New Watergate production. Sam cast Helen Cherry, a leading actress, married to Trevor Howard. Tim Seeley, a young actor who had recently left RADA, had played the part of the schoolboy for the New Watergate production, and repeated the role for Sam, as well as playing in Sam's *A View from the Bridge.* The other parts were strongly cast, including Norman Wooland, a stalwart of Laurence Olivier's productions and films, who played the apparently macho husband. This production, too, was praised. One critic (*Evening Express*) wrote that it was 'played with a sensitivity which is rare nowadays.'[29]

By the time, *Tea and Sympathy* opened in December, the Chief Constable had passed the task of investigating the New Shakespeare to one of his constables, who obliged with a full report of his discoveries. He pointed out that the Membership Secretary of the Club 'is a staunch Conservative, is a woman of private means, and is connected with a number of local and national charitable works.' He reported that members of the Merseyside Unity Theatre (known for its radical tendencies) had associated themselves with the Club, but Sam Wanamaker 'is not at all anxious to develop any local contacts with left-wing political organisations',[30] and had declined an invitation to address the Unity Theatre Club. The constable included a brochure about the New Shakespeare Club, the programme for *Tea and Sympathy*, a full programme of the plays, children's plays and films, adult films, jazz and other concerts, and art exhibitions being mounted, and cheekily enclosed a Club application form, so that Special Branch could participate in the new venture if they wished. When the Security Service received the report, the most that the Director General could muster in response was to write that the report 'confirms what we expected i.e. that any venture of WANAMAKER's would attract a certain number of Communists and Communist sympathisers, however much WANAMAKER himself might seek to avoid becoming identified with such persons.'[31] After that, little else of importance about Sam's activities was reported to MI5.

Sam was aware that the political climate was changing in America. In the programme note for *Tea and Sympathy,* he pointed out that while the play 'appears to deal frankly with the problems of homosexuality, it goes much deeper and reveals how people who are "different" can be condemned and pilloried by people who do not understand them.' He explained that the play was written 'after the wave of mass hysteria associated with McCarthyism and Senate Committees which swept America a few years ago had subsided.'[32] But he remained careful not to associate himself openly with any political affairs in Britain. A few months later, he was writing to Wayland Young, a journalist who campaigned against theatre censorship, who had asked him to sign a protest when Theatre Workshop received a summons over an unlicensed performance:

Unfortunately, as I am an American citizen, and have pledged to the Home Secretary that I would not participate in any activities which may be construed as political or having to do with the internal affairs of the British Government … I regretfully must tell you that I am not in a position to sign the letter.[33]

Sam knew that the Christmas production would have to compete with the traditional British pantomime. The Empire was presenting *Babes in the Wood*, the Royal Court had booked rock'n'roll star Tommy Steele to star in *Goldilocks and the Three Bears*). Sam chose *Finian's Rainbow*. In this modern fairy tale, set in Rainbow Valley, 'Missitucky', Irish Finian and his daughter Sharon arrive with a crock of gold stolen from the leprechaun Og, and try to help a group of black and white tobacco sharecroppers, whose land is threatened. It had run for over twenty months on Broadway, but its mixture of Celtic whimsy and political comment had not attracted an audience in London's West End. Sam judged that it would suit Liverpool audiences better, offering family audiences a refreshing alternative to 'panto'. It was his first venture into directing a musical comedy, though it had some qualities in common with *Purple Dust*. He asked Sandy Wilson, famous for writing the successful musical *The Boyfriend*, to take the first rehearsals in London, which began while he was still working on *Tea and Sympathy*. Bobby Howes, father of Sally Ann Howes, was cast as Finian (and was later acclaimed when he took on the role again in a Broadway revival), Shani Wallis, already an experienced musical theatre actress (later to create the role of Nancy in *Oliver!*) played his daughter, and Harold Lang, a character actor who had appeared in Sam's production of *The Lovers*, played the leprechaun. The production had good reviews and ran right through January.

The stage director, Maurice Stewart, like the actors, travelled up from London to work on *Finian's Rainbow*. Years later, he recorded his impression of working at the New Shakespeare. At first he had found the project of creating a prestigious repertory theatre questionable, since there was already a good repertory company at the Liverpool Playhouse. But Sam's idea was different, in that he wanted to get 'star names' to come up: 'he put on a very well mounted season of very good productions'. Stewart did not get on particularly well with Sam: 'He actually said later on "You know, there are people you respond well to, and there are people you don't respond well to," … but you know it was a working relationship – it worked. He was running a very, very good theatre, and he did it beautifully if you accepted that he was a performer running the theatre, he *acted* running the theatre.' Stewart felt that there was a need for 'a working-class theatre for working-class people' and that the New Shakespeare was not it, because it was 'a

Victorian theatre, completely refurbished, doing ex-West End plays ... so it was very prestigious.' It attracted 'a slightly snobbish audience because it was the latest thing.'[34]

Sam's viewpoint was a little different. He believed that working-class people deserved a beautiful, comfortable, prestigious theatre centre just as much as the well-heeled, or the 'slightly snobbish'. 'We aim to make this a Community Theatre,' he had written in the opening programme, '... we hope that Merseyside will take over the initiative and treat this theatre as its own.'[35]

7

'A Lifetime Occupation'
1958–59

By end of 1957, Sam could feel proud of the start they had made. On New Year's Eve, Charlotte and he attended the Chelsea Arts Ball, at the Hoffnungs' invitation. Early in January, he gave a talk at the Bristol Old Vic. Nell Moody, wife of John Moody its director, wrote to say how much she had enjoyed it, but Sam replied that it was not as good as he wanted, because he was exhausted. Over the last three months he had launched the New Shakespeare, with all its activities, and directed three major productions. Now free of passport restrictions, he took a recuperative holiday, skiing in Austria, before embarking on the next stage of the enterprise.

Back in Liverpool, there were two pieces of good news. The Education Committee agreed to subsidise schoolchildren coming to the theatre in school time for a performance by Caryl Jenner's English Children's Company. Then Anna decided to take a thirty-five-year lease on the theatre, investing £60,000, and putting the whole scheme on a much more permanent footing. The lease was in her name, and she granted an underlease to WW Productions. Sam wrote to his parents in Los Angeles: '… [it] looks like I shall have a lifetime occupation, which pleases me very much.' Knowing that this might not be quite so pleasing to them, he added, 'It doesn't mean, however, that I will have to live in Liverpool or even in this country for that matter, in future, because we hope that the theatre will be able to operate without my official presence later on.'[1]

The first production in 1958 was a revival of *The Rainmaker*, a simpler task than the first three productions, as he had already directed and acted in it in London. This time a Canadian actress, Barbara Kelly, played Lizzie Curry, the part first created by Geraldine Page, while Sam repeated his own performance as Starbuck. Kelly was best known as a lively panellist on the popular television show *What's My Line?* and seemed an unlikely choice for the role of the plain, nervous and unconfident heroine, but she approached the task gamely, surprising her television fans by dyeing her naturally blonde hair dark brown for the four-week run, and presenting the character as a 'sympathetic hoyden'.[2]

As usual, Charlotte came up for the opening night, while remaining in London the rest of the time. In the autumn, Sam had rented a flat in Liverpool, but he had given it up at the end of the year, and now travelled up and down from London as required. During the week he stayed at the Adelphi Hotel, often taking the midnight train on Saturday night, spending Sunday with the family, and returning to Liverpool on Monday.

In the spring, not wanting to carry the responsibility for every production, Sam had invited three visiting companies to the New Shakespeare. An Irish company, led by the actor Cyril Cusack, came from Dublin, and companies from the Oxford Playhouse and the newly-opened Belgrade Theatre, Coventry, also performed there. On the spur of the moment, Sam took fifteen-year-old Abby on a whirlwind, weeklong holiday to Copenhagen, Amsterdam and Brussels. They went by train, then boat across the North Sea, without reservations or foreign currency, Sam using his persuasive powers to get his personal cheques cashed. They visited Expo58, the Brussels World Fair, which reminded Sam of the Chicago World Fair over twenty years earlier, but was 'much more imaginative and architecturally brilliant'.[3]

The next production was something of an experiment. Sam had been sent a script by a new young writer, Beverley Cross. *One More River* was his first play, and was based on his experience in the merchant navy. It was set on a 7,000 ton British freighter, anchored on the estuary of an African river, on New Year's Eve, the crew unable to join in festivities as they wait for a berth at the nearest port. The Captain has recently died, the First Officer has taken over and is determined that his ship shall be as spick and span as its age will permit, despite protests of ill-usage by the crew. The men take the law into their own hands, with terrible results, despite the Bosun's attempts to conduct a fair 'trial' of the First Officer. Sam hoped that it would appeal to the naval community in Liverpool, bringing in a new audience.

It was the first original play, and the first English play, he had chosen. As with every production, he needed to get Anna's approval, but was beginning to have problems getting her agreement over the plays and the budgets he presented to her. On one occasion, when he sent her a list of thirteen possible plays, she ticked only one. She delayed giving her approval for *One More River*. He wrote to her in London, explaining that it was difficult to get clear decisions when she objected, as she sometimes did, at the last moment, after he had started negotiations: 'It puts me in an embarrassing position with agents, actors, authors and other managements, as they naturally feel they have been wasting their time.'[4] He was anxious to keep the peace between them, and wrote again after he had spoken to her: 'I believe now all the misunderstandings about the above play have been wiped away'[5] He still needed her to agree to its production at the beginning of May. Some actors were awaiting contracts.

The Theatre had now been running for six months. Before Christmas Sam had written to Cliff Carpenter: 'Anna has not stinted in pouring money into the project, but, of course, now it will have to be self-sufficient. Whether we can make it so or not, we will find out in the next few months.'[6] But WW Productions was not yet making money. In March, the accountant and he agreed that it was 'unrealistic to expect any of the activities to immediately make a profit'. But Sam had complained that he had not received clear information about *which* of the many activities were incurring a shortfall. The accountant wrote that he thoroughly appreciated that Sam wanted 'a pattern of book-keeping which will show you where the profits or losses are made or incurred, and this should be running satisfactorily in the immediate future.'[7] He did not explain why such a pattern had not been in place from the beginning. In April he reported that WW Productions was overdrawn by £1600, but he still did not submit weekly running cost reports.

There was also some confusion about authorization of expenditure outside the production budgets. Anna wrote to Sam: 'I am not prepared to pay for any work that is done, unless it has been agreed to in writing by me,'[8] and he replied: 'I quite agree that expenditure has been large and I myself have been surprised at the recent additional amount.'[9] Early on, they had had problems with unauthorized purchases made by Major Neville-Willing, who had swiftly taken his departure from running the restaurant. (At one point he threatened to sue Sam for assault, after Sam elbowed him out of the restaurant during a row.) Robert Lush, who had undertaken the refurbishment of the Theatre, and was still on a retainer, had also put work in hand without reference to Sam. He himself made a substantial reduction in running costs by re-organizing his office at the Theatre so that he could eat and sleep there, instead of staying at the Adelphi Hotel.

Anna's dissatisfaction with affairs at the Theatre became focused on Lovat Fraser, the General Manager and Administrator, against whom she developed a strong antagonism, but she was not the only one to find him unsatisfactory. At the beginning of April, Sam wrote him a three-page letter: 'If the truth were to be told, I have had a long series of complaints from almost everyone with whom you have been in contact on business matters. I tell you this only because you refuse to admit your own mistakes and failures. It is no good pretending that those things do not happen.'[10]

He wrote that he had frequently defended Fraser from Anna's attacks. Eventually, Fraser tended his resignation, and Sam set about finding a replacement. His luck was in, because Beverley Cross's father, George, was an experienced stage director, who, hearing exciting reports from his son about the New Shakespeare, expressed his interest and was appointed. Lovat Fraser left during the run of *One More River*. His departure was announced diplomatically in *The Stage*: '[He] feels that he has done all he can to launch the new venture.'[11] George Cross began a few days later, and proved to be a loyal and efficient administrator.

Sam approached Beverley Cross's play with his usual thoroughness. The enclosed world of the ship offered a microcosm of a hierarchical society. Besides the Bosun and the First Officer, the all-male cast consisted of four seamen, one of whom was ex-Royal Navy, a deck-boy, an apprentice, the carpenter, the cook and two 'greasers', one white, one West Indian. Beverley Cross wrote a note on the characters: 'They are not caricatures. They are not a dozen assorted character men displaying their skills with all the stage dialects from Tilbury to Tipperary. Let them speak plain, audible English, neither emasculated Oxford nor exaggerated Cockney, but a rough and vigorous English.'[12] Sam, taking a popular term of the time, described each as being, in his own way 'an angry man'. He was at pains to achieve realism in the setting, taking his designer (Robert Clatworthy, better known as a sculptor) and the stage staff to visit the Liverpool and London docks, to get the atmosphere of a working ship, and acquiring rails and a winch from actual ships.

The cast was a strong ensemble, including Norman Wooland as the Bosun, and Robert Shaw as the First Officer. The West Indian greaser was played by Thomas Baptiste, a Guyanese-born actor and singer who had worked in Joan Littlewood's Theatre Workshop. The other greaser was played by twenty-five-year-old Michael Caine, who had already gathered experience in repertory and television, but had not yet made the break he aspired to. In his later recollections of that time, he described the Merseyside buzz that was just beginning; he had heard the teenagers John Lennon, Paul McCartney and George Harrison, who had formed the Quarrymen band by that time.

Sam hoped that this play would attract a working-class audience to the theatre. 'It is appropriate,' he wrote in the programme note, 'that the world premiere of this new play should be staged in Liverpool during the celebrations of the Mersey Docks and Harbour Board's centenary year.'[13] He contacted all the local trades unions. When someone wrote to protest at the unsympathetic portrayal of some of the crew, he replied: 'I myself have tempered my early prejudices that the working class must never be shown in a negative light, or that negroes [sic] are all intelligent, or that the working class does not have bullies and hard drinkers among them.'[14] Advance bookings were slow, and the play did poor business throughout its two-week run. An untested script, with no major stars, did not attract the audience Sam had already built up, but nor did it bring in a new audience. He was beginning to realize that it would take longer than he had hoped to persuade the working population in and around Liverpool that a play could be relevant to their lives.

Beverley Cross, who went on to a successful writing career, was grateful: 'Believe me, it's been a magnificent lesson to watch you work – and for an author with a first play, the best possible start.'[15] The following year, he managed to get it on in London, in a new production presented by Laurence Olivier at the Duke of York's Theatre, with Robert Shaw repeating his performance as well as several other members of Sam's cast, not including Michael Caine.[16]

It was ironic that when Charles Marowitz, a burgeoning director, wrote to Sam around this time, asking for £500 towards the setting up of an experimental club theatre in London, he described the New Shakespeare as 'a commercial success', and suggested that Sam had created 'a commercial form of West-End-ism, which is fine, as long as you realise that is what you are doing'[17]. Unsurprisingly, Sam took issue with the word 'commercial', and maintained that 'the productions we shall do could in some cases easily fit into the experimental and artistic frame which you seem to have set yourself'.[18] Truthfully, he did not dare suggest anything that Anna, with her taste for light comedies, would consider too outlandish. She could well afford to cover present losses, but she was volatile and likely to make decisions on a whim. He offloaded the difficulty of dealing with her in a frank letter to Bill and Edith, his brother and sister-in-law, referring to 'my millionairess partner, who is a little bit off of her rocker.' She was 'an example of too much money being a curse, because it has ruined this woman mentally and physically'.[19] In what sense she was 'ruined', he did not explain. Anna was in Spain at the time, recovering from illness of some sort. Although he had got on well with Terese Hayden in New York, he found it difficult that this enterprise, so dear to his heart, was dependent on a successful woman of strong opinions.

Sam's next production was more in line with his previous strategy. Tennessee Williams' *Cat on a Hot Tin Roof* was another play banned by the Lord Chamberlain for its reference to homosexuality. The New Watergate

Club had presented it at the Comedy Theatre at the end of January, directed by Peter Hall, best known at that time for bringing Samuel Beckett's *Waiting for Godot* to London. Premiered on Broadway in 1955, and already filmed with Elizabeth Taylor, Paul Newman and Burl Ives, it tells the story of a dysfunctional Southern family, including Big Daddy, unaware that he is dying, his son Brick, distraught over the death of his friend Skipper, and his wife Maggie, the 'cat'. Sam lured Kim Stanley, who had played Maggie for Peter Hall, to star in his production for a three-week run. She had trained at the Actors Studio and starred in several Broadway plays. In June, Sam could write to a friend: '*Cats*, as you have probably heard from Kim, is playing to packed houses now, and it's a pity that we are unable to play it here longer. Kim is superb in it.'[20]

Sam hoped to welcome his former leading lady, Ingrid Bergman, to visit Liverpool that spring. She had been *persona non grata* in America when she left her husband and daughter for Roberto Rossellini, the Italian film director. But in the same way that the political climate was beginning to thaw, Hollywood and the public had 'forgiven' her offence against conventional morality. She had made a successful return to make the film *Anastasia*, and was now in North Wales, filming *Inn of the Sixth Happiness*, about Gladys Aylward, the English missionary in China. Sam had seen her in London, and invited her to come over to Liverpool from Wales, dine in the restaurant and address members of the Theatre Club. (The Club had already welcomed Vivien Leigh, Claire Bloom, Flora Robson and Tommy Steele amongst its guest speakers). Bergman protested 'Dear Sam, No, no, no. I won't come if I have to be guest at some party.'[21] Sam replied: 'So I only asked. Will sneak you into the theatre through a side door and put an umbrella over the table'.[22] But by the end of June, when she had finished filming, she wrote regretting that she had not managed to get to Liverpool.

Perhaps Charlotte, based in London, looking after the girls, was secretly relieved to hear that, remembering that they had been close in New York. A gossip columnist had recently asked Sam about the ladies in his life: 'My wife was the first girl I ever embraced,' he told her, before listing a number of leading ladies he had kissed: '... Ingrid Bergman, Lilli Palmer, Madeleine Carroll, Jeannette MacDonald, ... Luise Rainer, Eva Bartok.'[23]

For the next production, Sam invited Caspar Wrede, a young Finnish director, to mount a new production of *The Potting Shed*, by the novelist Graham Greene, which had played recently on Broadway and in the West End. Wrede had trained under Michel St Denis at the Old Vic School, and, with others from the School, had set up the Piccolo Theatre, at Chorlton-cum-Hardy, in Manchester, a short-lived enterprise. Sam's invitation could be seen as part fulfilment of the request six years earlier that he should help continue the work that Michel St Denis had done. A year earlier Sam had starred in a television production of Greene's *The Power and the Glory*, and had considered bringing that to Liverpool. It might have been a better proposition than this psychological drama, which critics felt was trapped in the structure of the well-made play.

Still, as the Club membership rose to 21,000, and George Cross settled into his role as General Manager, Sam had reason to feel confident that the New Shakespeare was becoming an established feature of the Liverpool arts scene. The plays and films for children were popular; there, perhaps, lay his hope of building a new theatre audience. The following year, Caspar Wrede would go on to co-found Theatre 59 at the Lyric, Hammersmith, and later, the 69 Company in Manchester, pursuing a goal similar to Sam's, to mount first-class productions outside the West End.

For the summer, Sam presented a 'Comedy season of Broadway successes'. The first was *Reclining Figure* by Harry Kurnitz, a light-hearted piece about the forgery of a Renoir painting, for which all the cast were English except himself. The second was *Will Success Spoil Rock Hunter?* a showbiz take on the Faust legend, written by George Axelrod, who had written screenplays for two Marilyn Monroe films. Bonar Colleano played the naive hero, and the director was Dick Lester, who had worked with Peter Sellers and Spike Milligan, and would later direct The Beatles in *A Hard Day's Night*. The third play was *King of Hearts* by Jean Kerr and Eleanor Brooke, which had won a Tony Award in 1954. It was directed by John Dexter, then Associate Director of the English Stage Company, whose first great success would be the following year, directing Joan Plowright in Arnold Wesker's *Roots*.

Sam had planned the summer season to allow him to join the family for a holiday in France, leaving the cast of *Reclining Figure* when it toured to Streatham. He rented a house in the Alpes-Maritimes, above Nice and Cap d'Antibes. But the break was sadly interrupted for him when, after the final performance of *Will Success Spoil Rock Hunter?*, Bonar Colleano crashed his Jaguar sports car, while driving Michael Balfour, another cast member, and himself, back to London. He was killed, and his passenger was seriously injured. Sam flew back to deal with the aftermath of the disaster. (He reported to Zoë the exciting news that he had met Tommy Steele on the plane.) The rest of the family finished the holiday staying with Norma and Ben Barzman near Cannes.

The autumn season at the New Shakespeare began with a new production of *Epitaph for George Dillon*, which John Osborne had co-written with Anthony Creighton before he wrote *Look Back in Anger*, and which the English Stage Company had presented earlier in the year. This was followed by Sandy Wilson's musical *Valmouth*, based on Ronald Firbanks' decadent novel, preceding its London run at the Lyric Theatre, Hammersmith.

Sam was putting his main effort into another string of significant American plays. He was eager to direct the British stage premiere of William Inge's *Bus Stop*. Inge had refused to grant the rights for a London production of this Broadway success, because he already had one play on in the West End. To Sam's annoyance, he had given the first provincial rights to the unlicensed Leatherhead Repertory Company, where it had played earlier in the year. He was also annoyed that Anna was so slow in agreeing to the production that he was in danger of losing the rights, and eventually obtained them on behalf of his own company, Sam Wanamaker Productions Ltd. He announced his production as the first production in a leading British theatre.

The play, substantially different from the 1956 film starring Marilyn Monroe, is set in a roadside café in Kansas, where a handful of bus travellers are stranded by a snowstorm. They include Cherie, a young night club singer, and Bo Decker, a rancher from Montana, whom he is carrying off to marry. Sam had hopes of persuading Kim Stanley, who had played the part of 'Cherie' on Broadway, to make a second star appearance for him. His next choice was Diane Cilento, who had had much success in film and theatre since appearing in Sam's production of *The Big Knife*. He finally cast Shani Wallis, returning to Liverpool after her success in *Finian's Rainbow*. The production was praised, especially its atmospheric setting; later in the autumn it toured to Golder's Green and other venues..

Early in the autumn, Anna took against George Cross, and suggested to Sam that he should be replaced by Bertie Meyers, best known at that time for mounting Enid Blyton's *Noddy in Toyland*. Sam managed to dissuade her: 'I don't think we should change George Cross. He has done a really wonderful job so far, and I think he is just probably overtired. He has certain weaknesses, as do all of us, but I think a change at this stage would be bad'.[24] He pointed out that Bertie Meyers was over eighty years old, and hard of hearing. The truth was that George Cross was worried about the continuing shortfall. A few weeks later he tendered his resignation to Sam, on the grounds that WW Productions was not in a position to meet its financial obligations: 'It is with great regret that I take this step, particularly as it means breaking my association with you, which has been such a happy one'.[25] But he resolved the situation on his own initiative, persuading Anna to invest a further £10,000 immediately, and continuing in his post.

While Sam continued with plans for the rest of the autumn and for the winter, he was approached with an exciting offer away from Liverpool: to play Iago opposite Paul Robeson as Othello, in the 1959 season at the Shakespeare Memorial Theatre in Stratford-upon-Avon. It would be Robeson's third crack at the role that he – and many others – felt he was born to play. His last ten years had been frustrating and unhappy. In 1949, he had spoken at a World Peace Conference in Paris. His pro-Soviet words were considered deeply unpatriotic, and his passport was withdrawn the following year.

For Sam, the withdrawal of his passport had meant he could not return to America because he would be unable to leave again; for Robeson it meant that he was already trapped, unable to travel. Throughout the following years, he received much sympathy from his friends in Britain, including many in the arts and entertainment world. In 1957, British Equity had got up a petition for him to have his passport returned. Glen Byam Shaw, director of the Shakespeare Memorial Theatre, made the first attempt to have him play at Stratford-upon-Avon, inviting him to play Gower in *Pericles*, to be directed by Tony Richardson in 1958. Robeson and Richardson met in New York, where Richardson was directing John Osborne's *The Entertainer*, but Robeson's application for a passport was again refused. At last, in June 1958, the Supreme Court decided – by five votes to four – that the Secretary of State had no right to deny a passport to any citizen because of his or her political beliefs. When that was announced, Glen Byam Shaw immediately cabled an invitation for Robeson to open the season at Stratford in 1959, playing Othello, directed by Tony Richardson. The idea of inviting Sam to play Iago opposite him was Richardson's; he thought that an American Iago would be a good sparring partner for an American Othello.

After Peter Hall took over as artistic director at Stratford-upon-Avon in 1960, expanded its work to London, and had the name 'Royal Shakespeare Company' incorporated, the years before him were rather forgotten. But the period when Glen Byam Shaw ran the theatre, from 1952 to 1959, first as co-director with Anthony Quayle, then in sole charge, were memorable and glittering, with stars such as Michael Redgrave and Peggy Ashcroft in *Antony and Cleopatra*, Vivien Leigh and Laurence Olivier in *Macbeth*, *Twelfth Night* and *Titus Andronicus*, and John Gielgud in *The Tempest*. In the 1930s, the director Ben Iden Payne had run the annual season for eight years, following his work at the Globe Theatres in Chicago and Cleveland. (The architecture of the theatre had meant he could not pursue his idea of Elizabethan staging.) Sam had been in touch with Byam Shaw and Quayle a few years earlier, with the idea of filming the productions and distributing them in America, but the scheme had come to nothing. To play a leading part there would be a great boost to his acting career. It would be his first leave of absence from Liverpool. He had had such a possibility built into the original terms for WW Productions, and was eager to accept the offer, even though it would mean a substantial time away, and necessitate delegating many of his responsibilities.

Negotiations through Al Parker raised some difficulty over the salary Byam Shaw was offering, £50 per week; in Liverpool he drew £100 for mounting a production and £50 a week while it was playing. Eventually it was agreed that he would receive £2500 for the whole engagement, from February to November, with all his expenses paid. By mid-October, all was agreed, including official approval at a meeting of WW Productions. Richardson wrote: 'I am so delighted that everything is fixed for Iago. I think it will be thrilling.'[26] Sam wrote to Robeson: 'I presume you know that I am to play Iago with you at Stratford next season, which fills me with great delight and excitement.'[27]

The next production at the New Shakespeare was Eugene O'Neill's mammoth drama *The Iceman Cometh,* set in a dilapidated bar in downtown New York. Its British premiere had been at the Arts Theatre in London, early in the year. Making his London debut in that production was a young actor, Toby Robertson, who had understudied John Gielgud in *The Tempest* at Stratford-upon-Avon the previous summer. Sam learnt that he wanted to direct, and gave him *Iceman* as his first professional production, which also played at the Belgrade, Coventry. David Knight, an American actor beginning to make his name in British theatre and film, played the lead. The production was designed by Hutchinson Scott, better known for elegant Belgravia settings, and the production was not thought to be as successful as Peter Wood's in London, though a local journalist, writing at the time of the city's eightieth anniversary year, thought the production 'must surely rank among the finest shows of the whole eighty Liverpool years'.[28]

Robertson's time with Sam may have inspired his belief that 'the best theatre was not synonymous with London'.[29] He would go on to found Prospect Productions, which toured classics around Britain, and later Theatr Clwyd, in Mold, North Wales. Sam could consider Casper Wrede, John Dexter and Toby Robertson all in the frame to stand in for him during 1959.

His own standing as a producer and director was now high amongst theatre aficionados. In October he took part in a radio programme about 'The State and the Theatre' on the BBC Third Programme. The other participants were the Drama Director at the Arts Council, founded more than ten years earlier, the General Manager of Salisbury Playhouse, the director Tyrone Guthrie, and Henry Sherek, the discussion chaired by the treasurer of the English Stage Company. Having lived now for eight years in a 'welfare state', Sam thought the state *should* support the theatre, just as it supported schools, libraries, music 'and institutions of culture and learning generally'. (In July, he had thanked the critic Harold Hobson for 'including me in a short list of management people whom you consider would make good use of subsidy.')[30] He took issue with one participant who thought that unemployment helped an artist to be 'on their toes'. Sam knew from personal experience the stress of worrying about 'how I am going to pay the rent and feed my family and pay the school fees' and felt that that caused a 'sort of division of concentration away from art [that] is very bad and destructive'. He believed that subsidy should be locally controlled, directly related to individual theatres, and administered by theatre people 'not some local businessman who happens to sit on the Council telling an artistic director what to play.' He described the difficulties he faced in Liverpool, where he was trying to bring 'West End quality to a provincial city,'[31] but could not manage financially unless every seat was taken for five to seven weeks. He explained that they were trying to make the theatre building itself a community centre, and that it was a slow process weaning people back to the theatre, when they could be sitting at home watching television, and when travel from outlying areas was time-consuming and expensive. Having noticed the dearth of children's theatre in Britain, compared with America, he raised the question of subsidy for that, and also wondered if subsidy might be directed towards improving theatre buildings, lighting, costumes and scenery, and, thinking of the box-office failure of *One More River*, towards taking risks with new playwrights. The whole discussion was wide-ranging and touched on many topics still relevant to British theatre.

In Liverpool, Sam now focused on the third American play of the autumn season, the British stage premiere of Tennessee Williams' *The Rose Tattoo*, which he had been wanting to present for over five years. He had managed to obtain the rights in the spring, but because of Anna's delays, had again taken them on behalf of his own production company instead of WW Productions. The play tells the story of Seraphina delle Rose, an Italian/American dressmaker in Mississippi, who, after the death of her husband, rhapsodizes about the rose tattoo on his chest, withdraws herself from the world and expects her daughter Rosa to do the same, until the arrival of Alvaro Mangiacavallo, a hunky truck-driver, who reawakens her sexually and spiritually. Maureen Stapleton had created the role of Seraphina on Broadway, in 1951. Tennessee Williams had wanted the Italian actress Anna Magnani, but she did not feel her English was good enough. However, by 1955, she had felt ready, and played the role in the film, with Burt Lancaster as Alvaro, in the role created by Eli Wallach.

Sam wanted to obtain a licence to present the play as a public production, and entered into a lengthy correspondence with the Lord Chamberlain's office. The word 'bugger', was objected to, and also the moment when Alvaro drops 'a rubber preventative' out of his pocket, both of which, the Assistant Comptroller asserted, would 'even in these sophisticated days … cause embarrassment to the average theatregoer'.[32] That piece of stage business had already caused a problem when the play was presented in Dublin the previous year. On that occasion the theatre was invaded by the police, and the director arrested. But Sam could present the play as a Club performance. He approached both Maureen Stapleton and Anna Magnani to play Seraphina, and then had the inspired idea of approaching Lea Padovani, his Italian co-star in *Christ in Concrete*, who had won three awards playing Maggie in *Cat on a Hot Tin Roof* in Italy and had also played Blanche in *A Streetcar Named Desire*. Tennessee Williams had told him that there were only three women in the world who could play Seraphina, and they did not include Lea.[33] However, Sam persuaded him. He approached Eli Wallach and the Welsh actor Stanley Baker to play Alvaro, then decided to play the role himself. For the daughter Rosa, he cast Catherine Feller, who had made a success in his production of *A View from the Bridge* the year before. As usual, Sam took pleasure in creating the local colour needed, using folk music specially recorded by villagers in Southern Italy and Sicily to provide an authentic sound tapestry.

The play opened on 4 November, but Sam remained in correspondence with Tennessee Williams and the Lord Chamberlain's office, and it was finally agreed that Alvaro would *not* drop the contraceptive. The ban was lifted on 21 November, and Sam arranged a second, public opening night. At last, he had succeeded in presenting the British premiere of a major American play. The next step was to arrange a transfer. While several New Shakespeare productions had played outside Liverpool, none had yet played in the West End. This, being a premiere, had a much better chance, and Sam was soon in negotiation with Donald Albery, who ran the New Theatre (now the Noël Coward). *The Rose Tattoo* opened there in January 1959. John Osborne was at the first night, with his wife Mary Ure, as well as Sam's ex-colleague, Luise Rainer.

Afterwards, Jack Perry wrote to Charlotte that his wife Doris had spotted her in a back row 'inconspicuous, hiding from everybody, anxious and tense,' but he assured her that 'Sam's integrity and dedication is beginning to obtrude'. He believed that Sam's career had been hampered by 'envious contemporaries', but that 'his character and honesty is forcing his critics to re-evaluate him'.[34]

The professional critics inevitably compared Sam's production with the film, and some thought that Lea Padovani could not match Anna Magnani's performance. But Philip Hope-Wallace (*Manchester Guardian*) was one of those who saw past that:

> Lea Padovani ... though at first overshadowed by our memories of Anna Magnani in the film ended in a personal triumph, having radiantly played the long and exhausting part. The absurdity of the woman, the primitive rage, and the desolation, were most movingly conveyed. She well deserved the ovation which saluted her at the end.[35]

Harold Hobson (*Sunday Times*) was not so enthusiastic. He greatly admired the play and Sam's performance and acknowledged that there were cheers at the end, but he was critical of Padovani, he thought many of the other performances were poor, and he believed that Sam had misinterpreted the play:

> He has chosen to see the play, except now and then, in his own part, as a comedy, even as a farce. He allows the scene, which should flame with heat, to be illuminated by a positively Arctic sun. The children who run across the front of the stage from time to time and furnish a kind of chorus to the play are not integrated into the mood of the production. The sounds of the players' voices are not in aesthetic harmony with the plentiful off-stage music. And Mr Wanamaker permits Seraphina to inhabit a home which is too spacious, too airy, for a play of such breathlessly fleshly excitement.[36]

Sam was furious at this review and sent Hobson a long telegram:

> Your review of Tattoo vicious, distorted, cruel, vindictive and above all destructive. Destructive of me personally of the New Shakespeare Theatre venture of a brilliant talented actress incomparable in this country and of a company of hardworking talented actors whom you bitterly insult. Am convinced you must retire as a critic since such a destructive force can only do great damage to the theatre and

those of us who give our lives and sincere efforts to it. As result of your vicious piece New Shakespeare Theatre may close. I am withdrawing from producing at Edinburgh Festival and most likely shall return to America.[37]

Hobson responded immediately:

Astounded by your telegram. Read the article again. Its effect will be the exact opposite of what you think. It is critical, which is part of my job. It is also very lavish in praise which again is part of my job but also my pleasure. Beg you reconsider decisions of last part of your telegram. They involve enormous loss to British Theatre.[38]

Sam then wrote a 600-word diatribe against the review, which he perhaps intended to publish, but his harsh words were in reality a displacement activity, substituting for his rage at someone quite different. Some weeks before, Anna had suddenly withdrawn her entire support for the New Shakespeare. The very day of Sam's outburst to Harold Hobson, he was back in Liverpool, chairing a meeting of the Club members to discuss ways and means of keeping the theatre open.

There are no private papers that throw light on what actually went on between the two partners. According to her friend and colleague, the producer Peter Cotes, Anna 'threw tantrums but never really hated.'[39] But she had, over the last months, taken against Lovat Fraser and then George Cross. Now, she turned against Sam. Perhaps she was disappointed that, through being dilatory about the rights in the spring, she was not as involved in the success of *The Rose Tattoo*, as she might have been. She had refused to co-produce the transfer, and retreated to America. Another American donor, Mrs Gilda Dahlberg, an actress who occasionally dabbled in production, had stepped in to partner Donald Albery, with Sam Wanamaker Productions.

For the next few weeks, while re-rehearsing and then performing, Sam had pulled out every stop to keep the theatre afloat. He proposed to run the theatre through his own company during February and March, and to set up a non-profit making company in the next financial year. The staff were given notice, but in the hope that that was a formality. Local support began to arrive. At the Club meeting, there were pledges of £512. The *Liverpool Daily Post* reported on 'the remarkable spectacle of some 200 theatre lovers, congregated on a Sunday afternoon, [vying] to give money away in defence of what has quickly become a cultural institution on Merseyside.'[40] A young woman reportedly walked into the theatre and handed a cheque for £1000 to George Cross. Sam received other pledges of £1000 towards the £4000 he would need to continue with a new production. At one point the Arts

Council offered £5000 if Liverpool Corporation would match it, but their grant would have to wait until the new financial year.

He sent a press release to the local papers:

> I am desperately trying to keep this theatre alive. The scheme has proved an outstanding success and should be in a position to begin to show a profit in another year or so. Should this theatre close down now, it will mean not only shutting down one of the most beautiful theatres in Great Britain, but it will damage the cause of the whole provincial theatre, which has found encouragement and stimulus in the example of the New Shakespeare.[41]

He drew attention to 'A New Pattern of Patronage' – a recent Arts Council report on support for the arts from commerce and industry, hoping there might be a source of funding from that quarter. *The Times* reported on 'Liverpool's Bid to Keep the New Shakespeare Open.'[42] *The Stage* newspaper was supportive, covering the story of the 'Wanamaker Campaign' as a news item, and featuring a sympathetic article by theatrical journalist R. B. Marriott, under the heading: 'New Shakespeare Theatre: Pioneer Experiment and Pattern for the Future', illustrated with a photograph of Sam and Charlotte at their London home:

> ... there is no doubt that the New Shakespeare has set a standard and is forming a pattern which may well influence the theatre in the provinces for a long time.

Sam explained the expenses involved in establishing the theatre and centre. 'Two, or three or even four years are required before one can hope to see a solid foundation.' He pointed out that 'having a social centre, with a theatre, films, an art gallery, concerts, children's productions and other activities, had never been tried out ... we have become stronger every month. Audiences have increased and are more regular – so far as the children's section is concerned by five hundred per cent – and people have become aware that this lovely theatre is for *them* – not only for a small coterie ... Putting the New Shakespeare on the map through advertising, and getting the Liverpool public familiar with all its activities, entailed an enormous amount of work and expense, but results have been achieved and things in this direction are now running far more smoothly.' He admitted that there had been too few plays by new British writers, but claimed that it was imperative to play safe at the beginning, and that it was a problem to get audiences in the provinces to a new play by an unknown writer. Marriott concluded: '... with a good average attendance, and several big successes, the children's theatre and film and art gallery sections justifying themselves, there is good reason to be optimistic.'[43]

Believing that the best way forward was to keep planning a future for the New Shakespeare, Sam announced that, at personal financial risk he was putting a new production into rehearsal. But Anna became vindictive. She revealed in a transatlantic call that she was putting W W Productions into liquidation, and Sam would have no access to the theatre without going to court. The petition for liquidation was presented on 7 January, even before *Rose* had opened in London and the order was made a month later. She issued a statement through her English solicitors, to the effect that she was not receiving any benefit from the current production, and that her position was simply that of a creditor, along with other creditors, of W W Productions. Sam made his own statement putting the blame for financial failure on her unpredictability, on poor administration by Lovat Fraser, the first General Manager, and on poor accounting.

Sam and Anna never worked together again. She continued to back single productions for some years before her early death, aged forty-three, in 1963. At one time she suggested to Peter Cotes that they might run the New Shakespeare together 'where her past losses had been so tremendous.'[44] It was true that WW Productions was making a loss, but she could afford it far better than Sam. He had recognized, quite early on, that the Theatre was not going to make a profit for some time, but he failed to persuade her to stay with the project for the long haul, or to give wholehearted support to his choice of plays. He had worked his charm on her at the beginning, no doubt promising her an enhanced reputation in the British theatre, but, being himself volatile and sometimes abrasive, he had not managed to create a satisfactory working relationship.

Sam continued for many months to pursue ways the New Shakespeare might be saved. One person who helped in his efforts to re-open it was the Head of English at Liverpool Institute High School for Boys. (One of his A-level students was Paul McCartney, who had happy memories of visits to the New Shakespeare.) They failed, but a few years later the teacher went on to be the driving force in the creation of the Everyman, a Liverpool theatre which did succeed.[45]

Sam's achievement was nevertheless considerable. In the thirteen months of the New Shakespeare, he oversaw a repertoire of sixteen productions of significant modern plays, and two musicals; he directed nine productions, each individually cast with a range of fine actors, and he acted in four; he brought in directors for five more productions, together with four in partnership with other companies. His correspondence shows that what appeared upon the stage was the end product of negotiations with playwrights, directors, designers, technicians, agents, actors and theatre managers, only some of which came to fruition. He discovered that he enjoyed administration, and that he enjoyed being part of the Liverpool community. Maurice Stewart, stage manager on *Finian's Rainbow,* commented in his retrospective interview that Sam enjoyed the 'schmoozing', and the press exposure that the role of Artistic Director entailed. That was true, but it was also true that he paid careful attention to less prestigious colleagues and associates. One letter he wrote in the spring of 1958 was to a theatre manager he knew, asking him to look out for a position for the man who had been Sam's dresser in all his London productions, and who had fallen on hard times. When it became clear that the Theatre was not going to reopen, he was assiduous in making sure that those who had made a contribution to keeping it open, had their donations returned to them, especially those who had given £10 or less.

Comparing the New Shakespeare repertoire with a modern theatre season, one difference stands out, and that is the comparatively low profile of women in the companies. While several of the plays featured women in major roles, there were no women directors, no women designers and no women stage directors. Only one play required the employment of a black actor; Sam remained on good terms with Thomas Baptiste, with whom he had fruitful discussions about the possibilities of colour-blind casting.

Most importantly, Sam pioneered a new kind of arts venue, by offering a range of activities under one roof. By establishing a Club, he not only circumvented censorship, but created a core group of loyal supporters, numbering over 30,000 by the end. By presenting children's plays and films alongside the adult entertainment, he cut through a generation gap and made further links with the local community. In later years, he would claim 'Liverpool' as his greatest achievement, and was proud when he encountered those who cherished memories of their visits to the New Shakespeare.

But for an actor, the final exit brings closure, and he is soon on the lookout for the next entrance. In February 1959, Sam left the cast of *The Rose Tattoo* to begin work in Stratford.

8

'Anything and Everything'
1959–1962

S am's dismay at the closure of the New Shakespeare was tempered by the challenging prospect that lay ahead. It was Byam Shaw's final year, and the centenary season at the Shakespeare Memorial Theatre. He had put an impressive repertoire together as well as *Othello*, with Charles Laughton playing Lear, and Bottom in *A Midsummer Night's Dream*, Laurence Olivier as Coriolanus, with Edith Evans as Volumnia, and also the Countess in *All's Well That Ends Well*. For *Othello*, Mary Ure, who had played Alison in *Look Back in Anger* was Desdemona, and Byam Shaw's wife, Angela Baddeley (later to be famous as Mrs Bridges in *Upstairs Downstairs*) was a strong Emilia. The cast included several who would soon be leading actors themselves, including Albert Finney as Cassio and the Australian actress Zoe Caldwell as Bianca. Vanessa Redgrave understudied Mary Ure; she and Diana Rigg were supernumeraries.

Just as Sam was beginning to prepare the role of Iago, he took a phone-call from Byam Shaw, who broke the news that Paul Robeson and his wife had both been taken ill while on their first visit to Moscow since he was free to travel. He would not be able to play Othello. Byam Shaw assured Sam that he was looking for a replacement – perhaps Fredric March, or a black actor, William Marshall, who had made his Broadway debut in *Carmen Jones*, and whom Sam may have known from the Actors Studio. Fredric March was unavailable, and William Marshall flew over. Sam swallowed his disappointment, and arranged to meet him and begin working on some scenes. To his great relief, by the beginning of February, Robeson's health had improved and he was eager to fulfil his Stratford engagement. Marshall returned to New York. (Three years later he played the Moor, for the first of many times, at the Dublin Theatre Festival, and was thought by Harold Hobson to be 'the best Othello of our time.') Byam Shaw thanked Sam for the way he had dealt with the setback:

> I know what a bitter disappointment it was to you when I told you Robeson couldn't play Othello, and your attitude ever since has been marvellously unselfish and helpful. I don't know what I should have done without you – that you should

have troubled to rehearse privately with Marshall, and act those scenes with him when you have had so much to do and so many worries of your own, is something I shall never forget, and for which I shall always be deeply grateful to you.[1]

For the first few weeks of rehearsal, Sam stayed at a company house just outside Stratford, and was looked after by a housekeeper. Julian Glover, who was understudying Robeson and playing Montano, attended the first blocking rehearsals in his place. Robeson arrived, frail and nervous. Tony Richardson encouraged Sam to work with him privately. Robeson was apt to 'sing' his lines, creating a beautiful sound, but not filling the words with real content. Sam encouraged him to explore the emotions underlying the lines. They improvised the situations in their own words, working especially on Othello's jealousy. Sam thought that Robeson succeeded in combining the musicality of the language with dramatic reality, and they achieved a close rapport, on and off stage.

He approached the role of Iago with his usual thoroughness. He had contacted Martin Holmes, curator at the Museum of London, who was an expert on Shakespearean stage history. Holmes pointed out:

> Iago has it all his own way for the first half of the play, but it is no use his trying to steal the second half from Othello. It can't be done ... When Edwin Booth alternated the part with Irving, each of them, as Iago, played the other one's Othello off the stage ... neither of them had the sheer naked passion that the part of Othello requires.[2]

Sam created a back story for Iago, broke the play into units, defined the given circumstances, Iago's objective and the appropriate physical action, invented improvisational situations, and made notes about costume and props. He liked Tony Richardson's approach, which he defined as 'a naturalistic approach which makes the drama easily understandable by the public in terms of today.'[3]

The play opened in April, with a starry first night party, including Diane Cilento and Sean Connery, shortly to be married to each other. The notices were mixed. Cecil Wilson thought it 'a freakish production and grossly maimed text', Philip Hope Wallace thought that Sam's performance was 'loaded down with a great deal of tiresome naturalistic detail'. One critic complained of Sam's 'cold nasal voice, sharply twanged off,' but admitted that he had 'a certain glib charm'. He was soon nicknamed 'Iago from Chicago'. The best review was by W. A. Darlington (*Daily Telegraph*). He felt that Robeson now had the authority that he had lacked in 1930, 'he is completely in control of his followers, of Cyprus and of himself. Only Iago can shake him,' but he felt that, although Robeson had a sincerity, 'he leaves one's heartstrings untouched'. He had much praise for Sam:

> Only a degree less impressive is Sam Wanamaker's Iago, a subtle rogue with a confidence trickster's plausibility which he can shed at will for the benefit of the audience.
>
> We see him as a man at odds with himself whose only compensation for ignobility of character is pride in his magnificent cleverness. This must be the first time that two Americans have appeared together in England in these two great parts. Their countrymen can be proud of them.[4]

When the girls' schools broke up for Easter, Sam rented Mary's Acre, a Cotswold stone house in Broad Campden, Gloucestershire, about fifteen miles from Stratford. They stayed at weekends during the following term, and then for the summer holidays, enjoying an idyllic time during a warm summer. *Othello* had opened the season, playing two straight weeks; as the other plays opened and joined the repertory, Sam had more time off. The current family dog was a blonde Afghan hound called Pasha, who eventually had to be given away, because he kept running out of the garden into a field of sheep. Members of the company visited – Albert Finney, Vanessa Redgrave, Tony Richardson (not yet married to each other), Julian Glover, Ian Holm, Roy Dotrice and his family. Bill Wanamaker came over with his wife, son and daughter. 'Char worked so prodigiously hard,' he wrote after their visit, 'I would like to strike a gold medal in her honor.'[5]

Sam enjoyed being part of a company without the responsibility of running it. He read up about Frank Benson, the actor-manager who ran the Festival over a period of twenty years, and was as keen on how well the company played cricket, as how well they acted. In imitation, Sam organized team-games for his fellow-actors, who responded with varying degrees of enthusiasm. It was a long time since he had played a part for more than a few weeks. He could absorb himself in the world of the play, and enjoy the small changes that made each performance different, either through audience response or through actors making some subtle variation. He encouraged Robeson to vary his performance night by night, but found him too insecure, happier to do the same thing each night. Nevertheless, Sam felt that it was 'a great and defining performance'.[6] The season ended in November; afterwards Byam Shaw wrote gratefully to Sam:

> Thank you so much for all you have contributed to this season, both on and off the stage.

It has been a very special pleasure for me that you have been here during my last year of office.

Your influence in the company has been of real importance and has certainly helped to make it the best that I have known in eight years.

It has been fascinating to see and hear how you have developed and enriched your creation of "Iago", which from the start was brilliantly original and true.[7]

What was he to do next? During that autumn, Sam was still exploring ways of reopening the New Shakespeare. In May, Bernard Miles, an actor and director who shared Sam's idea that a theatre building could be more than a venue for productions, had opened his Mermaid Theatre in Puddle Dock in London, where its restaurant and bar soon became a popular venue, day and evening. He invited Sam to write an article about Liverpool for the programme of the official opening. In it, Sam had stressed the quality of the New Shakespeare building, the many activities it housed, with the plays themselves taking first place, with strong casting and quality productions. 'The New Shakespeare,' he wrote, 'represents a big single stride in a prevalent trend towards a de-centralisation away from the bright lights and glamour of the West End.'[8] But none of the schemes to reopen came to fruition, nor was he offered anything in the theatre that compared with the satisfaction of running his own. The alternative was radio and television, or a film role.

Ever since Sam settled in London there had been broadcasting work, as in his early days in New York. He had grown familiar with the three BBC radio stations. There was the Light Programme (now Radio 2). When he was invited to broadcast a play of his own choice he had suggested a suitably 'light' play, *The Pirate*, a burlesque by S. N. Behrman. The Third Programme (now Radio 3), offered him more highbrow drama, such as *Brothers to Dragons: A Tale in Verse and Voices* by Robert Penn Warren. The Home Service (now Radio 4) did not offer drama, but he was sometimes invited to 'guest' on a 'talks' programme.

His first appearance on BBC Television had been in 1954, *A Tragedian in Spite of Himself*, a one-act play by Chekhov. He followed it with several more plays. Independent Television had begun in 1955, and Sam was in an ITV play with Catherine Feller the following year. In 1957, he played the meaty part of the 'whisky priest' in a BBC TV production of Graham Greene's *The Power and the Glory*. During the Stratford season he appeared with Patricia Neal in a Clifford Odets romantic play, *Clash By Night*, already presented on American television. His performance in *The Velvet Alley*, a play originally done on American television, unfortunately elicited a review headline in

Upper left: Molly Watenmaker; *Upper right:* Morris Watenmaker
Lower: William and Samuel Watenmaker (All ©Bison Archives Photographs)

Upper left: Charlotte Holland, Chicago, c1938 and *Upper right:* Sam Wanamaker,
Chicago, c1938 (©Maurice Seymour); *Lower:* Sam and Charlotte 1940s

Upper left: Jan Sterling, Sam, Ralph Morgan in *This Too Shall Pass*, 1946; *Upper right*: Sam and Charlotte, New York, c1947; *Lower*: Sam with Ingrid Bergman, *Still Life*, 1947. (All ©Bison Archives Photographs)

Upper left: Make-up test for *My Girl Tisa*, Hollywood , 1947 (©Bison Archives Photographs); *Upper right:* Buried in liquid concrete for the filming of *Christ in Concrete* (*Give Us This Day* in UK, *Salt to the Devil* in USA) (Trinity Mirror / Mirrorpix / Alamy Stock Photo); *Lower:* Directing *Caesar and Cleopatra*, with Lilli Palmer, Cedric Hardwicke, Sy Oakland, Nick Joy, William Cayton, Ralph Forbes, Ivan Simpson, Arthur Treacher, New York, 1950 (©Bison Archives Photographs)

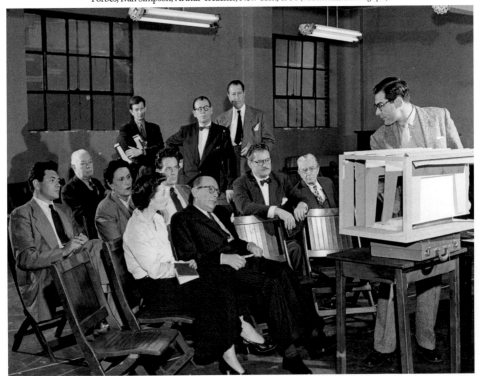

Upper left: With Michael Redgrave in *Winter Journey*, London, 1952; *Upper right:* With Googie Withers in *Winter Journey*, London, 1952. (*Left & Right* ©Mander & Mitchenson/University of Bristol/ArenaPAL); *Lower:* With Geraldine Page in *The Rainmaker*, London, 1956 (©David Westen/Associated Newspapers/Shutterstock)

Upper: Sam, Abby, Charlotte, Zoë Wanamaker, London, 1952 (©Bill Johnson/Associated Newspapers via Shutterstock);
Lower: Abby, Sam, Jessica, Zoë, Charlotte, London, c1957 (©Bison Archives Photographs)

Upper left: Directing *The Threepenny Opera*, London, 1956. (©Julie Hamilton); *Upper right:* With Anna Deere Wiman, Liverpool, 1957. (From the Sam Wanamaker Collection, Howard Gotlieb Archival Research Center at Boston University.); *Lower:* The New Shakespeare Theatre, Liverpool, 1957. Brochure for The New Shakespeare Theatre (Courtesy of Liverpool Record Office, Liverpool Libraries)

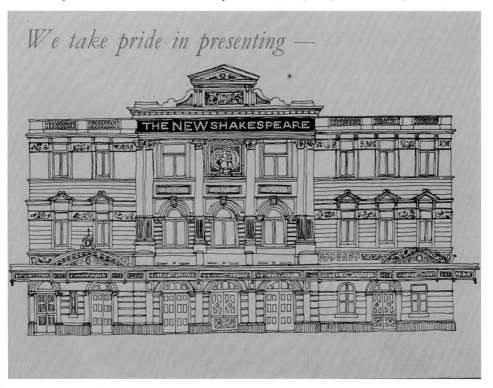

Upper left: As Iago in *Othello*, Shakespeare Memorial Theatre, 1959; *Upper right*: As Iago with Paul Robeson as Othello, Shakespeare Memorial Theatre, 1959. (Both ©Angus McBean/Royal Shakespeare Company); *Lower left*: As King Henry VIII in *Royal Gambit*, Chicago, 1961 (©Chicago Public Library, Special Collections, GTA, PHF, Photographs, 46/31); *Lower right*: As Dr Breuer in *A Far Country*, New York, 1961 (©Bison Archives Photographs)

Upper: 1967 revival of the 1962 production of *King Priam*, Royal Opera House, with Victor Godfrey as Hector and Forbes Robinson as Priam (©Donald Southern/Royal Opera House/ArenaPAL); *Lower: Macbeth*, Chicago, 1964

(From the Sam Wanamaker Collection, Howard Gotlieb Archival Research Center at Boston University.)

Upper left: As Macbeth, Chicago, 1964-65 (©Chicago Public Library, Special Collections, GTA, PHF, Photographs, 54/12);
Upper right: 'Love Story' - 'The Rainbow Man' 1964 (©ITV/Shutterstock); *Lower:* Riding his horse along a beach in preparation for a role in his forthcoming film, *Taras Bulba.* (©John Silverside/Associated Newspapers/Shutterstock)

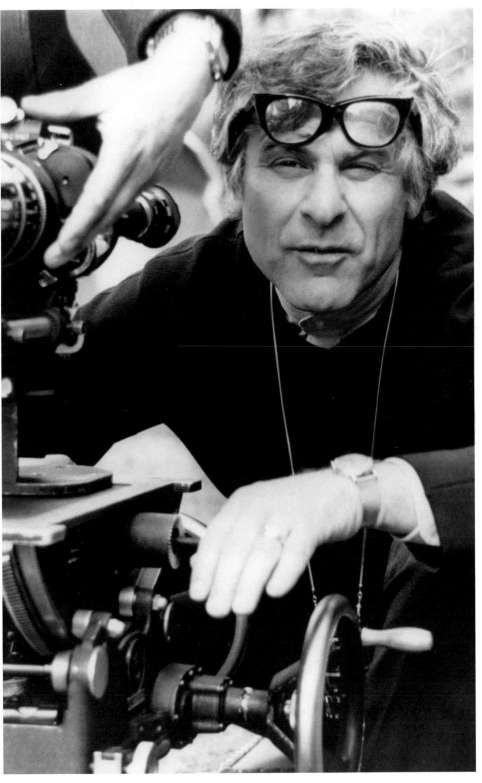

On location in Spain, directing Yul Brynner in *Catlow*, 1971 (©Bison Archives Photographs)

Upper: The Bankside Globe Playhouse, 1973; *Lower left:* 40 Bankside, 1973;
Lower right: In the Bankside Globe Playhouse, 1973. (All ©Bison Archives Photographs)

Upper left: With Charlotte, fundraising for the Globe. (©Bison Archives Photographs); *Upper right:* 1970s, at Trinity Street with Yashmak. (©Ian Tyas/Stringer); *Lower left:* Directing *War and Peace* for Australian Opera, 1973 (©Opera Australia); *Lower right:* Sam in front of a portrait of Shakespeare (©Dezo Hoffman)

Upper: The Australian Opera Chorus in *War and Peace*, Sydney Opera House, 1973 (©Photo by John Walsh, Opera Australia);
Lower: Margaret Price (Aida), Simon Estes (Amonastro), Kevin Langan (King of Egypt), Stefania Toczyska (Amneris),
Luciano Pavarotti (Radames) in *Aida*, San Francisco Opera 1981/2 (©Photo by David Power/San Francisco Opera Archives)

Upper: With model and plans of the Shakespeare Globe Centre (©Bison Archives Photographs);
Lower: With agreement for the Globe site, 1986 (©Photo by Alan Butland)

With the first oak bays of the Globe, 1993 (©Terry O'Neill/Iconic Images)

the *Daily Telegraph*, 'Spectacular Flop for Mr Wanamaker,'[9] though he also received several fan letters about his performance as a failing scriptwriter. 'It was one of your finest performances,' wrote Michael Barry, Head of Drama for BBC TV, 'Anger has been expressed at the savage comment made.'[10] Soon after the Stratford season ended, Sam played Willie Loman in Arthur Miller's *Death of a Salesman* on the BBC Third Programme. More lightheartedly, when he was asked to voice the husband in a nine-minute two-character cartoon, *I Wanna Mink*, for ABC Television, Charlotte voiced the wife.[11] A few months later, they were again together in *Miss Lonelyhearts* on the Third Programme, a black comedy set in the Depression. 'How very splendid you both were,' wrote their friend Eileen Atkins.[12]

The Liverpool seasons had raised Sam's profile as a spokesman for the British theatre. As well as the discussion programme on 'The State and the Theatre', he took part in a radio conversation with Sir Donald Wolfit (famous for his Shakespearean tours, and later portrayed in Ronald Harwood's play, *The Dresser*). The two actors talked about the way they created their roles, including their views of the Stanislavsky system. That must have been a lively discussion, since they came out of completely different acting traditions and both had strong opinions. During the time Sam was still confident he could keep the New Shakespeare open, the Third Programme broadcast 'Talking of Theatre', in which George Devine, Artistic Director of the English Stage Company, Joan Littlewood, Director of Productions at Theatre Workshop, and Sam explored ways and means of running non-commercial theatres. During the Stratford season, he was on the Brains Trust, a discussion programme in which a panel responded to questions from the public (like *Any Questions,* now on Radio 4). A few months later, he took part in a 'Producers' Seminar' at the British Drama League. But invitations of that sort soon dried up when it was clear that he no longer ran a theatre.

Towards the end of 1959, Joe Losey offered Sam a film role. Losey had settled in London in 1953, had little success in the theatre, but then made several films in England, of which the most successful was *The Gypsy and the Gentleman,* starring the Greek actress, Melina Mercouri. Sam had been in touch with him at various times, always hoping they could work together. Losey was now to direct the Welsh actor Stanley Baker in *The Criminal,* a tough crime story. Baker played Johnny Bannion, a dominant figure in the underworld, a topdog in prison, where much of the film is set. He plans to mark his release from prison with a racetrack robbery. In a large cast, Sam played a supporting role as Mike Carter, a sophisticated American corporate criminal, who informs Bannion that crime is now a business: '... your sort doesn't fit into an organisation. So we can't have you running about, messing things up, now can we, John?'[13] After the robbery, Bannion buries the stolen money in the middle of a field, but his former girlfriend informs on him, and he is arrested and sent back to prison. He escapes, falls into the clutches of Carter, and is shot as he goes to retrieve the hidden money. Carter cradles him in his arms as he lies dying in the field, trying to get out of him where the trunk of money is buried.

The original screenplay was by Jimmy Sangster, who had scripted *Dracula* and *The Curse of Frankenstein* for Hammer Films, but Losey got a budding Welsh writer, Alun Owen, to help rewrite it. Filmed in black and white, it presents an unusually graphic picture of life in a British prison, there is a haunting theme song by jazz composer John Dankworth, performed by his wife, Cleo Laine, and the final shots are particularly evocative, as the camera soars up above the field where Bannion dies, and then returns to a long shot of the prison. Losey's directing was skilful, but like many who worked with him, Sam found him uncongenial. He was 'morose, bitter, very interior – self-absorbed. Something of an intellectual snob.'[14] The film was released in Britain in October 1960. The same week, Karel Reisz's *Saturday Night and Sunday Morning*, also opened, heralding a new wave of British cinema, creating a new star in Albert Finney and somewhat overshadowing *The Criminal*. Losey would have to wait longer for a big success. (The film was not released in America until mid-1962, as *The Concrete Jungle*.)

With no exciting opportunity in the theatre, Sam was eager to begin directing films and television drama himself. In the first months of 1960, after completing *The Criminal*, he put out many feelers, and so did the agents in Al Parker's office. He explored the idea of a film based on a story by Robert Louis Stevenson. One actor he approached was Kenneth More, who was not interested but wrote a cheering reply: 'ONE SHOULD ALWAYS TALK ABOUT ANYTHING AND EVERYTHING, WHETHER IT'S IMPOSSIBLE OR NOT'.[15] Sam set up a meeting with the Head of Drama at the commercial television company Associated Rediffusion; he made contact with the Drama Supervisor at ABC Television; he asked MCA and the William Morris Agency in New York for teleplays he could offer to these companies:

> Plays of an hour length or more, international in subject and story dealing with human relations of a universal nature. Comedy or Drama. Nothing too exclusively American in idiom or requiring a knowledge of intimate American attitudes or ideas.[16]

But the scripts they suggested were unsuitable, and he had to make do with taking part in an episode of *Danger Man,* a series which featured Patrick McGoohan as a secret agent, and in a one-off play for Armchair Mystery Series, a spin-off from the more prestigious Armchair Theatre, for ABC.

At last, in August, the Head of Drama at Associated Rediffusion offered Sam a play to direct for ITV Television Theatre, *A Young Lady of Property.* It was set in Texas and concerned a fifteen-year-old motherless girl whose father wants to sell the family house which she loves and owns. An American production had already been broadcast, as part of the anthology series, Playhouse 90. The drawback was that, as Sam was new to directing on television, he was humiliatingly assigned a 'technical advisor', who was eventually credited as 'Director', while Sam was credited as 'Producer', a less hands-on role. In the hope of getting some public credit for his work, he wrote to the television critic of the *Sunday Times:* 'I would value your critical judgment as to whether I have any real contribution to make, as a television producer/director'.[17] But the letter does not appear to have elicited a reply, and the play did not have any great impact when it was shown. (He did receive a letter from a 'John Miller', possibly the man who would eventually become chief marketing officer at NBC in America, saying: 'May I say how thankful I am you have come into television'.[18])

Sam was frustrated that his career seemed to be at a virtual standstill. As usual, his mind was full of possible projects – he had an option to present a stage version of the Soviet film *The Cranes Are Flying,* which had won the Palme d'Or at Cannes in 1958, and he was interested in a Russian play – but neither was a practical proposition. He started to think seriously about venturing back to America. On his behalf, Al Parker began sounding out the situation. In September he asked Arnold Weissberger, a New York lawyer well-versed in all aspects of show business, what were the likely prospects of getting Sam into film or television there. Weissberger replied: 'the procedure would be to offer him for commitments, and if the motion picture companies evince an interest but question his political affiliations, the appropriate statement can then be made.' He explained that television was much more sensitive than motion pictures, because of the sponsors: 'I think it would be extremely difficult for Sam to get on television at this time.'[19]

Weissberger was right in his assessment that working on a 'motion picture' might now be possible. That autumn, Stanley Kubrick's film of *Spartacus* opened in New York. The screenplay was by Dalton Trumbo, one of the Hollywood Ten. He had been living in Mexico ever since he finished his prison sentence and had written thirty scripts under pseudonyms. But Kirk Douglas, star of *Spartacus*, insisted that the screenplay should be attributed to him by name. Two months later, Otto Preminger's *Exodus* opened, also listing Trumbo as screenwriter. Cliff Carpenter wrote to Sam that several other blacklisted writers and directors were finding Hollywood doors at last beginning to re-open to them; Ring Lardner Jr had just gone there for a script conference.

Meanwhile, Sam began to investigate theatre opportunities in New York. He had a new agent there, Milton Goldman, who was supportive. In September Goldman wrote: 'Rest assured, Sam, I want very much to bring you to New York and I will do all in my power to do it as quickly as possible,' and a week later, 'We are working very hard to come up with a plan for you.'[20] Sam was in correspondence with his previous co-producer, Terese Hayden. What about an off-Broadway production of the recent British musical, *Expresso Bongo*? But its main character, a rock-'n'-roll singer, was too close to the hero of the American musical, *Bye Bye Birdie*, based on Elvis Presley, then playing on Broadway.

While Goldman continued to look for an opportunity to bring Sam back to America, a new and exciting possibility had at last arisen in England. The only snag was that it was for eighteen months ahead. Sam had been asked to meet the composer Michael Tippett, whose opera *King Priam* was scheduled for its first performance in the spring of 1962. The invitation had come about through John Pritchard, who was principal conductor of the Royal Liverpool Philharmonic throughout Sam's time at the New Shakespeare, and had been impressed with his productions. Tippett's first opera, *Midsummer Marriage*, had had a mixed reception. This, his second, was to have its premiere in Coventry at an arts festival to mark the reconsecration of its Cathedral after rebuilding. Sam was surprised to be asked. He thought that perhaps the controversy aroused by *Midsummer Marriage* had made other directors reluctant to approach Tippett's work, and that he was invited as a last resort. He had come late to opera-going, having been put off by the poor production of *Die Walküre* which he had seen in his teens. 'To a person of fifteen, it was just awful and it put me off for many years. Eventually I became an opera-goer, if not an opera buff.'[21]

Unusually for Sam, he at first demurred at taking up this new challenge, telling John Pritchard that since he was not a musician and did not read music, he did not feel confident enough to take it on. But Pritchard persuaded him to talk to Tippett, and they hit it off. 'I'm so pleased about yesterday,' Tippett wrote in a postcard, 'and excited into the bargain.'[22]

When Sam continued to have qualms, Pritchard assured him 'Michael will be there with you.' So he signed up for his first opera production. But that did not solve the immediate problem: he had no current project that would earn him good money, give him artistic satisfaction and/or enhance his professional reputation.

Out of the blue came a real chance to work in America again. Sam was invited to be guest artist at his *alma mater*, the Goodman Theatre in Chicago. The background to the invitation was that, three years earlier, the head of the School of Drama, Maurice Gnesin, had died, and David Itkin, Sam's first acting teacher, had retired. Their successor was Dr John Reich, an Austrian director, who had studied under the great Max Reinhardt, directed Austria's national theatre, and emigrated to America before World War II. He had taken the post on condition that the theatre re-establish a professional company. Over the next few years, he built up a list of subscribers, just as Sam had done in Liverpool. In 1959, he was one of ten American directors who received a $10,000 Ford Foundation grant – the sort of sum that would have helped Sam keep the Liverpool theatre going. Dr Reich decided to use the money to bring in professional actors to star alongside students. The role that he offered Sam was quite unlike anything he had attempted before. He would star in a German play, *Royal Gambit* by Herman Gressieker, a surprise success off Broadway in 1957. It presented King Henry VIII of England in relation to each of his six wives. The part was challenging, as it showed the king at every phase of his life.

Milton Goldman was in favour of Sam accepting this offer.

One: it would get him into America. Two: he could meet with some of the television people here in New York and some theatre people about possible theatre work. It's important to be on the scene. Let them see him again. It's been too long since any of them have seen him.[23]

Within a week, Sam had agreed, and John Reich was issuing a press release, linking Sam's name with other Goodman graduates, Geraldine Page, Karl Malden and Ralph Alswang. He managed to get it into the *New York Times* as well as *Variety*, the foremost entertainment magazine.

Sam had three weeks to prepare for his departure. He would be away from the family for Christmas, leaving Charlotte in charge of their plans for a new home. Cliff Carpenter had sold the Connecticut farmhouse for him, and Sam had entered into another joint property scheme. Jack Perry already held some property in north London, and had found an unmodernised Victorian villa in Highgate, which he proposed to pull down, and replace with a new building, in which Sam and Charlotte would have two floors to design as they wished. There was no doubt in his mind that London was his home, but this trip would allow him to see how things now stood in the country of his birth.

Sam flew into New York and had a reunion with Cliff and Mac Carpenter, staying with them on Riverside Drive, reporting to Charlotte that Cliff had grown a moustache and put on weight. He saw Milton Goldman, but had little time to meet many friends, before flying in to O'Hare Airport, the replacement for the overcrowded Midway Airport, lying fourteen miles from Chicago city centre. The weather was freezing. He managed to find Christmas presents, sending Abby a dress (too small) and Zoë a skirt. Charlotte and he had already arranged to buy Jessica a birdcage, which would later hold a budgerigar called 'Basil'. He had ordered a small car for Charlotte to drive herself around London. Then he was plunged into rehearsals, and only several weeks later had the chance to give Charlotte his impression of the city.

He was excited by the Art Institute, which had been entirely redone. There was now a well-established opera company in the city, with a growing international reputation. The Dan Ryan Freeway had cut through many of the old immigrant areas, and the city was dominated by automobiles. Most of the Jews now lived in clean suburbs. Sam noted that the accents of Europe and the ghettos were almost all gone. 'They still eat their corned beef sandwiches, and lox and bagels on Sunday – but after all, who can give that up?' But when he was driven round his old neighbourhood, he found that it was still one vast slum, inhabited by 'Mexicans, Negroes and other depressed people' and he was appalled. 'It all came back to me with renewed revulsion. How ugly and horrible it was – I knew it then and hated it then – the dirt, the ugliness – now more so ... I shall never, ever want to see it again – or have anyone live like that again.' There were various relatives to meet, but he found it difficult to keep up with them all: 'aunts, uncles, cousins, second and third cousins, children, grandchildren etc. But I got most of them over in one crack.'[24] He spent more time with Charlotte's family. Her brother Ernie had died in 1954, and her sister-in-law Eleanor was bringing up two daughters on her own, Ann and Aviva, for whom 'Uncle Sam' soon became a great favourite.

Rehearsing in the Goodman brought back vivid memories. He wrote to eleven-year-old Zoë: 'It is very strange to be back in the place I went to school and to walk through rooms where Mommie and I first fell in love – it all seems so long ago – like a dream.'[25] At first he was frustrated at the standard of acting by the students, at one point describing the young women playing the six queens as 'RANK amateurs', although he was impressed with the student who was playing Katherine of Aragon. He complained that he had had to find the music, and help with the lighting; he was glad he had insisted on hiring costumes for himself from the Old Vic in London. He missed having Charlotte there to boost his morale, and knew that she found the separation difficult. He was unusually pleased when his brother Bill flew in to be with him. Only when the play opened and he found himself basking in praise, did he admit how depressed he had been feeling during the previous months: 'I guess my insecurity had hit a new low these last months in London. The fears of money, of career, of feeling unwanted and untalented, of being boxed in were so great that if the play had flopped it would have staggered me. You know my decision to come to the States was motivated by sheer desperation.'[26]

The two-week run, in January 1961, was the hit of the Goodman season. The chief Chicago critic, Claudia Cassidy, whose reviews were read widely, gave the production a thumbs up, praising Sam's performance as 'a rich, full-blooded characterisation that expands to fill first the eye, then the imagination. It is a brilliant, resourceful, often hilarious piece of work.'[27] John Reich wrote delightedly to Gressieker's American agent: 'I think you will be pleased to know that *Royal Gambit* was the greatest artistic success the Goodman has had since I took over three and a half years ago.' He included copies of the reviews 'by leading Chicago critics, which you may know are generally much more severe than Broadway critics.'[28] The part of King Henry was demanding, as the character was only ever offstage long enough for Sam to change his make-up, and re-enter, having aged. Many who came backstage were particularly impressed with that aspect of the role, which to Sam was merely external, though he did admit that the changes themselves were a challenge, leaving no time to breathe or smoke a cigarette. He was better pleased at the praise he received from Danny Newman, press agent for the Chicago Lyric Opera, who remembered him from when he was a student and later recorded his impression of the performance:

> I recall those magic moments of Sam's monologue spoken on his knees as, in the role of King Henry VIII he pleads for heaven's intercession ... Only such a magical actor as Jacob Ben-Ami, one of the fabled greats of the international Yiddish stage, could so instantly evoke such eviscerating emotion in an audience.[29]

Excerpts from the play were televised as a showcase on a Chicago channel, and Sam was able to obtain a 'kinescope' – a recording made, before the use of magnetic tape, by literally filming the screen.

In an interview for the *Chicago Sun-Times*, Sam talked expansively about his ideas for the future of theatre, going further in the direction that his experience with Brecht had led him. He now looked forward to a kind of theatre that combined 'dance, music, art, costume, spectacle, literature, movie screens – an amalgam of all the arts, with a purpose'. He contrasted it with a recent Broadway production, Jack Gelber's *The Connection*, one of the first productions mounted by the avant-garde company, Living Theatre, an experimental play-within-a-play that focused on a group of drug addicts. Sam felt that that had little to offer except 'mystic self-contemplation'.[30] In another interview, he was optimistic about plans for the Lincoln Center for the Performing Arts, already in construction on Manhattan's upper west side, as part of an urban renewal scheme; he hoped that such an initiative might be copied in other parts of the country.

While Sam was in Chicago, the moment came that Charlotte and he had 'both hoped and dreaded', when an opportunity arose to return to Broadway. The play, *A Far Country*, was about the young Sigmund Freud; Sam was offered the role of Dr Breuer, an older man who warns Freud about the dangerous territory he is entering, as he starts to use hypnotism to delve into the suppressed memories of a beautiful, aristocratic young woman. The title was based on a quotation from Heraclitus: 'The soul of a man is a far country which cannot be approached and explored.' Sam liked the play, he liked the part, it would be good money, and Milton Goldman thought that, although it was a supporting role, it might lead to work in England, as well as perhaps opening the door to television work in America. But Sam knew that prolonging his time away from London would place a huge strain on Charlotte, as she dealt with the three girls, the household and plans for the new flat, without Sam beside her, all the time aware that he was starting a new life that she was not part of. He knew that he too, having missed her encouragement while rehearsing *Royal Gambit*, would find it difficult to take on another demanding job without her beside him. He wrote:

> Now the biggest and most agonising problem – the separation. And darling believe me when I say that this for me too would be painful and terrible and almost too much to bear. Despite all the excitement, the small success, the new and stimulating experiences and people, I am more and more aware of the need of you and the children. I know all your hidden fears – that I might get to like

it, that I might want to live here, that I might find a pretty young girl and fall in love – all that has been going through your mind – it won't happen![31]

He accepted the job, flew to New York to discuss it with the producer, Roger Stevens, then to Los Angeles to see the family there, then back to New York to begin rehearsals. In early February, *Variety* carried a notice: 'Welcome and Thank You SAM WANAMAKER'.[32]

Eager as usual to research the character he was playing, Sam started a correspondence with a psychiatrist, about the real Dr Breuer. The production starred Kim Stanley, who had acted for Sam in Liverpool; it played in New Haven and Boston in March, before opening in April 1961 at the Music Box Theatre on Broadway. On the first night, Roger Stevens wrote gratefully to Sam, echoing Glen Byam Shaw's praise, eighteen months earlier: 'You have been a steadying influence over the less experienced members of the company.' Henry Denker, author of the play, wrote 'You're going to find out tonight how much the American theatre needs you. Now that you're back, do us all a big favour ... Stay!' Charlotte, returning from another stay at Mary's Acre with the children, sent a 'good luck' cable from JAZME,[33] the abbreviation for Jessica, Abby, Zoë and 'Me', which was how Sam and she usually signed off their letters to each other.

The play opened on Broadway at the beginning of April. It was well reviewed, including Sam's performance. Frank Aston (*New York World Telegram and Sun*) thought the part was 'suavingly and movingly played'. For Howard Taubman (*New York Times*), 'a fine American actor who too long has absented himself from this country, plays Dr Breuer ... with elegance and compassion'. Walter Kerr (*New York Herald Tribune)* wrote that 'The nuances Mr Wanamaker keeps inventing for the role are rich in dignity and strength'. A less prestigious journal, *Women's Wear Weekly* stated: 'A prodigal returned to Broadway ... illumes the play.'[34]

Cliff and Mac Carpenter attended the opening night. Mac wrote to Charlotte the next day to say how good Sam was in the play, and how much he was missing her. Sam had perhaps prompted her to write that, because Charlotte had just learnt that the danger she had most feared was perilously close: Sam's former lover, Jan Sterling, had been in touch with him. Sam wrote the same day to try and set Charlotte's mind at rest. He explained that he had meant to tell her when she came over from London to see the play. Apparently, when 'JS', as he referred to her, had first read that he was back in America, she had called him to say 'hello' and 'welcome back'. He had agreed to have lunch with her: 'I realised this woman had not grown up at all since I saw her last – despite a husband who drank himself to death and apparently a completely unhappy marriage.' Eighteen months earlier, her husband Paul Douglas had had a fatal heart attack, aged fifty-two, at their Hollywood home. Four years before that, she had had a son, whose father, according to rumour, was Charlton Heston. Sam wrote that when she hinted that she was romantically interested, he was 'surprised and shocked'. He told her that he had no intention of starting a relationship, considering the 'scars' left on his marriage by their earlier liaison. 'She said she understood and she seemed to mean it. We parted in a friendly way, wishing each other happiness and good luck.'[35]

Charlotte brought Jessica to New York on a short visit, and returned to London somewhat reassured. They continued to communicate through frequent letters, occasional transatlantic phone-calls and messages on reel-to-reel tape-recorders. The design of the Highgate flat preoccupied both of them, Sam sending samples from time to time that he thought would be suitable for furnishings. During this period, Charlotte was doing occasional radio work, that, to some extent, must have raised her morale. In May, Sam wrote her a love-letter, in celebration of their twenty-first wedding anniversary, describing how their marriage had come of age, from when it was 'tender and tiny and helpless' through its 'difficult adolescence' to what it was now, an adult 'strong, sure of itself, not unscarred – but loved and loving. Happy birthday, beloved, Sam'. [36]

Meanwhile, he was strengthening his position back in the American theatre. The press representative for *A Far Country* was Merle Debuskey, soon to become a close friend. He made sure that Sam's return to Broadway was given ample coverage. Sam omitted any political slant to his account of his years in Britain, in order to avoid any sense that he was not proud to be American. 'Wanamaker insists,' reported one interviewer, 'he didn't leave this country initially for political reasons, as has been intimated. It wasn't to have been a longterm move in the beginning, he says, only "a sort of holiday," a chance to work there and see the country.' He was 'building a home for his family in London, … but has no intention of giving up his American citizenship, and in fact hopes to divide his time in both countries henceforth, thanks to the jet age.' He described himself as 'a perpetual transient', explaining what life as an actor was like. 'You can't really plan anything. You have to take what comes your way when it comes and where it comes from.' His present job was typical. 'It happens to be a most attractive role … and it caught up with me at a moment when I had nothing to do right away.'[37]

Still nostalgic for what he had achieved in Liverpool, he wished there was something like the New Shakespeare in America:

> What I would really like to see happen would be for several American cities to have permanent year-round professional community theaters where actors, directors and writers could put down roots and stay permanently if they wished; become members of a community and not have to worry about whether they're going to have to rush off to New York or London or Hollywood in order to make a living in any given season.[38]

In another interview, held at Lindy's, the famous Manhattan deli, he talked about his future plans. These included a wish, perhaps deliberately provocative, to direct the Irish actor, Peter O'Toole (not yet the star of *Lawrence of Arabia*) in *The Ginger Man*, a dramatization of a novel by Irish writer J. P. Donleavy. The novel had originally been banned for obscenity; the play, produced in Dublin, had been closed for its offensiveness.

He spoke of doing some Shakespeare. He said that he had been asked to stage and act at the American Shakespeare Theatre in Stratford, Connecticut, and perhaps do a Shakespeare play in New York. He would not be drawn on whether English or American actors were better at handling the language: 'There is a basic unaffected speech for the English actor devoid of Oxford and Kensington, just as there is a virile American speech, devoid of southern or midwestern inflection.'[39] Danny Newman, having heard that Sam was to direct *King Priam* in London, tried to get him to direct a production for the Lyric Opera in Chicago. None of these plans came to fruition, but others had more basis in reality.

While *A Far Country* continued its successful run, Sam staged a production for the Theatre Guild. The play, *Ding Dong Bell*, written by two American women, had won a prize in *The Observer* playwriting competition, set up in England by the critic Kenneth Tynan. Sam had planned to stage it in Liverpool in partnership with Donald Albery, the manager who had helped him bring *The Rose Tattoo* to London. It was about a ruthless populist demagogue in a Southern community, like the controversial Governor Huey Long of Louisiana, assassinated in 1935. 'Idealism, that's the sand in the wheel of progress,' was the cynical motto of 'Abidah Bell'.[40] It played in Westport, Connecticut, but did not come into New York.

Milton Goldman then put Sam up for a guest appearance in an episode of a new CBS television drama series, *The Defenders*. Just as lawyer Arnold Weissberger had predicted, the big shots at CBS were unwilling to employ him, even in 1961. Sam produced the Affidavit he had presented to the

American Embassy in London, four years earlier. He also let them know that, because of his wartime service, he was a member of the American Legion, the veterans' association. The Legion had contributed to the creation of the 'blacklist' and staunchly supported McCarthyism. Its threat to boycott *Salt of the Devil* (the American title of *Christ in Concrete*) had meant the film had very little exposure in America. It was a pleasing irony that the Legion now indirectly helped convince CBS to employ Sam.

Mindful of the challenge that lay ahead of him back in England, Sam made a trip to Tanglewood in the Berkshire Hills in Massachusetts, to meet Boris Goldovsky, director of the opera department at the Music Center there. The visit was useful in two ways. First, he saw how he did *not* want to direct singers, since Goldovsky blocked them to move according to a musical phrase, while Sam was already thinking about ways to bring the human drama to life. Second, hearing a rehearsal pianist at work, he realized that the problem of not reading music would be solved by finding someone to play a piano version of the score to him.

The next hurdle for Milton Goldman was to get Sam back into motion pictures. That proved easier than for television. In the early autumn, Sam left the cast of *A Far Country*, made a quick trip back to London to see the family, and then flew off to Argentina, to take part in a Hollywood epic.

The film was *Taras Bulba*, based on a novel by Nikolai Gogol about a sixteenth-century Cossack leader from the steppes of Ukraine, and his battles with the Poles. It had already been filmed four times before, including a silent version, and a British version called *The Rebel Son*. This lavish American version was directed by J. Lee Thompson, a British film director who had recently achieved great success with *The Guns of Navarone*. Russian-born Yul Brynner played the eponymous hero and Tony Curtis played his son. Sam was 'Filipenko', a headman, bearded and moustached, resplendent in black and red uniform, complete with Cossack hat, under which he had to be bald. He learnt Cossack dancing, took riding lessons from a White Russian ex-cavalry officer, who taught him, among other tricks, how to jump off a horse backwards. His part involved a lot of macho shouting, and riding into battle. Sam was critical of the script, the organization, the directing and the star actors. He wrote to Charlotte that it should be 'Larger than life, but not phoney.'[41] But he made the whole experience pleasanter for himself by moving out of the hotel in Salta where the cast and crew were staying, to the nearby village of San Lorenzo, which reminded him of Portofino in Italy and offered a peaceful retreat. (The film was released a year later, and Brendan Gill, in the *New Yorker*, described it as 'a preposterous animated cartoon of a picture' with the actors 'looking very silly in native costume'.[42] It was popular with audiences but never recouped its large cost.)

When he finished filming, Sam spent four days in Mexico, then on to Los Angeles, and then New York, for discussions with producer Roger Stevens, and another television play, this time for NBC. Once again he was initially rejected. It was 'the old bugaboo', and he had to produce the affidavit once more, before he was given the role. At last, in March 1962, he flew back to London to start work on *King Priam,* his first job in England for eighteen months.

9

'BIG' or 'Marvellous'
1962–1968

S am had begun his preparation for *King Priam* by reading Homer's *Iliad* to get a sense of the world of the story. Then he studied Tippett's libretto in detail, and saw that it could be staged as a visual, theatrical, dramatic piece. Only then did he start on the music, playing a tape-recording of the piano score, and linking it with the development of the drama. The designer was Sean Kenny, also new to opera, best known for his creation of the slums of London in the musical *Oliver!*. For *King Priam*, he built a steeply raked circular revolving stage, with different ramps and levels allowing for a variety of scenic arrangements. There were elaborate back-projections, changing the colour and mood of the scenes; the costumes were classical, with individual modern touches.

The first performances were at the end of May 1962 in Coventry Theatre, conducted by George Solti, part of the Festival commemorating the reconsecration of the Cathedral. The venue could accommodate only half the set, but still allowed Sam to create patterns of movement on different levels. He found that, compared with rehearsing a play, he had very little time with the singers. John Pritchard had assured him that Tippett would be on hand to guide him, but in fact the composer left him alone, and he worked on his own with the company, first asking them to read the libretto aloud, to connect them with the reality of the story. When it came to the *sitzprobe*, the first orchestral rehearsal with the singers present, which Tippett conducted himself, he found the music a revelation, hearing for the first time the different contribution made by each instrument. After Coventry, the production moved to the Royal Opera House, where the full splendour of the set and production could be realized.

The reviews were enthusiastic. There was a sense that something new was being done. David Cairns (*The Spectator*) felt that the production marked 'a coming of age of operatic design in this country,' replacing 'the dusty parochialism' of what had gone before. He admired the colours which seemed 'both antique and new, evoking the ancient world in a fresh and utterly convincing way.' He picked out a moment when the radiant light matched 'the intense shimmer in the orchestra, as Priam … confronts Paris … (one of many superbly effective moments in Sam Wanamaker's production).' He felt that the steep rake brought the audience close to the action, and encouraged the actors '(if only out of regard for their own safety) to stay in their correct positions and acquire a more controlled, less loose and "operatic" style of gesture'. He ended with praise for the 'inspired fidelity with which the truth of the opera is realised, in action and symbol in the theatre.'[1]

Peter Heyworth (*The Observer*) praised:

> … Sam Wanamaker's lucid and vigorous production and Sean Kenny's sets, which adapt a quasi-Bayreuthian formula with virtuoso-like brilliance and individuality.
>
> This is one of the finest productions I have seen at Covent Garden. It marks a coming of age in a field in which our native operators have for too long been content with the inanely decorative. I hope that this remarkable team will be given a chance to try their hand at Wagner.[2]

Charles Reid (*Punch*) wrote that Sean Kenny and Sam, 'both making their debuts in the operatic field, attend to the eye with a nobleness of touch which makes all the contemporary opera productions I ever saw, and most other incursions from the straight theatre seem pretentious muddles by comparison.' Several critics noticed the quality of acting that Sam had drawn out of the singers. Andrew Porter (*Financial Times*) wrote that Sam's production was brilliant 'not only in its theatrical progress, but also in its realisation of the characterisations and conflicts that make up the living surface of the inner drama.' Another wrote 'Mr Wanamaker gets better acting from the half-dozen members of the repertory company than I – or I suspect, themselves – ever dreamed they were capable of.'

It was Sam's first chance to explore the fusion of different performance elements which he had defined, when talking about theatre while he was in Chicago. George Solti, the Hungarian-born conductor, musical director at Covent Garden since the previous summer, was impressed with Sam's work and saw the answer to a problem he had had been trying to solve since the beginning of the year. Verdi's *La Forza del Destino*, last staged at Covent Garden thirty years earlier, was scheduled for performance that October, but he still did not have a producer (the term still used at the Opera House for the director), having originally hoped to get Franco Zeffirelli. He asked Sam to take it on. He had already engaged the Italian tenor, Carlo Bergonzi, for the main role of Alvaro, but had some difficulty finding a singer for the heroine, Leonora. He eventually settled on Floriana Cavalli, who was 'as good a soprano as was available'.[3] Sam agreed to 'produce', even though it gave him less time to prepare than he would have liked for such a major work.

After *King Priam*, Sam returned to America to play two parts in a summer company at the Olney Theatre, Maryland. Not Broadway, but it gave him the opportunity to tackle a couple of substantial roles, the first as Berenger in Ionesco's *Rhinoceros*, the man who witnesses the transformation of all the townspeople into rhinoceroses. Eli Wallach had played the part on Broadway, Laurence Olivier in London. Sam was praised for his 'delicate, tasteful, warmly humorous portrayal of the distraught Berenger'. 'With skill born of imagination and experience, Wanamaker creates a memorable, quizzical fellow.' He followed this with Captain Bluntschli, the 'chocolate cream soldier' in Shaw's *Arms and the Man*. This was much more suited to him than pompous Sergius, the part he had played in 1950. 'A strong cast headed by Wanamaker give the old number a fresh look.' His portrayal was considered

> ... a brilliantly conceived Shaw hero. His scorn for the absurdity of military heroes and for the romantic and intellectual delusions of the Petkoff household is the more stinging for being always subdued. He dares to be off-hand with the play's most dazzling dialogue, to pit a crisp and tidy mind and soft voice against the primitivism of the Petkoffs.[4]

These positive reviews show the contribution Sam could make, acting in a repertory season such as he had attempted at the Festival Theatre. Later in the year, Milton Goldman passed on to him a suggestion that he should take over the Arena Stage, Washington. This was a not-for-profit theatre co-founded in 1950 and run by a Russian emigrée, Zelda Fichandler. It was the first integrated theatre in the city; she hired actors regardless of race or colour. She was ready to pass on the baton, and had thought of Sam. Goldman wondered if this might appeal to Sam as a way of continuing the work he had done in Liverpool. But, despite what he had said the year before, about wanting to see 'permanent year-round professional community theaters' in American cities, he does not seem to have given the idea any considered thought. It would have meant an enormous upheaval in family life, and perhaps he was not attracted to the idea of following in someone else's footsteps. Instead, Fichhandler stayed on for nearly thirty more years.

Back in London in the late summer, Sam continued to prepare for his second opera production. As with *King Priam*, he had begun by studying the libretto. This time there were commercial recordings of the work that he could listen to. Musically rich, *La Forza* is a long and unwieldy dramatic work, with eight different locations. Sam's idea, which Solti approved, was that, instead of the usual heavy-handed romantic sets for each location, the design should be spare and presentational, so that each scene could flow musically into the next, the changes made in full sight of the audience. He soon ran into difficulties with the appointed designer, Renato Guttoso, who was first and foremost a painter. Sam wrote to him:

> I had envisaged different planes for each scene, by rearranging two or three basic platforms in different positions. Projections – to make comments on the action of the story and not to be a pictorial representation of the scene. I don't mind using pictorial projections on the cyclorama to define place, so long as we have foreground projections on scenes in the form of hanging tapestries of flags, banners or hanging burlap[5]

When Guttoso sent sketches which Sam did not like, the designer 'felt obliged to withdraw though without any feeling of ill will';[6] the sketches were later put up for sale in a private London gallery. Sam contacted Michael Knight, who had assisted Sean Kenny on *King Priam*, and they designed the sets together, creating 'the sparsest sets they have ever used in the epic-minded Garden.'[7] '… we extract bits of reality from the whole work, and the composite makes up to total reality – a door without a wall, a church represented by a cross, candlesticks, a hint of stained glass'.[8] He used paintings by Goya as an inspiration for the costumes, and for some of the projections. He wanted to bring out the pathos of war that he saw forming part of the background to the story.

He worked out a specific character for each of the 150 members of the chorus. Rehearsing the principals, Sam again began by having the cast read the libretto out loud. He was pleased with the effect of this exercise:

> Many singers understood the content of what they were singing only after speaking the libretto. A still further revelation was that the spoken intonation usually matched the musical; where there were variations, these were found to be a matter of different emphasis and often shed light on the composer's intention as to meaning, thus illuminating a nuance not previously recognised.
>
> The singer now found that when he sang the libretto again, the effect on his interpretation was enhanced with shades and subtle variations … His total relationship to the music, the other characters, the situations in the story – all took on a new and immediate experience.[9]

At first, the cast were tentative and nervous, but most gained in confidence. The chief problem was that Carlo Bergonzi arrived only five days before the first performance, and attended only one complete rehearsal. Sam rehearsed with an understudy, then took Bergonzi through the blocking, and the duel. Partly because Bergonzi was never integrated into the production, partly because the cast was not, as with *King Priam,* drawn from the resident company, the ensemble did not achieve the same quality of acting. Nevertheless, James Lockhart, the répétiteur, wrote to him afterwards saying 'I have found you one of the most outstanding producers I've ever worked with. Gifted operatic producers are so rare that I hope you will continue in this field, and I hope I'll be working with you again in your next production.'[10]

On the opening night, the first hint of trouble from the audience came after Cavalli had sung the famous aria 'Pace, pace mio dio', when a stentorian voice from the audience demanded 'Where's Shuard?' referring to the English singer, Amy Shuard. Cavalli was 'often out tune, sometimes acid in tone, and generally dull in interpretation.'[11] Bergonzi sang beautifully. He ignored the staging, walked down to the footlights, faced the audience squarely to sing his arias, and received rapturous applause. For the duel, Sam seethed as he 'stood there and waved his sword like kids do.'[12] At the curtain call, he was greeted with enthusiastic cheers, Cavalli was greeted with savage boos, Solti was applauded, with a boo or two, and Sam, for the first time in his life, was 'vilely and violently booed'.[13] He smiled and bowed, while Solti smiled and took him by the hand.

There was much comment and correspondence afterwards about the booing, some believing there were 'claquers', many shocked at the audience behaviour. It may have been caused partly by antagonism at the ticket prices, which had been raised because of Bergonzi's and Cavalli's participation; her poor performance caused resentment as well as disappointment.

Sam's production was slated by some: 'I can hardly believe that the shoddily makeshift bits and pieces that we saw represent a considered attempt to stage a spectacular romantic opera.' 'Sets of an appalling ugliness'. 'Sam Wanamaker's tendentious staging, with its implications of political protest, and incorporating a large number of Goya projections, was apt to make points not merely irrelevant, but contradictory.' Andrew Porter, who had praised *King Priam,* also took exception to the Goya, and believed that Sam had wrongly imposed social comment on the opera. But others praised his work. Frank Granville Barker (*Music and Musicians*) wrote: 'Sam Wanamaker, in a production of remarkable clarity and intelligence has done everything to hold the sprawling work together.'[14] He later wrote to Sam: 'Thank you for a smooth, splendidly atmospheric production that let the opera flow from beginning to end. I've seen it a couple of times before, but it has always seemed scrappy and disjointed – but you've really made it clear and unified.'[15] Another enthusiast wrote to Sam: 'Needless to say I'm not among the carpers at "Forza" – I thought the whole company (bar the tenor) acted wonderfully, and the whole scheme a clear, lucid exposition of an all-but-insoluble problem.'[16]A critic in Germany commented: 'In England ... generally speaking the public approaches operas with the mentality of the last century.'[17]

The influential theatre director Peter Brook, in an article about the role of the critic, felt that the music critics had missed the point. In his view, Sam had achieved:

> a quite strikingly high level of production, where so often things have been loose and untidy and messy. He did something which, from all standpoints of view of the theatre and opera, was an improvement, imaginatively done. Stupid intervals were replaced by a more modern and more intelligent use of scenery, and so on.

Some critics, he thought,

> were not aware even that as a whole this represented something which for the medium was a step forward. Their irritation that the soprano's voice wobbled, that they looked at images on the stage which were unfamiliar and annoying, led them to a sort of anger by which the entire production was demolished.[18]

Cavalli withdrew from the last few performances; Bergonzi was not scheduled to sing them; Sam stayed away from opera for the next ten years. He had been invited to direct *Die Zauberflöte* at Glyndebourne the following season. After *Forza*, he wrote to the General Manager there to say that he was now unavailable.

Sam had a number of jobs to look forward to in 1963. He was cast in several plays on British television, and a film. He was in negotiation with Irwin Shaw to direct one of his plays in America and perhaps in London as well. He started the year playing in another episode of the American series, *The Defenders*.

But before any of that happened, the family at last moved, before Christmas, into their new 3000 square-foot duplex in a small custom-built modern block in North Grove, Highgate. It had been designed and built entirely to Charlotte's and Sam's specifications. Downstairs, was a large reception room with a central fireplace, divided by floor-to-ceiling stained-glass doors from a smaller room, and a kitchen-dining room. Other doors opened onto a large terrace leading to the rear garden. A floating stairway led to the upper floor, with a master suite including a bathroom and dressing-room, three more bedrooms and two bathrooms. These rooms led onto a walkway overlooking the rear garden. The move, however, took place in a freezing, snowy winter, before there was central heating, or carpets on the concrete floors. For the first few weeks the family shivered.

At the same time that Sam started work on *The Defenders*, Abby left home to study at UCLA, staying with her Uncle Bill, Edith, Marc and nine-year-old Lisa, with whom she had to share a room. The arrangement was so impractical, that she was back home after one semester, at which point Sam arranged for her to go to Israel, and stay on a kibbutz. When she returned, Sam had enrolled her on a speech therapy course. He had firm ideas about what his daughters should be doing. Zoë continued at King Alfred's, and Jessica at the Lycée Française.

In New York, Sam started to rehearse the Irwin Shaw play, *Children From Their Games*, which he co-produced with Roger Stevens. (He had the rights, Stevens put up the money.) 'Stevens has been marvellous to me –' he wrote to Charlotte, 'he stays away'.[19] (The company was flabbergasted when Jacqueline Kennedy walked into one of the rehearsals.) It was a strange title for a comedy that did not quite work, about a misanthropic writer who tries to persuade a close friend to kill him, but is frustrated by the arrival of a number of eccentric characters. The leading actor was Martin Gabel, who had started his career in radio, working with Orson Welles, and had recently won a Tony Award in another comedy. The play opened in New Haven, Connecticut, where Sam's staging, Gabel's performance and the design were admired, but when it came to Broadway in April, it closed after only four performances, criticised for an 'improbable situation' and 'unprobable people'. Walter Kerr (*New York Herald*) found it inventive, but 'The evening's conceit keeps wavering.' The actor Gene Hackman, soon to begin his film career, played a small part, and won a Tony Award for Outstanding Performance as a Newcomer. Martin Gabel wrote that he had found working with Sam 'a revelation':

> I never knew a play to benefit so much from a director's invention. Really. I'm sure there will be many plays offered to you here – because many people, including the staff of the Stevens plays factory, know how well you did for them.[20]

Later that year, Roger Stevens did indeed offer Sam another play to direct. As usual, Sam had another project in mind as well. In preparing to direct *King Priam*, he had read Robert Graves' translation of the *Iliad*, published as *The Anger of Achilles*. He learnt that Graves was adapting it into a three-part radio drama. Sam thought it would also make an impressive film, and wrote to the poet in Mallorca, suggesting he turn it into a screenplay. Graves expressed some interest, but nothing came of the idea at that point. It stayed simmering in Sam's mind, to re-emerge at a later date. Roger Stevens' offer was less lofty. Henry Denker, the author of *A Far Country*, had written a play based on a famous libel trial, when a journalist had sued a right-wing columnist for calling him 'yellow' and accusing him of being an 'absentee war correspondent'. The journalist was represented by a well-known attorney, Louis Nizer (who also represented John Henry Faulk in his suit against AWARE), and won the biggest award ever made up to that point. Courtroom dramas were proving popular on television, including *The Defenders*, the series that Sam had already played in, and *Perry Mason*, then in the middle of its successful nine-year run. Van Heflin, an actor successfully combining a theatre and film career, played the lead in *A Case for Libel*. Sam found him difficult to work with; when given private notes 'he just keeps dissing everyone else'.[21] And he could not improvise in rehearsal, as Sam wanted: 'I'm no good at making up lines – I cut whatever I can. But,' he wrote on opening night, 'I'll never delete or tamper with lines that might express my gratitude and sincere feeling for you.'[22]

Sam was not completely satisfied with Henry Denker's script, but he researched court procedure in order to make the trial as authentic and dramatic as possible. After opening night, he cabled Charlotte:

NOTICES LUKEWARM TO GREAT CONSENSUS WE HAVE A HIT BUT PERSONALLY CAUTIOUS BUT OPTIMISTIC ARRIVING BOAC SUNDAY CANT WAIT LOVE ME[23]

The consensus was right. Most critics found that the production and acting created enough suspense to overcome the problem that most of the audience already knew the outcome of the trial. After a few weeks in London, Sam flew back to New York to film another episode of *The Defenders*, and to keep an eye on the production, which ran well into the following year.

Thus, he was in a television studio in New York on 22 November, 1963, when the news broke that John F. Kennedy had been assassinated. Sam described to Charlotte how someone in the company had a transistor radio, and heard it reported 'first as a wild rumour, then that he was wounded, then that he was dead'. From that point on, no one could think of work and the afternoon petered away inconclusively. 'We all went our separate ways – still disbelieving – still hoping it was some kind of hoax.' The theatres all closed. Sam watched television until 2.00 am, feeling the same 'shock, horror, sorrow, outrage,' as most of the world.[24]

Where exactly was Sam's career going? He wrote to Charlotte at this time: 'I could do lots of things but I'm not going to unless it pays BIG or is so marvellous I'd love to do it.'[25] His contract with Roger Stevens gave him $5000 plus 2% of the gross box office, rising to 3% once costs had been recouped. If he had accepted the offer to direct *Die Zauberflöte* at Glyndebourne that year, he would have received a one-off fee of just £750. It was difficult to balance the wish to earn good money, with work that would satisfy him artistically. Michael Tippett wanted him to direct his next opera, *The Knot Garden*. Edward (Ted) Downes, who had conducted some of performances of *King Priam* and *La Forza*, wanted him to direct Stravinsky's *The Rake's Progress* in Australia. A few months earlier, Sam had filmed an episode of *The Twilight Zone* in Hollywood, a series that ranged through science fiction, horror and fantasy. He had no objection to these popular genres, but:

> I see so much MEDIOCRITY around here doing well – like Denker – and these TV people and in NY – that I know I have more than that. But something is lacking – I know that – judgment – shrewdness – staying power – business sense – and erratic talent – sometimes good, sometimes lousy – no consistency.[26]

He was unsure if the fault lay in him, or the different worlds in which he sought employment.

It was especially difficult for him to find work in England that was either satisfying or lucrative. His productions in the 1950s had helped to inject the theatre there with a new energy, both in London and Liverpool. The director Richard Eyre would later describe the influence of American theatre in that decade, creating, 'a voracious appetite for a sinewy and passionate language used with unembarrassed enthusiasm'.[27] But in the 1960s, British playwrights of a new generation were finding their voices, developed out of their distinctively British experience: Harold Pinter, John Osborne, Shelagh Delaney, Ann Jellicoe, Arnold Wesker, Joe Orton, Brendan Behan. Producers looked for British directors and actors to interpret them. There was the occasional television episode to direct or play, but he had still not directed a feature film in Britain – or indeed in America.

Sam began the year 1964 directing for three producers he had not worked with before: Jeff Britton, M. J. Boyer and Nan Lawrence. *A Murderer Among Us* was a French play set in a small town in Provence, about a man wrongly convicted of murder, who decides, after serving his sentence, that he is 'owed' a crime. It was translated by George White, who had written the English version of *Royal Gambit*. Its theme bore comparison with Friedrich Dürrenmatt's *The Visit*, in which a wealthy woman returns to her home town and offers a large donation, if the townspeople kill the man amongst them who made her pregnant and then jilted her. Perhaps the producers were looking for the sort of success that play had had when Peter Brook directed the well-known acting couple, Alfred Lunt and Lynne Fontanne, on Broadway in 1958. It is not clear how Sam got involved. The translation was wordy and confused, there were no stars to attract advance booking and critics found Sam's over-busy direction tried to encompass too many theatrical worlds, from zany farce, to mordant comedy. It previewed for twelve performances, but closed after opening night.

For some months after that, Sam pursued a surprisingly different project, in collaboration with the actor Richard Burton. They had worked together filming John Le Carré's *The Spy Who Came in From the Cold*, in which Sam had one scene, as an East German intelligence officer. Burton's extra-marital affair with film star Elizabeth Taylor, begun two years earlier, had brought the couple enormous publicity. They had made one film since then, *The VIPs*, which closely mirrored their private lives; they wanted to work together again on something different. The idea that interested Burton, Taylor and Sam was a film based on the Great Train Robbery, which had hit the British headlines the previous summer, when a gang of robbers stole £2.6m from a Royal Mail train. In April, Burton, Taylor and Sam announced their plans to form a production company to make it. Arnold Weissberger outlined to Sam the business arrangement they would need to make:

> I take it that each of you will have a two-fold relationship: Richard, Elizabeth and yourself as co-owners of the production company; Richard and Elizabeth as actors, employed by the company, and you as directer employed by the company.[28]

Burton suggested fellow Welshman Gwyn Thomas as screenwriter, perhaps as a sop, since he had agreed to appear in a play of Thomas's about Aneurin Bevan, and that project had come to nothing. Presumably, Burton was to play Bruce Reynolds, nicknamed 'Napoleon', leader of the gang, and Taylor his wife. Gwyn Thomas called on Sam, and left with the impression that this project was going to be 'very big indeed'.[29] The two of them had several productive meetings. Gwyn Thomas never knew, and Sam did not record, how and why this project also collapsed. But the real-life drama of Burton and Taylor continued to make headlines.

Sam now pursued a project that was definitely on the 'marvellous' side of his career, as it would not earn him much. John Reich was eager to lure him back for another guest appearance at the Goodman. At the same time as Sam was making plans with Burton and Taylor, he was in correspondence with Reich about directing and starring in *Macbeth*, which would be his first Shakespearean role since playing Iago. He wrote that it would be 'a labour of at least six months preparation,'[30] and he was anxious not to miss out if a lucrative opportunity arose in the meantime. Reluctantly, Reich agreed to Milton Goldman's request that the contract include a get-out clause. Sam signed in early May, the fee would be $1000 – less than he would have got directing *Die Zauberflöte* at Glyndebourne. Reich appointed a staff director to assist, who could, if necessary, take over if the get-out clause was invoked, Sam began correspondence with the Goodman chief designer.

His ideas for the production were influenced by the operas he had directed. He envisaged a 'Scotland' that was barbaric, but with modern connotations. He wanted to use projections, as at Covent Garden, and consulted Ralph Alswang and Eddie Kook, another close friend, who was a lighting designer. Alswang had recently used projections that integrated live action with motion pictures in a process which he called 'Living Screen'. He recommended someone in Chicago, who might help create such projections. Reich took fright, as Sam's ideas grew:

> My friendly advise [sic] is to forget the projection system ... Please make it an actor's not a designer's play.

He pointed out that '[e]verybody in the US' was now greatly influenced by the bare, thrust stages built at Stratford, Ontario (completed in 1957), at the Chichester Festival in England (completed in 1962) and at the Guthrie Theatre in Minneapolis, which had opened the previous summer. 'And we do have some actors who can really speak',[31] he assured Sam. By June, he was still trying to persuade Sam to use the architecture of the building to differentiate the various scenes, and hoped he would use 'as small a cast as possible'. He advised double casting, 'rather than use beginners in small parts'.[32]

His advice fell on deaf ears. In line with Sam's ideas, the Goodman resident designer created a set consisting of a revolve, on which an elaborate series of planes, ramps and stairs were built, made of harsh, industrial materials, so as to be 'strong, violent, full of strains and stresses'.[33] The costumes were 'a monochromatic scheme of all shades of black and white, the red of blood being the only splotch of colour.'[34]

Sam arrived in October, and ensconced himself in a suite at the Astor Tower hotel. His private rehearsals and dramatic outbursts there caused pandemonium. One of the maids reported 'There's a madman up there.'[35] Later, Charlotte joined him, and they spent time with her sister-in-law and her daughters. Her family noticed how much he relied on her guidance, and the extra boost to his confidence she always gave him.

The Assistant Director wrote a programme note: '*Macbeth* is a story of the night. There is a pervasive barbarism throughout the play wherein human destruction is matched by chaotic disorder in Nature.'[36] Sam had set himself a huge task in managing the production at the same time as undertaking a notoriously difficult role. The set was so difficult to negotiate that he broke his ankle on it in rehearsal and had to miss two performances. There was a complicated sound plot, as if he was trying to create the equivalent of an operatic score: the witches issued their prophecies through off-stage recordings; Macbeth's own imaginings were accompanied by a piercing whistle; each murder was followed by a series of loud clangs. In rehearsal, he worked on appropriate reactions from the student cast, moment for moment, but did not succeed in fully motivating them. After one performance the Assistant Director wrote a stern memorandum accusing them of 'dullness and self-indulgence',[37] while admitting that it had not been an easy rehearsal period.

Reviews for the production were mixed. Roger Dettner (*Chicago's American*) was impressed:

> Mr Wanamaker and his associates have gone the Bayreuth route, so to speak, to make *Macbeth* cosmic ... This *Macbeth* has imagination, gaudy daring and a European willingness to put aside clichés of tradition in search of heightened dramatic expression.

But Richard Christian (*Chicago Daily News*) thought that the effects 'take away from the drama' and that the evening was 'frenetic with invention'. The most influential critic, Claudia Cassidy (*Chicago Tribune*) liked the opening effect, but when the lights went up she saw 'a sleek, shiny and clumsy revolving trap for actors in slippery sandals, who scramble up and down its ramps and ladders'. Dettner thought that Sam had 'the outline of a powerful characterisation in hand, but not the nuances. His change from the gentle warrior to a crazed and bloodthirsty monarch is compelling theatre, but doesn't quite arouse compassion'. Cassidy found him 'an intelligent Macbeth, of voice and stature, and a curiously soft streak of self-pity that can make the bloodbath a self-indulgence'; Christian wrote that he sometimes became 'so strangled with acting emotion that he is impossible to understand.'[38]

While this production proved too complicated to be completely successful, Sam was also finding complications in his personal life. Jan Sterling had not taken him at his word, and stayed away. She continued to maintain contact, and made it clear that she wanted their love affair to start again. For some time, Sam resisted. While he was in Chicago, he wrote to tell her that they had no future:

> Once again and finally I want you to understand that you must never write to me, phone me or try to see me.
>
> I love Charlotte deeply and forever and there never has been nor ever will be any possibility of my leaving her or being separated from her or my children.
>
> She has discovered, as was inevitable, that we have been in contact at times during my trips to the States. And this has caused her anguish and has made me deeply regret that I have allowed such contact between us.
>
> Whatever impels you towards me and motivates you must be examined by you in the light of clear and unequivocal understanding on your part that I love Charlotte and will never leave her.[39]

But this letter remained among his personal papers, perhaps drafted to reassure Charlotte. Some time later, the affair resumed, on what 'understanding' between the two of them, can only be guessed at.

His career, too, was taking another turn. *Macbeth* was not only the one Shakespeare production Sam directed, it was also his last role in the live theatre. He was now offered work directing on American television. First he directed an episode of *The Defenders*, then, in 1964, four of the thirteen episodes of *Coronet Blue*, a series that grew out of it. The series was not aired until 1967, and was succeeded by *N.Y.P.D.*, with the same leading actor.

Over the next couple of years, Sam was cast in supporting roles in several major feature films. In 1963, he had played an army major in *The Man in the Middle*, a World War II film set in India. After *The Spy Who Came in from the Cold*, he had a small but colourful part in *Those Magnificent Men in Their Flying Machines*, the popular comedy about an international air race, caricaturing the national stereotypes, and including footage of genuine planes. Later, he appeared in another Hollywood film, *Warning Shot*, and then in *The Day the Fish Came Out*, written and directed by Michael Cacoyannis, the Cypriot-born director who had made Anthony Quinn into a major star with his *Zorba the Greek*. The shooting of it gave Sam a pleasant time on location in Greece. Another, *Danger Route*, which he made in 1967, was a British spy story, an attempt to cash in on the success of the early James Bond films. These films, in which Sam turned in a succession of competent performances, showed how eminently employable he was. The cast lists, all predominantly male, show how much easier it was for a man than for a woman, to stay gainfully employed as an actor.

In the second half of the decade Sam established himself further as a television director. He directed Burt Reynolds, near the beginning of his acting career, in *Hawk,* a series about a New York police lieutenant of Iroquois blood. It ran for only one season, and was perhaps before its time, paving the way for such series as Telly Savalas's *Kojak,* in the 1970s. He directed Burt Reynolds again in the pilot of *Lassiter,* about an undercover magazine journalist. After that, he directed the pilot for three Westerns, *Lancers, Custer* and *Cimarron Strip,* as well as one episode of *Dundee and the Culhane,* a one-off summer series which reunited him with the English actor John Mills, playing a frontier lawyer.

In working on pilots, the try-out episode for series which might or might not be taken up, Sam was able to have his cake and eat it. They built his reputation as a successful director. All had 'the benefit of his energy and dramatic conviction,'[40] but they did not tie him down for whole series working with scripts that did not excite him. He was getting well-paid work in Hollywood, without totally committing himself to its commercial values. He wondered, in one letter to Charlotte, if he should get himself a publicity agent, and 'put out for the big sell', but went on 'it's no substitute for being really creative – for searching out ideas – for reading and thinking, for being fertile, alive and aware.'[41] She consoled him by suggesting he should 'Make SILK from the dung – you're the magician who's done it before – time and time again.'[42]

In his personal life, too, Sam was having his cake and eating it. When in Hollywood, he was based in his parents' house, free to visit Jan Sterling's apartment whenever he wanted. Their liaison soon became common knowledge there, with the result that one day, a friend from Los Angeles mentioned it to sixteen-year-old Zoë. Charlotte had tried to keep the truth from the girls, as she did not want them to turn against their father. Zoë, at boarding-school, where she had been sent after her 'O' levels, refused to speak to him for many months; her sisters did not learn about the affair until later.

Sam's letters to Charlotte during 1965 show his determination to keep her in his life. In one, he admitted that their sex life had never been completely fulfilling, but assured her of his 'deep, deep, strong unbreakable love'. He had considered whether they would be happier apart, 'but I could not – nor can I <u>ever</u> – SELFISHLY – give you up.' He knew that it was up to him to break with 'JS' – as he always referred to her when writing to Charlotte – and admitted that it was his own weakness that stopped him doing so. But he was aware that 'JS's' feelings, too, and her need for him, were real. 'I've got to do this so as not to destroy another person.'[43]

Early the following year, with the personal situation unresolved, Sam turned his attention to a long-term project that would feed his artistic hunger, the adaptation of Robert Graves' *The Anger of Achilles*. Instead of a film, it should be a spectacular theatre piece. Ever since his first return to New York in late 1960, Sam had been excited by the new Lincoln Center on the Upper West Side. In October 1965, the Vivian Beaumont Theater opened, as part of the complex. Sam approached Schuyler Chapin, the Vice President of Programming, with the suggestion that the Center should commission a script from Graves to be produced there. He asked Beverley Cross, by this time an established playwright, to work with the poet. He also involved Jo Mielziner, one of the foremost American theatre designers. Graves had completed the radio version, which the BBC broadcast in 1964. On reading the script, Mielziner wrote: 'the more I think about this challenge the more excited I get' and he found Beverley Cross's version 'full of intriguing ideas, and problems too.'[44] Late in the year, Sam tried to get Yale Drama School to mount a preliminary test production, but it was not feasible as part of their programme.

In February 1967, the Lincoln Center paid Sam and Robert Graves $5300 to develop the project. Sam's idea was that the design would be along the lines of Ralph Alswang's 'Living Screen', with the gods entirely on screen, and the humans played by live actors. He remembered that the Czech scenographer, Josef Svoboda, had created a multimedia installation, Laterna Magika ('Magic Lantern'), using similar ideas, for the Brussels World Fair, which he had visited with Abby in 1958. Svoboda combined projections with elaborate architectural sets on several levels. He had already designed for the National Theatre in London, and was working on the Czech pavilion for Expo67 in Montreal. When approached about designing the *Iliad*, he showed interest, and flew to New York in May, to see the Vivian Beaumont Theater. In June, he was temporarily out of action, having fallen eight feet from one tier to another on his own set, while working on the Covent Garden production of Richard Strauss's, *Die Frau Ohne Schatten*. (Shades of Sam's fall while rehearsing on his *Macbeth* set.) But he was soon up and active again. Mielziner gracefully withdrew: 'I am truly sorry we couldn't make our association practical on this project.'[45]

In the autumn, Sam's personal and artistic lives came to a crisis. During the summer, he had told Jan Sterling that the affair must end. He had then spent some time with Charlotte in London, at which point Sterling suffered some kind of breakdown. When Sam returned to Los Angeles at the end of September, he found her 'wan and ill', and under sedation on doctor's orders. According to the account he gave to Charlotte, he explained how he had come to the point of trying to end their relationship, and 'JS' had tried to explain and justify her own state of mind and behaviour. She made the extraordinary suggestion that Charlotte should come and live in Los Angeles, where they would work out some sort of *modus vivendi*, the two women sharing their time with Sam. 'As soon as I know where the hell I am with the career', Sam continued, 'we will make further decisions, and you will come here if necessary, so that we can sort things out here.'[46]

Since it was clear he had not followed through with his decision to break with Sterling, and since the *modus vivendi* idea outraged Charlotte, she assumed that she had lost the battle. But three weeks later, Sam was writing to her again: 'Darling, I do not accept your conclusion that all is decided – my need for you and the kids is as great a need – and perhaps greater than whatever this is here.'[47] He wanted her to consider moving to California. Perhaps he convinced himself that if she were there, he would find it easier to end his affair.

By that time, the two older girls were no longer 'kids'. Abby had completed her training as a speech therapist, and was working. Zoë was at the Central School of Speech and Drama. She had nursed the ambition to act ever since the summer in Stratford-upon-Avon. Sam and Charlotte had done their best to put her off, fearing the fierce competition and rejection she might have to face. But a year at Hornsey College of Art had not deterred her, and so the next step was to send her to secretarial college, so that she had 'something to fall back on'. Only then was she allowed to audition for drama school.

In mid-November, Sam flew from Los Angeles to New York, to make a presentation about the *Iliad* to the Board of the Lincoln Center. Charlotte was to meet him there, and then accompany him back, where she could 'get the feel of it – see the folks if you want – see the housing situation.'[48]

Svoboda's model arrived, a series of blocks, levels and screens, with graphics and live action photographs that showed how projections, film and live action would be combined. Sam thought it 'a staggeringly exciting concept which surpasses every expectation and hope that I have had'.[49] Drawing on the Robert Graves/Beverley Cross script, he gave the Board an eloquent account of how the epic piece would work. He would have to wait for some weeks to hear if they would put it into production.

Whatever transpired when Charlotte and he were in California, it led to a drastic decision. Copper Beech was put up for sale. 'After sixteen years in London, the last four of them in Highgate,' ran a press announcement, 'Sam Wanamaker, the American director and producer is selling his maisonette in North Grove, to return to Hollywood permanently ... Mrs Wanamaker is sad at moving: "I know it sounds marvellous and glamorous to say you're going to live in California ... but I would prefer to stay in Highgate. We love it here"'.[50]

In January 1968, Sam heard that the Lincoln Center had decided not to proceed with the *Iliad*: 'the price tag, as far as we are concerned, is simply too much.'[51] But at last he was offered a feature film to direct, *The File of the Golden Goose*, a spy film starring Yul Brynner. Sam thought the screenplay was 'lousy', but his agents at IFA (International Famous Agency) urged him to accept. It was to be filmed in London, starting that July. Nearly twenty years earlier the filming of *Christ in Concrete* in England had brought Sam's affair with Jan Sterling to a decisive end. Now again, his career carried him away from her. Copper Beech was withdrawn from the market.

10

A New Scheme
1968–1973

S am enjoyed being reunited with Yul Brynner, though he was no great admirer of his acting in this later part of his career. Brynner played Peter Novak, a Secret Service agent who comes to England on the trail of a counterfeit operation. Edward Woodward, then playing an English Secret Service agent, Callan, in a popular British television series, played a Scotland Yard detective, and Charles Gray was the gay villain. There were many London locations, perhaps the reason Sam was asked to direct it. They included Heathrow Airport, the Festival Gardens in Battersea Park, the Royal Festival Hall, Burlington Arcade, New Scotland Yard, the Old Vic Theatre and Smithfield Market, as well as scenes filmed at Shepperton Studios. The film turned out to be as 'lousy' as Sam had feared. The poster announced that the 'golden goose' was 'A DIRTY BIRD'. 'There's not much to know about Novak' it went on, 'they killed his girl and now he sleeps with his gun!'[1] It contributed to the downward spiral in Yul Brynner's career. But at last Sam had broken into directing a feature film.

His next film, *The Executioner,* produced by Charles H. Schneer, was more successful, and brought him into contact, for the first time, with this independent American producer, who had settled in London some years before. 'Charlie was always so difficult to work for and quite irascible,' wrote one of his secretaries, 'but one couldn't help loving him nevertheless.'[2] A comment that could well have applied to Sam.

It was a Cold War spy thriller, with a screenplay by Jack Pulman, a successful English television writer. George Peppard starred as an MI5 agent who believes his colleague, played by Keith Michell, is a Russian agent. Filming began at the end of March 1969, and locations included Athens and Corfu as well as London. Peppard, an American actor playing a British spy, was considered wooden in the role, but the rest of the large cast was strong, including Joan Collins, Judy Geeson (Sean Kenny's partner), Charles Gray again, Nigel Patrick, George Baker and Peter Bull. When it was released in 1970, the reviews were favourable: 'A classic unravelling with a tortuous plot'; 'This spy film deserves a fairly high mark; it lacks neither pleasure nor punch'; 'A very beautiful job'; 'completely absorbing' (*LA Times*).[3] Sam was praised for keeping the pace tight (*Films and Filming*).[4]

In June 1969, Sam revived the possibility of getting the *Iliad* off the ground again, writing to Robert Graves: 'Now that I have finished my second film, I have some time to continue working on this most marvellous project.'[5] But he was also thinking of dumping the Graves/ Cross script, and working from the best-known American version of the *Iliad* by Richmond Lattimore. He wanted to get Leonard Bernstein to write music, and have Roger Stevens present it at the John F. Kennedy Center for the Performing Arts, then in construction in Washington DC. Perhaps it could be done in association with the Lincoln Center, where Svoboda's model and sketches still resided. But in September, Schuyler Chapin wrote that he doubted the possibility of a joint production. Reluctantly, Sam put his grand scheme aside, although three years later, a letter to Graves showed that he was still hankering after it. 'I am pushing the *Iliad* with the Kennedy Centre as hard as I can.'[6] But by that time, he was involved in a *new* grand scheme.

Earlier in the year, Sam's brother Bill had come over to London to attend a medical conference at the Royal Festival Hall. Accompanying him to register, Sam took the opportunity to walk him eastwards and show him the plaque on the site of the Globe theatre, which he had first visited himself twenty years earlier, and which he still considered an inadequate memorial to Shakespeare. He had not been there for some time. He saw that some of the old riverside warehouses near the site were being pulled down, exposing a magnificent view across the river, and revealing the remains of the medieval Winchester Palace, with its beautiful rose window. If the area was being redeveloped, he thought aloud, was not the time ripe for a permanent *working* memorial to Shakespeare, which could enliven the whole area? Bill suggested that if Sam wanted that to happen, he should do something about it himself. Sam went home fired with the idea of a new Globe, to be built on or near the site of the original playhouse. He began to explore the whole district more thoroughly.

At the time of his first visit in 1949, Bankside, the area on the south side of the Thames between Blackfriars and London Bridges, had been distinctly shabby, with run-down workshops, poor housing and bomb sites. But the riverside itself had been busy, its wharfs full of lighters, loading and unloading from the ships anchored in midstream, its warehouses full of goods to be transported east or west, its cranes rearing up like sentinels along the bank. But with the advent of container ships which docked further downriver at

Tilbury, and the lack of sufficient rail and road links, the warehouses had become redundant; many were empty and derelict.

Tramping the local streets, Sam began to dream of how, starting with a new Globe, Bankside could thrive again, drawing on its sixteenth century history to create a lively cultural district attractive to tourists, and on its nineteenth century prosperity to create a modern trading centre. This was different from working on a theatre design, or a film set, or the Highgate duplex, or even an arts centre in Liverpool. It was about urban regeneration, bringing a whole area to life, with a living monument to the world's greatest playwright at its centre. The idea appealed to Sam, with his memories of the Chicago slums and the Lower East Side of New York, and his admiration for the Lincoln Center. Who should he talk to? Who was in charge of development and planning? His first stop must be the local authority.

Bankside was in the Borough of Southwark. With the chutzpah that his children knew from the times he had marched them through doors marked 'Private', Sam approached the Labour-led Council and introduced himself to the Chairman of Planning and Development, to the Chief Executive and to the Leader. They must have been a little startled at the American showman standing in their office, conjuring up a complete vision that was already clear in his mind. After some hesitation, they began to make noises of approval, although, as Sam was soon to discover, they were already in discussion about a similar proposal, spearheaded by someone else.

Sam approached the Greater London Council, and had some encouragement from the Leader and from the leader of the Labour group. He soon learnt that the idea of developing the cultural potential of the area had been mooted more than once before. The Abercrombie Plan, drawn up with considerable optimism in the middle of WWII, contained the suggestion that an area stretching westward from London Bridge 'might well include a great cultural centre, embracing, amongst other features, a modern theatre, a large concert hall and the headquarters of various organisations.'[7] A Greater London Development Plan had just been published, the first strategic plan of its kind, encouraging culture and housing in the area, rather than industry.

Sam's mind went back, of course, to the replica playhouse he had seen at the World Fair in Chicago, and acted in at the World Fair in Cleveland. He decided to approach the academic world next. Surely Shakespeare scholars would support the idea of a third Globe, and give credibility to his scheme. (The first Globe, which opened in 1599, had burnt down when a cannon that was fired during a performance of *King Henry VIII* in 1612, caught the thatch on the roof. No one was hurt, but one man's breeches were set on fire, and doused with a bottle of beer. The second Globe, built the following year, was prudently roofed with slate.)

Sam soon learnt that one of the authorities on Elizabethan theatres was Dr Richard Southern, at the University of Bristol. He approached Professor Glynne Wickham, Head of the Drama Department there and an eminent theatre historian himself. He was enthusiastic. In July 1969, Sam arranged a meeting at his home in Highgate with Glynne Wickham, and Professor Terence Spencer, Head of the Shakespeare Institute at the University of Birmingham. These two soon became stalwart supporters of the idea, and another early supporter was C. Walter Hodges, author of *The Globe Restored: a study of the Elizabethan Theatre*.

Sam now wanted to present his ideas to architects. He discovered that there was to be a meeting of the Architectural Association to discuss the development of the South Bank. He went off to Shepperton Studios, where the studio shots for *The File of the Golden Goose* had been filmed, and persuaded technicians there to build what was virtually a 'white card' model of his scheme, such as scenic designers used at an early stage of their work. The 'Bankside Development Plan', as he called it, stretched along the riverside between the two bridges, with a Globe playhouse at its centre. One of the people present when Sam made his presentation was Theo Crosby, a South African architect who had settled in England after the policy of Apartheid was introduced. Crosby liked to claim later that the model was so poor – 'a lot of shoe-boxes spread all over the Thames'[8] – that he felt sorry for Sam, and kindly approached him at the end of the meeting, offering to design a brochure. But in fact, he was hooked, and would soon find himself designated as 'official architect'. Another architect who helped was Ove Arup, a near neighbour in Highgate, who agreed to build a more substantial model of Sam's scheme.

Meanwhile there were films to direct. Sam's next project was not about resurrecting the past, or improving the present, but about the distant future. An undated press release from 20th Century Fox, in 1970, announced that he had been signed to direct *Kyle*, a suspense thriller set in the year 2026. The history of this production was complicated. Charles Juroe, an executive producer, had acquired the rights to the screenplay, originally a novel, about a detective who has to outwit a 'computer' – a futuristic word in itself at this time – to defeat a bunch of villains. Juroe took the project to producer Arthur P Jacobs, who had had a great success with *Planet of the Apes* in 1968. Jacobs, in his turn, went to Richard Zanuck at 20th Century Fox (son of Darryl Zanuck, its founder), who gave the go-ahead to the tune of £1m. Perhaps on the recommendation of Charlie Schneer, Sam was signed, despite having only two films to his credit.

Juroe and Sam set off for Montreal to reconnoitre the site of the World Fair Expo67 as a possible location, where they were treated royally by its mayor.[9] They chose its spectacular geodesic dome to be the setting for much of the action. Studio work would be done in London, where Sam and William Kaplan, the Production Supervisor, started exploring ways of creating a total look for what the future might look like, involving fashion designer Pierre Cardin and hair stylist Vidal Sassoon. The search took them to the Royal College of Art, to draw on the students' ideas for furniture, ceramics, glass, textiles, clothes and vehicles. Edward Paoluzzi, pioneer of Pop Art, attended a preliminary meeting. Kaplan wrote to Richard Zanuck's office describing a recent graduate, they had met, Zandra Rhodes: 'This girl is not only something of a genius in design, but she is probably one of the most far-out characters one could hope to meet, with her green-dyed hair ending in feathers, and crazy make-up to match. Underneath that far out exterior, though, she has a real brain, and is very articulate in discussing fashion and everything.'[10] Margaret Casson, in charge of interior design at the College, earmarked some likely students to work on the project. There was talk of starting a merchandising franchise to make toys and games as by-products of the film.

By late August, Sam was back in Montreal, ready to start ten days' shooting in September, when a message came through from 20th Century Fox, that the production of *Kyle* had been suspended. That autumn, a new film magazine, *Cinéfantastique*, announced, under the heading of forthcoming films, that *Kyle* was in production, directed, not by Sam but by Guy Hamilton. It never appeared. Like many film projects, *Kyle* sank, without any further information as to how, why or when.

Underneath the announcement about *Kyle* in *Cinéfantastique* was news of another forthcoming film, to be directed by Sam. *Last Place Left* was to be co-produced by Charlie Schneer and Sam. It was based on a novel by Marshall Pugh, whose best-known work was *Commander Crabbe*, the true story of a British officer who learnt deep-sea diving, to thwart Italian frogmen who were sabotaging British naval forces during World War II. *Last Place Left* was a grim novel, published in 1969, about chemical and biological warfare, and the environmental pollution it creates. It was to be shot in the Hebrides, in a suitably bleak landscape, but the project was not sufficiently developed for filming to start that year.

The positive outcome from the aborted *Kyle* was that Sam had met Lady Casson, and her husband, Sir Hugh Casson, architect, Principal of the Royal College of Art, and designer of the Festival of Britain in 1951. He buttonholed them to talk about his Bankside scheme, and they became keen supporters.

During the rest of 1970, Sam focused on his new project. There was no immediate prospect of implementation, but he wrote to many of the great and good, to get their endorsement. He had a beautiful brochure designed and printed, which took as its title a quotation from Ben Jonson, *'The Globe, the Glory of the Banke.'* George Djurkovic, designer and architect (an associate of Sean Kenny), drew an elegant imaginary view of the development, on which was superimposed a tracing of Claes Visscher's equally imaginary view of the Thames c1600. The new Globe was provisionally sited by the existing Anchor Inn, just east of Southwark Bridge, surrounded by historic houses which would be relocated from other parts of the country.

Sam's visionary plan included a conference and trade centre, flats and offices, four hotels, a museum, a 'mixed media entertainment building', pubs, restaurants and coffee-shops, adventure playgrounds, car parks, and a 'travelator' across the bridge at Blackfriars. Winchester Palace, home of the Bishop of Winchester in Shakespeare's time, now in ruins, was to be restored. It would house what Sam boldly called the 'World Centre for Shakespeare Studies', for which, thanks to an enthusiastic presentation by Terence Spencer at the biennial Shakespeare Conference in Stratford-upon-Avon, he could already list nine more academics as 'associates', besides Glynne Wickham, Spencer himself, Richard Southern, Walter Hodges, The Shakespeare Institute, The Shakespeare Association of America and the Modern Language Association. The brochure quoted numerous expressions of support and listed fifteen planning advisors and eleven 'econo-political' advisors. Sam was yet to learn that fine words butter no parsnips.

The Bankside Development Plan was no more than that, a plan. It required property developers and planners to bring it into existence. His own part of the scheme would be the Globe. Sam soon became aware of earlier projects to rebuild Shakespeare's theatre, besides what he remembered of Chicago and Cleveland. First was William Poel, who had founded The Elizabethan Stage Society in 1895, in reaction to the scenic extravagances of productions by West End managers such as Sir Henry Irving and Sir Herbert Beerbohm-Tree. Poel had encouraged the formation of the Shakespeare Memorial National Theatre Committee, under whose auspices Sir Edwin Lutyens created a half-sized replica of the Globe in

1912, for the exhibition 'Shakespeare's England' at Earls Court. At that time, the two ideas, a Shakespeare Memorial and a National Theatre, were closely linked. WWI had brought that project to an end, but Ben Iden Payne, with whom Sam had worked at Cleveland, was an associate of Poel and had implemented many of his ideas.

In the 1930s, another scheme had been dreamt up by the Globe-Mermaid Association, an Anglo-American organization aiming to build a third Globe, a Mermaid pub and a museum and library for Shakespeare studies. This scheme, supported by Joseph P. Kennedy, then US Ambassador to London, Herbert Hoover in America, and Lord Bessborough in England, was partly inspired by a fake story that Shakespeare and Ben Jonson had shared convivial evenings at the 'Mermaid' tavern on Bankside. Their plan was to build on the site of the Bankside Power Station, built in 1891 between Blackfriars and Southwark Bridges, and considered to be too old and polluted to be useful. WWII brought that project to an end, after which a new Power Station was built, designed by Sir Giles Gilbert Scott. It was in construction when Sam first visited the area in 1949; he would have seen the Victorian many-chimneyed edifice, still operating, while the new single-chimneyed building was in construction alongside. This Globe was to have been twice the size of the original, and roofed in glass. After the War, when the Festival of Britain was being planned, with Hugh Casson as its chief architect, there was some idea of including a replica of the Globe among its new buildings. The idea was dropped, partly because the original concept of an 8-sided Globe had recently been demolished and there was no consensus as to what the playhouse had actually looked like.

All these schemes were in the past. But when Sam began to approach the most likely theatre people to support his project, he discovered that there was another actor, George Murcell, with a similar idea. He knew Murcell; he had played alongside Warren Mitchell as one of the cuthroats in Sam's production of *The Threepenny Opera*. His career included Old Vic seasons with Tyrone Guthrie and Michael Benthall. The year before Sam began his project, Murcell had set about the purchase of a redundant church in Islington, which he proposed to convert into a roofed Elizabethan playhouse. Guthrie became Chairman of his company, St Georges Elizabethan Theatre Ltd. Sam had thought that Guthrie, who had long been interested in playing Shakespeare on an open stage, would be interested in *his* scheme.

At first, it seemed that the two enthusiasts might work harmoniously along parallel lines, but Sam discovered that Murcell was not confining his scheme to Islington. He was already in negotiation with Laing Development

Company about a scheme to acquire a chunk of land by Southwark Bridge, and build an office tower, a revamped Anchor Inn and a replica Globe theatre. A representative from Laing had even discussed the scheme with Southwark Council and the GLC, before Sam had approached their members and officers. Already, Sam realized, there were developers eyeing the area with a view to demolishing the old buildings and replacing them with lucrative offices. Guthrie wrote: 'The sensible thing is for all interested parties in a Bankside Theatre to get together. There are really so few who give a damn'.[11] But Sam was not prepared to collaborate with another passionate, hot-headed man, and the press enjoyed working up the rivalry between the two schemes. It was an indication that while Sam was eager to recruit an army of supporters, he wanted to be recognized as the only begetter of a Bankside Globe.

He was finding less support than he had hoped from actors, directors and managers. Quite apart from Murcell's rival scheme, there was a general feeling that Shakespeare and his contemporaries were well served by the Royal Shakespeare Company, which performed at the Aldwych Theatre on the Strand, as well as in Statford-upon-Avon. There were preliminary plans for a purpose-built theatre for the Company in the Barbican Estate, an urban regeneration scheme in the City of London. Sam received some realistic advice about his long-term goal from Lord Chandos, Chairman of the National Theatre, which would soon be in construction east of Waterloo Bridge:

> Of course I wish you well, but I think the task – with three theatres on the South Bank, and the Barbican scheme, all in being – is an immense one.
>
> It is not only the building of the theatre, but a large annual subsidy is necessary to keep any theatre in being. This will prove the principal obstacle.[12]

Perhaps America, where Sam had first been enthused by the idea of a Globe theatre, would provide more fruitful ground. He began to moot the idea of a company that would tour to various theatres there, including the Old Globe in San Diego (which was built from the Cleveland Globe timbers), ending up on Broadway, or at the Lincoln Center, and forming the nucleus of a company that would in due course make the rebuilt Globe their permanent home.

As in the 1950s, when he wanted to produce in New York and then in the British theatre, he needed a business partner. He thought of Alexander Cohen, a producer who mounted shows on both sides of the Atlantic, and had an office in the West End as well as on Broadway. Cohen had been responsible for an immensely successful revival of *Hamlet*, six years earlier, in which John Gielgud had directed Richard Burton, as part of the quarter-centenary Shakespeare celebrations. It had run on Broadway even longer than Maurice Evans' *G I Hamlet*. Sam was acquainted with Cohen, but before paying him a call, he decided to get Burton on board. He visited him on the set of *Villain*, a forgettable film in which Burton was playing a gangster along the lines of Ronnie Kray. Burton expressed enthusiasm and they arranged to have dinner a few days later. Burton cancelled, but meanwhile, Sam made his first approach to Cohen, who expressed interest. He then outlined his plan in writing, and suggested that they meet.

This letter shows Sam at his most confident and ebullient:

> I will undoubtedly have had a meeting with Sir John Gielgud and persuaded him he ought to participate in this marvellous project. I have no doubt that the idea of a tour next season with Gielgud and Burton in two Shakespeare plays in which each starred, and in which each directed the other, could be a great success … There is enormous enthusiasm for this project, as well as enormous obstacles. The financial ones are the least important since if I can overcome the acquisition of land problems, everything else will fall into place, and there is no question that on the basis of the concept, this theatre would be self-supporting. However, it would probably be formed as a non-profit-making trust, to enable it to secure large building grants from major foundations such as Ford and Rockefeller.[13]

To make his bid to Cohen more convincing, Sam wrote on the same day to David Brierley, manager of the Royal Shakespeare Theatre in Stratford, to ask for a set of figures that would help him draw up a realistic budget for a season in a projected Globe playhouse.

The first person to puncture Sam's enthusiasm was Burton, who did not reply to two of Sam's letters following their aborted second meeting. Sam dictated a furious third letter:

> To <u>totally</u> ignore my correspondence is a contemptuous affront to me personally. If this is your intention you can be assured it only demeans your own stature as an actor, a fellow "professional", and more important as a human being.[14]

Burton's response is not recorded. Undaunted, Sam pursued his idea of an American tour. He wrote to the director of the Shakespeare Festival in Ashland, Oregon, which had been presenting plays in an outdoor Elizabethan-style theatre since 1935, and to the director of the Old Globe in San Diego. He wrote that the company would 'undoubtedly include such people as John Neville' – who did indeed say that he did not think his official support for George Murcell would preclude him from acting or directing for Sam – 'and Alan Badel, with even a vague possibility that Sir John Gielgud would be involved.'[15]

At the same time as planning an American tour, Sam began exploring the idea of a season of plays on Bankside. Thinking of how the Festival Theatre in Stratford, Ontario, had been launched in a tent theatre, he contemplated 'a temporary and inexpensive structure such as a tent', to prepare the way for a permanent Globe. He wrote to Toby Robertson, whose first production had been *The Iceman Cometh* for Sam in Liverpool. Two years after working for Sam, Robertson had founded Prospect Productions, which later became the Prospect Theatre Company, a touring company with a base at the Arts Theatre, Cambridge. In 1969 he had had a great success directing Ian McKellen as Shakespeare's Richard II and Marlowe's Edward II, in productions which started at the Edinburgh International Festival, transferred to Bernard Miles' Mermaid Theatre, and then played in the West End. Sam hoped to persuade Robertson to tour Ian McKellen as Hamlet in America, bring it to a tent theatre on Bankside, and have Prospect become the nucleus of a permanent company there. Robertson was enthused by the first suggestion and the third, but rejected the idea of performing in a tent. Guthrie also warned against such an enterprise. He declined to direct, because of his position as Chairman of George Murcell's company, and, despite his experience in Stratford, Ontario, warned 'I should be very leary about a tent.'[16] Undeterred, Sam continued to pursue the idea of a temporary Globe. The year before, the Royal College of Art had created a spectacular tri-sail canopy, to cover an outdoor sculpture exhibition. Sam approached the College, through Hugh Casson, and negotiated a loan of the canopy, which could cover a temporary stage, if he could just find a Bankside site for it.

In January 1971, Sam registered a new company, the Globe Playhouse Trust, dedicated to building a new Globe. It would later acquire charitable status. He held a press conference to outline the aims of the Trust. But it was high time to set aside his new project, and confirm his status as a film director, after the collapse of *Kyle*. In the spring, Sam began shooting a film for MGM. Two years earlier, he had boasted that he had a contract with MGM to direct three films, but this was the only one that was made.

Catlow was a Western based on a novel by Louis L'Amour. The eponymous outlaw was played by Yul Brynner, the third time Sam and he worked together. He is pursued by Marshal Cowan (Richard Crenna), despite the fact they were comrades during the Civil War. Leonard Nimoy, famous for playing Spock in *Star Trek*, played a mercenary also pursuing Catlow, who robs a Mexican gold shipment and flees through dangerous territory. The story was set in Apache country, but it was shot in Andalusia, Spain, allowing for picturesque panoramic backgrounds. 'People like action adventure,' Sam told a journalist: 'We all like to do things we can't do – punch the villain, shoot the enemy out of his saddle at 100 yards, be quick on the draw, swagger down Main Street. Like Greek drama, the western expresses the elemental nature of man.'[17] It was not surprising that Sam, always looking for the human actions and emotions underlying whatever drama he was dealing with, made this comparison. He was eclectic in his taste, seeing no superiority in one kind of story over another – spy thriller, science fiction, Greek myth – so long as the script told it well. In describing the story of *Kyle* at the Royal College of Art, he had compared it to a classic Western.

But the days of the true classic Western were over. MGM perhaps hoped that *Catlow* would rival the success, two years earlier, of the 20th Century Fox *Butch Cassidy and the Sundance Kid*, which took a sideways look at the genre. But that had had the advantage of a witty screenplay by William Goldman, whereas the screenplay of *Catlow* had no such merit. Sam drew on his experience with television Westerns, and directed it with tongue in cheek, bringing out its latent comedy. Leonard Nimoy, who had a nude scene, in a fight with Richard Crenna, enjoyed his escape from *Star Trek*, and the period of shooting in Spain was pleasant for all concerned, but the film did little to build Sam's reputation.

He had left Globe matters in the hands of an 'administrator'. Ronan O'Casey, a Canadian actor, had been in the cast of *The Shrike*, and had taken over Sam's part when *Reclining Figure* transferred from the New Shakespeare to Streatham Hill Theatre in the summer of 1958. Now, he was literary head of a film production company, Commonwealth United Entertainment, which had recently produced a film version of Shakespeare's *Julius Caesar*, with a glittering Anglo-American cast. O'Casey was intrigued by Sam's plans and pursued the idea of finding a site for the canopy, and the stage which would sit under it. But he was soon discouraged. He wrote to a friend at the Phoenix Theatre in Leicester, who might be interested in bringing a production to Bankside, explaining that he was having difficulty finding a site, since '… those bastards Laing's [Laing Development Company] have refused permission.' Another possible site was too small to accommodate a theatre, so he was considering using the 'temporary structure' for an exhibition instead, but his main gripe was the negotiating he had to deal with, involving rival property companies, the Council, and George Murcell:

The infighting is tiring and debilitating, but I'm afraid it's part of the job. It's made even more depressing because it's unnecessary. I'm sorry to be so down.[18]

O'Casey struggled on through the next few months, but by September he was gone, and there was a new 'Acting Administrator'. It would not be the last time that someone started out full of enthusiasm, inspired by Sam's great plan, but then ran out of steam, leaving Sam to soldier on. He himself was never debilitated, but rather invigorated by whatever challenge his project threw up. Early in August he was writing to Sean Connery combining an enquiry about whether Connery would be interested in directing *Last Place Left* instead of him (to which the answer was YES), with a suggestion that Sean should play Macbeth on an American tour by the 'Globe Playhouse Company', with his wife Diane Cilento playing Lady Macbeth (to which the answer was NO).

At the end of that month, Sam's project received a boost which, while it provided no practical help, gave it cachet. The first World Shakespeare Congress was held in Vancouver, jointly sponsored by The Shakespeare Association of America and the International Shakespeare Association based in Stratford-upon-Avon, England. One of the main topics on the agenda was 'Shakespeare Playhouses' and two of the keynote speakers were Richard Hosley, from the University of Arizona, already an expert on Elizabethan playhouses, and Walter Hodges. Sam was not able to attend, as he was still filming *Catlow*, but Glynne Wickham described the plan they had agreed. The scheme now included, besides the Globe, a library and small museum, an international hostel, a pub, an office, a rehearsal room, storage spaces and adequate car parking. The exact form of the playhouse had yet to be decided. The Djurkovic drawing showed a building that was no more accurate a replica of the original Globe than what Sam remembered from Chicago; he mentioned to a journalist the possibility of 'a plastic roof that will close over the pit in bad weather'.[19]

Sam conveyed an impression to his academic supporters that the granting of a suitable Bankside site was imminent. Such a distortion of the truth was as much evidence of his optimism as of a deliberate attempt to deceive; after all, he did have a site firmly in mind. Hoping that the Laing/Murcell idea would come to nothing, he had looked for a property for his own scheme. On one of his walks around the area, he came across an empty site about 300 metres from the original Globe, looking over Windsor Wharf, west of Southwark Bridge. It was on Emerson Street – named after an Elizabethan dignitary, not the American writer. The street had been heavily bombed during WWII, and the site was empty except for a small dilapidated office.

Sam's enquiries led to the discovery that the site was owned, but no longer used, by Ready Mixed Concrete. He approached the company to ask if he could have a licence to occupy the office. It turned out that Ready Mixed Concrete had just sold the site to Town and Metropolitan Estates, a subsidiary of Freshwater, a large group of property development companies. He met Robert Buchanan-Michaelson, who represented Town and Metropolitan, and discovered that he had plans to acquire several more properties in the area. That gentleman agreed to give Sam licence to use the site office. He would thus have a presence in the area, which he felt was a distinct advantage. Adjoining it was Greenmore Wharf, owned by Southwark Council, housing a car park and a rubbish depot. His hope was that the whole site, with the adjoining properties, would become available.

400 scholars from 26 countries attended the World Congress and passed a motion encouraging the idea of a full-scale reconstruction of the Globe, which would be: 'of the greatest value to Shakespeare Scholarship and to the history of Theatre, as well as of widespread interest to people and to education everywhere in the world.' The statement went on:

> Because it is believed that a site very close to the original location of the Globe Theatre on Bankside in London may soon become available for development, this Congress wishes further to express its opinion that this site might be eminently suitable for such a reconstruction.[20]

That should put Laing Development and George Murcell in their place – if they happened to be reading the report of the Congress.

During the autumn, Sam obtained permission from Town and Metropolitan and from the Council to use the Emerson St site and the adjoining properties for a temporary theatre. He put an optimistic slant on this decision. After all, if they had agreed to that, it was tantamount to agreeing to a permanent structure. He wrote to director Peter Brook: 'The Globe Playhouse Trust has now received approval and planning permission to construct a 3rd Globe theatre near the original site on Bankside. This is very encouraging news and we have decided to go forward with a temporary structure, a kind of glorious tent belonging the Royal College of Art.'[21] He could start planning a season for the following summer.

Sam now took much more drastic action in pursuit of his longterm goal. He knew that companies like Laing, and Town and Metropolitan, wanted to acquire contiguous properties on Bankside, so as to gain ownership of large swathes of land for development. If Sam owned one such property, however small, within the area they coveted, he would have a bargaining tool. A year earlier he had formed another company, Bankside Globe Development Ltd, with the express intention of doing just that. Late in 1971, three adjoining warehouses were put on the market in the area that the partners of Town and Metropolitan had their eye on. The addresses, Nos. 1 and 2 Bear Gardens, and Nos. 1 and 2 Rose Alley, bore witness to their sixteenth-century history. Bear Gardens was on the site of a bear-baiting pit, later replaced by the Hope Playhouse, while Rose Alley stood a few yards from where the Rose Playhouse was thought to be. At first, Sam hoped that the Globe Playhouse Trust could acquire these properties, but fundraising was not the forte for the management team he had set up. Instead, he decided to fund the purchase by selling Copper Beech, and taking out a ninety-day bridging loan.

This was a much more major personal commitment, not to say sacrifice, than when, nearly twenty years earlier, Sam had lost money on the Sean O'Casey play, and moved the family, temporarily, into a smaller flat. Copper Beech was the home that Charlotte and he, with Jack Perry's help, had created for themselves. His decision to sell was a clear indication that the Globe scheme was becoming the most important project in Sam's life. Did Charlotte raise any objection? Apparently not. For years she had focused her life on helping to fulfil his ambitions; she was not about to thwart them now. '... Sam said we were going, so we went. What he wanted to do, we did ...'[22]

Where were they to go? Their friend Mai Zetterling was then living in an unusual house in Southwark, which she was about to leave. She had started directing films, and was contracted to direct one segment of a film about the Munich Olympics the following summer. Sam liked the idea of becoming a resident of the Borough of Southwark, close to Bear Gardens and Emerson Street. He agreed to take over the short lease. The house was at 42 Trinity Street, on the corner of Falmouth Road, just off Borough High Street, south of Bankside. It was an attractive early nineteenth-century building, which had been taken over in 1927 by Trinity House, a local charity, to rehouse its 'Surrey Dispensary'. It had only just been put back into use as a residence. So across the river they went, Sam, Charlotte, Jessica and a dog. Zoë, now well-embarked on her acting career, stayed there when she was working in London. But Zetterling had made only one room habitable. At first Charlotte had to cook on a Baby Belling gas ring. It was far worse than the first cold winter in Highgate.

Unable to cover the ninety-day bridging loan, Sam approached a personal friend, Roger Wingate, whose company, Chestergrove Properties

Limited, became joint owners with Bankside Globe Developments Ltd, of the properties at Bear Gardens and Rose Alley, with an option to sell the properties to the Globe Playhouse Trust in due course. There was talk of involving one of Jack Perry's sons, but that idea was discarded. Jack himself decided, early on, that he would play no direct part in Sam's new scheme. 'One big ego is enough,' he told a friend.[23] And he feared the Globe would turn out to be elitist, since he could not think that Shakespeare would ever be truly popular. Having acquired the buildings, what use should Sam make of them? He was quite clear about that. 1 and 2 Rose Alley would be rented out as workshops, and he would turn 1 and 2 Bear Gardens into a museum of Elizabethan theatre, which would eventually be part of the Globe centre.

By March 1972, the Globe Playhouse Trust was based in the Emerson Street office, the official address being 40 Bankside, recalling the houses that had once lined that section of the riverbank. Sam was now ready to organize a series of events that would help bring Shakespeare back to Bankside. The Arts Council of Great Britain had shown little interest in his long-term plan. Sam felt it was because he was an American. 'They assumed I was going to create a Disneyland, or that I was only interested in property development and personal profit.'[24] But the Arts Council and the Greater London Arts Association had grants for events and specific projects that he could apply for. First there was Shakespeare's Birthday. Southwark Cathedral held an annual Commemorative Service to mark 23 April. Sam organized a Gala Concert to follow it, attended by the Prime Minister, Edward Heath. There was a Hymn by Cecil Day Lewis, set to music by Lennox Berkeley, there was a new Shakespeare song by Robert Graves – perhaps the commission was compensation for the demise of the *Iliad.* There was a medieval play in the Cathedral precincts. The Arts Council helped fund a volume of *Poems for Shakespeare* commissioned from modern poets.[25] Besides a paperback run, one hundred copies were specially bound in half-calf, signed by the poets, to be sold for £100 each.

Just in case anyone should forget that Sam had a professional reputation to keep up, a press release from the office stated: 'small wonder that Sam Wanamaker is currently working nearly twenty-four hours per day, for he is still active as a film producer/director. *Catlow* is to be released by MGM later this year'.[26]

In May, Sam took Charlotte off for a short holiday – perhaps to give her some relief from the squalor of the Surrey Dispensary. But he was soon back in harness, making final preparations for the theatre season. At the beginning of June, he gave an interview in which he described what the whole venture meant to him:

> The curious thing about my career is that I have always had this need to be identified with something permanent, always had the feeling of insecurity, staggering from one thing to another without any sense of building something in a world where you are only as good as the last thing you did. That is why I did that summer season in New York, and why I ran the Liverpool theatre from 1957 to 1960 [sic]. I have the need to make a home and more than just the narrow thing of doing plays, making it part of the community, with activities from morning to night.

He pointed out that his idea of what a theatre should be had later been developed at Bernard Miles' Mermaid on the other side of the river, and at some provincial centres 'and is now most people's desirable aim.'[27] He was justified in claiming a part in the development of regional theatre in England. In planning the season, Sam approached several theatres which were being run along the lines he had established at Liverpool: the Belgrade in Coventry, Nottingham Playhouse, which had opened a new theatre in 1963, under John Neville's artistic leadership, The Crucible in Sheffield, which had opened the previous year, with Douglas Campbell as artistic director. He could also consider that the Chichester Festival Theatre, opened in 1962, as well as the National Theatre, were following some of the principles he had pioneered.

For his season on Bankside, Sam obtained £25,000 in sponsorship from John Player & Sons, the cigarette company, as well as grants from the Greater London Council and Greater London Arts Association. The programme he mounted was, not surprisingly for anyone who knew him, ambitious. He sought out existing productions appropriate to the venue, by subject matter or genre: two productions from The Crucible, Thomas Dekker's *The Shoemaker's Holiday,* with music by the American composer Dominic Argento, a lively production which had begun its life at the Guthrie Theatre in Minneapolis, and Robert Bolt's *A Man For All Seasons.* Douglas Campbell, stalwart of Stratford, Ontario, and the Guthrie, directed and starred in both. The Northcott Theatre in Exeter brought its version of the *Cornish Passion Play.* Toby Robertson brought a production of *The Beggar's Opera,* the score adapted by Carl Davis. Roy Dotrice performed *Brief Lives,* his witty one-man show based on the seventeenth century diarist, John Aubrey. There were performances of John Ford's *'Tis Pity She's A Whore,* a National Theatre Mobile production with Diana Rigg and Anna Carteret, and *Pleasure and Repentance*, Terry Hands' programme on love, created for the Royal Shakespeare Company. The Globe Playhouse Trust itself presented *Hamlet*, for five weeks at the end of the season, a modern dress production directed by Peter Coe, with Keith Michell as Hamlet, Helen Cherry as Gertrude, Ron Moody as Polonius and the 1st Gravedigger, and Donald Houston as Horatio.

The season had a tight schedule, and everyone worked valiantly to make it a success. But Guthrie and Toby Robertson had been right to warn against using a tent. The tri-sail canopy looked superb. It was held up by pylons, a modified thrust stage was built to sit below it and there was seating for 700. The artist John Bratby produced a series of Shakespeare-inspired paintings around its perimeter. But the summer was rainy, and the canopy had not been designed for theatre productions. Pools of water gathered in it, sometimes perilously close to lighting equipment. On several occasions, Sam had to call in the technicians who were maintaining it.

Besides the performances at the Bankside Globe, there was a wealth of other activities. Glynne Wickham and Terence Spencer persuaded forty of the finest Shakespeare scholars to lecture at a six-week summer school held in the Chapter House of Southwark Cathedral. Jonathan Miller and John Barton were amongst those giving master-classes and there were outings to Dulwich College and the Banqueting Hall at Whitehall. Sam had made an arrangement with Classic Cinemas and converted what was virtually a large shed into a temporary cinema on the west side of the site, where sixty-three Shakespeare films were shown, beginning with Kozintsev's *King Lear*. Unfortunately, the cinema had a corrugated iron roof, which thundered loudly when rain fell. Not only film performances became inaudible, but lectures too, which were given in the cinema when the Chapter House was unavailable. H. F. Kitto kindly recorded his lecture on *Aeschylus and Shakespeare* for later hearing, since no one had heard a word he said. Jan Kott, lecturing, appropriately enough, on 'The Tempest as Psychodrama', battled through a literal tempest as the roof reverberated under a heavy cloudburst, and a valiant audience of six tried to make out his Polish accent.

David Munrow brought his Early Music Consort to perform in the Cathedral; Glynne Wickham's students mounted a Tudor interlude in the yard of the George Inn, in Borough Road; Southwark Council mounted an exhibition, *In The Clink*, about the Bankside prison; local art students created a sculpture garden; children submitted entries for a painting competition; throats were slaked at the Bull Ring, a pop-up pub set up by Bass Charrington a local brewery, and there was a kebab stall beside it, wafting spicy scents in the direction of the playhouse.

It was a magnificent festival of entertainment and learning, but it took place in an out-of-the-way part of London that few tourists or theatregoers were used to visiting, let alone in the rain. By the end of the season, The Globe Playhouse Trust had a deficit of £9548. Remembering what the site had previously been used for, one wag in the office said: 'Working for Sam, you are required to prepare large quantities of ready mixed concrete to support castles in the air – and he hasn't the money to pay for the concrete.'[28] Not for the last time, Sam put in money from his own pocket to offset the deficit, which amounted to £6000. Still, Michael Heppner of John Player & Sons announced that 'the temporary Bankside Globe Playhouse has been a colourful landmark in what was formerly a wilderness of warehouses',[29] and promised an increased sponsorship of £35,000 for 1973.

After the summer season, the next task was the Bear Gardens building, which was almost derelict, but which, as a Museum of Elizabethan Theatre, could be the masthead of the project, until the Globe was built. Sam had acquired a few theatre models: the old discredited John Cranford Adams version of the Globe; the second Globe, designed by Walter Hodges; the Rose Playhouse from one of the American academics. In December, the Mayor of Southwark opened the Museum. At weekends, Charlotte was sometimes to be seen holding the fort at the reception desk, to greet the few visitors who made their way to this cultural outpost, in a street that otherwise housed old warehouses and small industrial premises, such as Porn and Dunwoody (Lifts) Ltd.

Sam made no artistic contribution to the tent season, either acting or directing. He kept his professional work separate from the whole scheme, not wanting it to be seen as a way of placing himself centre stage, or for it to be judged by whether or not *he* received critical approval. In the autumn, he was able to pursue his own career. When one enthusiast suggested a Globe winter season near the Tower of London, he wrote: 'My dear Peter, I love you, BUT I CAN'T. I'm spread too thin as it is.'[30] He went into rehearsal for a production of Brecht's *The Resistible Rise of Arturo Ui* for BBC2, the play that depicts Hitler's rise to power through making him a Chicago gangster like Al Capone. Sam appeared in one scene, playing O'Casey, chairman of the committee that investigates Dogborough (representing Hindenburg) for corrupt practices in the Cauliflower Trust. He could draw on his memories of Chicago in the 1930s.

Sam hoped that in 1973 there would be real progress on his grand Bankside scheme, although there was still no prospect of acquiring a permanent site and planning permission to build the Globe. Still, there was plenty to be done to keep the project alive. In January, he hosted a conference at the Royal Festival Hall: 'The Third Globe – Ancient or Modern', to which a range of academics and architects contributed. Richard Southern and Sam had parted company, not having seen eye to eye, but Walter Hodges was there, advocating the idea that it should be an accurate reconstruction of the second Globe, built in 1613, after the first Globe burnt down. There was more visual information about it, but it was not really *Shakespeare's* Globe, as he had more or less retired by the time it opened. Theo Crosby questioned whether an exact replica was 'either possible or even wanted'.[31] Hugh Casson thought that problems of official regulations and technical restrictions stood in the way of building a complete replica. Sam's contribution was characteristically ambitious: he thought that there should be *three* theatres on Bankside: a reconstructed Globe, a modern theatre, and a children's theatre on the site of the Swan playhouse. (At other times, he also suggested a Rose theatre, to present plays by Shakespeare's contemporaries.) But later in the year, at a second conference, there was 'a general feeling … that a completely authentic building should be constructed'.[32] Richard Hosley was confident that he could provide all the evidence that showed what the first Globe looked like.

Bankside events were along the same lines as the previous year. Another Gala Concert at Southwark Cathedral to celebrate Shakespeare's Birthday. The guest of honour was Prince Philip, Duke of Edinburgh. Hugh Casson had introduced Sam at the Palace, believing, rightly as it turned out, that His Royal Highness would be intrigued by Sam's eloquence and enthusiasm. There were more world premieres of music, and a second book of *Poems for Shakespeare*; Sam firmly believed that Shakespeare should inspire *new* work.

In progressing his new scheme, Sam was developing some of the characteristics of Bill Starbuck, the 'rainmaker' he had played so effectively sixteen years earlier, building up expectations that he could not fulfil. For him, the vision of what might be was so clear, he could almost taste it; he *knew* what a regenerated Bankside would look like. Not surprising for a director of stage and screen, whose job is to bring a drama to life out of words on a page. Sam had long ago proved that he could do that. But he also had the power to conjure up what he saw so that others started to share his vision. For many months, he had drawn so vivid a picture of how the New Shakespeare Theatre in Liverpool might thrive, that Anna Deere Wiman had continued to invest money in it, even though she did not really like his artistic policy. In projects he had tried to make happen, most notably the *Iliad*, his eloquence had inspired potential colleagues.

Since he had begun to promote the idea of a new Globe in a revitalised Bankside, he had enthused hundreds of people sufficiently that they were prepared to endorse the scheme publicly. Some, once they discovered how far Sam was from fulfilling his mission, faded away, disillusioned, disheartened or disappointed. But gradually, he started gathering some individuals who were prepared to graft away, despite the gap that existed between the dream and the reality. People who believed that Bill Starbuck, or Sam Wanamaker, or perhaps the spirit of Shakespeare, just might make it happen, and meanwhile, they were prepared to survive the drought.

Some enthusiasts set up a temporary exhibition in the Museum. They mounted *The Stewes of Bankside*, evoking the time when Bankside had been a 'red light' district, and the prostitutes were known as 'Winchester Geese'. Sam recruited Grace Golden, a local illustrator and historian, who knew Bankside intimately. She should be the official 'archivist'. He appointed a 'curator' on a small salary, Colin Mabberley, a young man just completing a course in museum management at Manchester University, having already read Drama there. Sam had scrounged a 'Frost Fair' exhibit on loan from the Museum of London. Golden and Mabberley found it plonked against a wall. They cleaned it up; she gave it a cover and made little figures for it. Mabberley mounted his first exhibition, *This Wooden 'O'*, tracing the history of the Globe.

The canopy and stage were set up again for a second John Player season. Two productions came from Nottingham Playhouse: John Marston's *The Malcontent* directed by Jonathan Miller, and Ben Jonson's *The Devil is an Ass* directed by Stuart Burge. Then *Twelfth Night*, a summery production directed by Gordon McDougall and Michael Attenborough, set in the 1920s, with a cast including Alfred Marks as Sir Toby Belch and Jeremy Child as Sir Andrew Aguecheek. Next came *Macbett*, a take on Shakespeare's play by Eugene Ionesco, which Charles Marowitz had adapted and staged at the Belgrade Coventry. It starred Harry H. Corbett, famous for the television comedy series *Steptoe and Son*, and the comedian Terry Scott. The last play of the season was *Antony and Cleopatra*, starring Julian Glover and Vanessa Redgrave, directed by Tony Richardson, her ex-husband, all veterans of Sam's Stratford season. The summer school was cut down to three weeks, but there was another season of Shakespeare films and a children's film festival.

There were a few rumblings of discontent. An article in the *Evening Standard* implied that people were leaving the *Macbett* company because of difficult relationships with Sam, but he refuted the facts. He was not on good terms with Vanessa Redgrave, initially because he had leaked the information that she would be in the season before she had actually agreed, then because the pay and conditions were below West End standards. By the time *Antony and Cleopatra* opened, Sam was out of the country, embarked on one of the most exciting productions of his career. Just before he left, he heard that the Laing development scheme no longer included a Globe reconstruction.[33] The way was clear for him to pursue *his* plans.

11

'Let's Make an Opera' – Amongst Other Things
1972–1981

Sam was off to Australia, to direct the opening production at the Sydney Opera House. The invitation had come from Ted Downes, who had conducted some of the performances of *King Priam* and *La Forza del Destino* in 1962. In 1970, Downes had become Music Director of Australian Opera, the company that was to make its home in the new opera house. In 1972, when it became clear that the long-awaited building was on the verge of completion, he set about planning its opening production for September 1973. But, as Moffatt Oxenbould (then PA to the General Manager, later General Administrator) recalled, this was 'hopelessly late when dealing with international artists'.[1] (They lost the opportunity to have their own Australian-born 'diva', Joan Sutherland, in the opening season.)

Downes chose Prokofiev's *War and Peace*, because 'it would be unexpected, creating considerable national interest.'[2] It also had the advantage that there were many principal roles, so that a large number of the established artists in the company would take part in the historic first night. Downes approached several directors and designers, but none of them had the time to devote to such a vast work at short notice. He remembered that Sam had taken on the task of directing *La Forza* with only a few months to prepare.

It was ten years since that controversial production. Sam had not responded to the invitations from Ted Downes and Michael Tippett to direct another opera, perhaps because he had more lucrative offers, or perhaps because he was wary of getting his fingers burnt again. He had ceased to be the first director they approached. But this time, Sam was tempted, and agreed to discuss it with Downes *in situ*.

The huge white shells of Sydney Opera House which dominate the harbour are now an icon for 'Australia' throughout the world, but when Sam flew into the city for the first time, the sight was startlingly new. Through his friend Ove Arup, he knew something of how it came to be built. It was a cautionary tale which must have given Sam pause for thought as he pursued his own building project. The idea had first been mooted in 1954, when the

174

conductor Eugene Goossens, then working in Australia, and the Premier of New South Wales, Joe Cahill, agreed that Australia needed a first-class opera house. The following year, Cahill announced an international design competition, and approved the site, on the south side of Sydney Harbour. The competition closed in December 1956, when over 200 entries had been submitted from twenty-eight countries. The winner was Danish architect, Jørn Utzon. The judges reported that his drawings 'present a concept of an Opera House which is capable of becoming one of the great buildings of the world'. Ominously, they also stated that the drawings 'are simple to the point of being diagrammatic'.[3]

Utzon had never visited the site; in July 1957, he arrived in Sydney (where, despite his proven track record, he was required to pass a professional architectural examination), and began to oversee the construction. The engineers were Ove Arup and Partners, one of whose tasks was to look for ways of creating the shells, which were of 'undefined geometry'.[4] For six years, architect and engineers went through a dozen or more possibilities, and eventually, through structural analysis and early use of computer-imaging, they came up with a scheme, based on each shell being designed as a section from a sphere. Whether the solution came from Utzon himself, or from Ove Arup's team, remains controversial. In general, the two men enjoyed a fruitful collaboration.

Problems arose in 1965, two years after the original completion date, when a Liberal government was elected in New South Wales. The new Premier was not a supporter of the project, and the new Works minister, something of a Philistine, began to make trouble for Utzon, portraying him as an impractical dreamer. Eventually, in February 1966, Utzon resigned, and an Australian architect oversaw the design until the final completion of the Opera House in 1973. A major change from Utzon's design was that the larger of the two main halls, originally intended to be multi-purpose, became purely a concert hall. The smaller hall, originally for play productions only, would stage opera and ballet, despite its small orchestra pit and limited wing space.

On Sam's first visit, he had some stimulating discussions with Downes, who followed up with copious notes. Downes already knew Prokofiev's opera well, having conducted its first English performance in a concert version, five years earlier. Sam's immediate thoughts, perhaps inspired by the opera house itself, were also influenced by the exciting design for the *Iliad* that he had worked on with Josef Svoboda; he hoped that they could work together again. But Downes was wary of a non-romantic, non-realistic treatment. He explained that there had been a fair amount of opposition to the idea of doing the opera, because it was not a well-known popular work, and because – though he wrote that this was not explicitly stated – it was Russian. They would be asking for trouble, he thought, if they made it 'far out in terms of conception'.[5] He needed some early decisions: whether Sam wanted to do it, whether Svoboda wanted to do it, and whether, if Svoboda did not, Sam would like the resident designer, Tom Lingwood. Svoboda, it turned out, was not available. Sam did want to do it, and was soon in fruitful correspondence with Lingwood, an English designer with considerable experience in television, theatre and ballet.

Straight after the first Bankside tent season Sam flew to Russia to research possible design sources. As well as visiting houses and museums in Moscow and Leningrad, he managed to make time to see members of his family he had never met before. He struck up an immediate rapport with 'Aunt Bassya', his mother's sister, and her family. She did not speak English, so they communicated in Yiddish. He described later how a beautiful blonde Russian woman started talking to him on a bus, and showed him some of the sights, but he decided she was spying on him, and stopped seeing her.

He returned with lots of books and visual material, and impressions of 'the character of the life and physical surroundings of the period of the 1812 war'. 'I was astonished,' Sam wrote to Lingwood, 'by the degree of opulence and was indeed further convinced that our approach in terms of glitter and mirrors, surfaces of gold and silver is absolutely correct.'[6]

By the time he was reporting this visit, he had seen the first staged British production of the opera by the Sadler's Wells company at the London Coliseum. It was directed by Colin Graham, an experienced opera directer, and was received enthusiastically by the audience and the press. He had used projections, which Sam and Lingwood had already decided to use. Sam reported that the ballroom sequence had been performed by members of Sadler's Wells Ballet, and that convinced him that their production would also need professional dancers 'to maintain the visual interest throughout the long scene.'[7]

In January 1973, Lingwood visited London and they continued to work on the design. By May, Lingwood had discovered the limitations that the theatre, not originally designed for opera, necessitated. The need to accommodate a large orchestra meant that they could not use a proper revolve, which was essential for the scene changes; they would have to use the main ramp section 'as a motorised and pivoted truck'.[8] In June, while preparing for the opening of the second tent season on Bankside, Sam sent four tubes of plans, and answered some vital questions: 'YES, additional footmen in Scene 3, YES Napoleon without his hat, YES Dolokhov to darken his hair, YES to sleigh bells, YES to wind machine.'[9] He was preparing a sound plot to include birds, country sounds, battle noises and bombardment, and would send some 1812 drawings he had bought in Moscow. In July, Sam had a research assistant sourcing further material from the Wallace Collection and the *Illustrated London News*. He was in touch with the Hermitage Museum asking for photographs from a 1812 book he had seen there. At last, at the end of July, Charlotte and he flew out to Sydney, via New York. (He wanted to fit in discussions about a possible transfer of Ionesco's *Macbett* to Broadway.) Rehearsals began in the first week of August.

There were bound to be teething problems opening a major production in a new theatre. Tom Lingwood said afterwards: 'It was incredibly difficult. The theatre was unfinished. The staff were not all hired and the stage was too small. It was a gamble pulled off by sheer willpower because it had to be. We all knew the eyes of the world were on us. A nightmare!'[10] Articles in the local newspapers made apocryphal comments about 'lavatory basins collapsing under stout actors and smells in dark corridors'.[11]

Because the set was under construction, the stage was often unavailable for rehearsal. The chorus, which had been increased from thirty-six to fifty for the production, rehearsed in a service tunnel in the basement. When the stage was available, Sam spent most of the time choreographing exits, so that these were executed swiftly enough for the following scene to begin, without the backside view of performers scampering down the stairs to the greenroom. But cast members recalled that his voice remained warm and calm throughout. When he was asked by a journalist about the size of the stage, a matter of great controversy, he replied diplomatically, that he thought it was 'good and adequate', despite the large scale of *War and Peace*, with its number of chorus members and supers. 'It's a question of logistics,' he said, 'as in any kind of major operation where you are using a lot of people and fitting them into movement and timing and so on. The opera company is giving me every facility with which to do the opera in the best possible way.'[12]

There were two particularly comical incidents during rehearsals. The first was when there was a fire in the kitchen, and the adjoining greenroom filled with smoke. Moffatt Oxenbould described the scene:

The room was crowded with choristers, dancers and principals, all costumed in imperial Russian finery for the ballroom scene, milling around in the smoke, confronted suddenly by eager security guards and firemen, astounded to encounter these apparent ghosts from a bygone age.[13]

The second was during a dress rehearsal, which was being filmed, the reel flown to London for transmission on BBC2, on opening night:

[A] bush-tailed possum made an unexpected appearance … It came down from the flys [sic] above the stage and stopped downstage just in front of the flat rail dividing the orchestra pit from the auditorium – scampered along the rail to stop a metre or so from Ted Downes.[14]

Perhaps these incidents helped Sam maintain his cool when, in early September, he received the news that there had been a huge rainstorm during a performance of *Antony and Cleopatra* on Bankside, that the canopy had had to be split, to avoid a deluge of water falling onto the audience, and that the last few performances had been cancelled. The full story would have to await his return.

War and Peace opened on 28 September, and was as great a success as could have been hoped. A Melbourne newspaper announced: 'Overseas critics were lavish in their praise … When the curtain came down on the spectacular final scene, bravos rang out from every section of the audience, and the cast was given a ten-minute standing ovation.' Many commented on the cramped stage and orchestra pit, but thought that Sam and Lingwood had overcome the problems well. 'Despite all the drawbacks, [the theatre] managed to house a spectacular and ingenious version of *War and Peace* produced by Sam Wanamaker and designed by Tom Lingwood, as its opening venture.' (Fred R Banks, *Musical Times.*)

Tom Lingwood had created twelve impressive scenes, depicting Russian country homes and ballrooms in St Petersburg, military retreats and triumphs, and there were back projections, to convey the horror and carnage of war. His costume designs identified the main characters elegantly and clearly. William Mann (*The Times*) described how the 'revolve', for so he described the pivoting ramp, was used effectively for the transformation from the Rostovs' villa, to the first ball scene and the final tableau. He was impressed with 'the multi-level scene before Borodino with its duckboards and procession of shuffling refugees' and thought that 'strength through simplicity seems characteristic of Wanamaker's quality as a producer'.

The singers were praised and the theatre was 'acoustically superb'. An American critic, Irvin Kolodin, picked out Tom McDonnell, 'an Andrei to the life, imported from the London production to complement such home-grown artists as Eilene Hannan, a most promising lyric soprano, as Natasha [in fact, McDonnell was also Australian] ... Each [singer] has the voice for the music, and the frame to support Tom Lingwood's evocative costuming.' He reserved special praise for Neil Warren-Smith as Kutuzow, who had sung with the company since 1956, and the way Sam had staged the final moments of the opera:

> Not many stage directors would conceive of the possibility that the marshal's anguished outcry: "When, oh when, shall we see the end of this terrible strife?" could terminate with Kutozow immobile, lost in thought as the orchestra performed Prokoviev's closing commentary. Wanamaker dared it and Warren-Smith did it, to the credit of both.

Edward Greenfield (*Manchester Guardian*) found it 'a marvellous production in a marvellous theatre which Australia has always deserved'. He also commented on the fact that the opera house had become, in the popular press, 'a music-hall joke on a par with mothers-in-law', but thought that 'reactions will change once the pill of the price has been digested as well as swallowed.'[15]

In December, back in London, Sam went to Covent Garden to hear Ted Downes conduct a revival of *La Forza*, restaged by Ande Anderson, the resident producer. Afterwards, Sam wrote to him: 'It was a difficult experience for me to see it again, but you made it easier'.[16] While one critic carped at his memories of 'Sam Wanamaker's tendentious staging', William Mann (*The Times*), having praised Sam's work on *War and Peace*, also remembered the earlier production warmly:

> Mr Wanamaker rejected it as Grand Opera but gave us a big monumental opera, simply but spaciously produced with much emphasis on the nastier aspects of crowd psychology ... Mr Wanamaker's conception was fine and illuminating to this opera. It was too pioneer for British opera goers then, whether those who held that opera and theatre were worlds apart, or those noisiest spectators who were motivated by personal philistine spite. I reviewed this production enthusiastically and have often since mentioned it as a highlight of the Solti decade. Thank heaven the sets still exist and the production book, but with new found confidence, Covent Garden revived *Forza* last Friday. And Anderson produced it much in the Wanamaker spirit ... Mr Wanamaker's sets will offend few 1973 operagoers, nor, I suspect, would his sharp production if he had restaged it himself.[17]

Sam's main preoccupation, on his return from Sydney, was to deal with the aftermath of the disastrous end to the second Bankside season. For anyone else, this might have been the point to give up on the Globe project. He had given it his best shot, but, just like the *Iliad* idea, or the many film subjects he had suggested over the years, or the theatre productions he had tried to set up, it had not proved possible to bring it about. But that was not how he saw it. This was a scheme he had no thought of abandoning. Over the next decade, he worked with dedication and energy to acquire a site for the Globe and establish it as an artistic and educational centre of local, national and international importance. Until that could happen, he would make sure the idea was kept alive on Bankside, through activities on the site of the tent seasons and in the Bear Gardens Museum. Alongside those efforts, described in the next chapter, he continued to pursue his busy career.

It was still sometimes a question of juggling the 'BIG', the jobs that would bring him good money, and the 'marvellous', the projects that would give him artistic satisfaction. Although he had deliberately turned away from becoming a regular television director in Hollywood, he still accepted single episodes of successful American television series such as *Hart to Hart*, *Colombo*, and its spinoff, *Mrs Colombo*. He continued to act in films, and was in two British films, neither of them particularly memorable: *The Spiral Staircase* a remake of an American suspense film, and a spy film, *The Sell Out*.

Some years before, when Sam first returned to America, he had pointed out that jet travel made it possible to have a career on both sides of the Atlantic. He now relied on BOAC, Pan-Am, QANTAS, Aeroflot and other airlines to carry him between London, New York, Los Angeles, Sydney, Moscow and wherever else the work took him. It also allowed him to compartmentalize his life. He continued his liaison with Jan Sterling while remaining firmly wedded to Charlotte. In England, 'family' meant Charlotte, Zoë, who was often out of London, working in provincial theatre, and Jessica, who was studying at the University of Bristol, as well as the Perrys, who were as close as family. Abby had gained an MA in Speech Pathology at the University of Southern California, and, after a short-lived marriage, was working at Stanford University in San Francisco. In October, 1974, Sam's mother suffered a fatal heart attack. His father was left alone at North Croft, but with Bill and his family close by.

The projected film *Last Place Left* was never made, but in 1975, Sam was offered a completely different film to direct, *Sinbad and the Eye of the*

Tiger, the third Sinbad film, made for Columbia Pictures. The first had been *The 7th Voyage of Sinbad*, in 1958, the second, *The Golden Voyage of Sinbad*, in 1973. They were both the work of Charlie Schneer and Ray Harryhausen, who together created a stream of fantasy and science fiction films. Harryhausen was a pioneer in special effects. He invented a process which he called 'Dynamation', which allowed live actors to interact with animated creatures, in reality small-scale models which he built himself, manipulating them frame by frame against a projection of the actors.

Harryhausen put the story together, with Beverley Cross, Sam's previous collaborator, and it had all the basic elements of a fairy story. A wicked witch, Zenobia, transforms Prince Kassim, the rightful Caliph, into a baboon. His sister, Princess Farah, appeals to Sinbad for help, and they sail in search of the wizard Melanthius, and then, with his daughter Dione, on to the ice-bound land of the aurora borealis, where they meet a friendly trogladyte and enter the stronghold where the spell on the baboon can be reversed. Other creatures, all to be created by Harryhausen and his team, included a giant walrus, a minotaur look-alike who serves Zenobia, a seagull, into which she transforms herself in pursuit of Sinbad, and a sabre-toothed tiger that must be defeated at the end. The screenplay by Beverley Cross has touches of wit: 'Archimedes would shit himself with envy', 'That's telepathia'.[18] It was a kind of spoof of the epic ideas that Sam had had in mind for the *Iliad*.

In April that year, Sam was in New York and Hollywood to discuss casting. Sinbad was played by John Wayne's son, Patrick. The English actress Jane Seymour played the Princess, Melanthius was Patrick Troughton, famous as the second 'Dr Who'. Locations were in Jordan, Spain and Malta, with studio work at Shepperton and Pinewood. The shooting schedule was complicated, with a mixture of animation and live sequences.

At the end of May, Sam flew to Petra. Cast and crew were offered hospitality by the Bedouin tribesmen, fierce, proud warriors. Sitting around the fire, on priceless rugs, eating mutton and rice, talk turned to the American support for Israel. 'You're an American, aren't you?' the Chief asked Sam. Sam admitted that he was. 'And are you a Jew also?' to which Sam replied 'Who, me? Absolutely not!'[19] While they were shooting in Wadi Rhum, King Hussein flew out to visit them. When Sam mentioned that he needed to make an urgent call to America, the King ordered one of his men up a telegraph pole, to set up an immediate connection so that Sam could make his call there and then.

In June, they moved on to Spain, where they found, amongst other problems, that the boat was not being built according to the design. But in July, Charlie Schneer reported good progress to Columbia, at Burbank Studios:

> We have moved from Spain to Malta, endeavouring to wrap up principal photography by mid or end of August ... Patrick Wayne makes the best Sinbad we have ever had. Jane Seymour is a stunning Princess and the rest of our cast fit their parts exceedingly well. Wanamaker is doing an excellent job and my only hope is that we will eventually be able to recapture some of our lost time and that the final film will be contained within the appropriate budget that has been approved.[20]

At first, Sam found it strange to direct actors in a scene to which visual effects and animation would later be added, and he was uneasy at not being in control of how the scenes would look, since Harryhausen's work was out of the hands of the director. He commented at one point that 'the work with trained seagulls slowed progress'. At another point, he needed 'thirty more extras, to make a total of eighty, two additional horses, a flock of sheep and two mules'.[21] Delays in Spain meant that some sea scenes were filmed in a tank in Malta. He ended up impressed with Harryhausen's inventive work. Despite setbacks, the film, though not considered the best of the three 'Sinbads' made by Schneer and Harryhausen, came in on time and on budget. Sam received a bonus which he spent on a new Jaguar car. Working in a completely new way, for Charlie Schneer, with whom he got on well, and in beautiful parts of the world, some of which he shared with Charlotte when she joined him on location, it had elements of both 'BIG' and 'marvellous'. *Sinbad* turned out to be the last feature film that Sam directed, though he continued to develop ideas for film projects.

In the early weeks of 1975, before embarking on *Sinbad*, Sam was busy on another theatre project that was as exciting in its way as the *Iliad*. As early as 1972, Carol Fox, General Manager of Chicago Lyric Opera had decided to commission a new opera to be performed in 1976, as part of the American Bicentennial celebrations. The Polish composer Krzysztof Penderecki was her first choice, and by April 1973, he had agreed. Both Danny Newman, her press agent, and Fox hoped Sam would direct it, and after the success of *War and Peace* later that year, he felt ready to undertake another opera. In the spring of 1974 he visited Penderecki in Kraków and they discussed what grand work of literature the opera should be based on, soon agreeing on Milton's *Paradise Lost*. Harold Bloom, professor of English at Yale University, where Penderecki also taught, was to write an English libretto that would include some Hebrew elements. But the composer was disappointed with Harold Bloom's libretto, so Sam suggested commissioning the English playwright Christopher Fry instead. To design the opera, Sam thought of Svoboda once again. There was an intensive week of meetings in January 1975, when Carol Fox and Penderecki were both in London. Svoboda agreed to produce preliminary designs by April.

The design that Svoboda and Sam came up with was multimedia, with five giant screens incorporating stills and film of disasters and human misery throughout history, as predicted by Archangel Michael to Adam. A choreographer was appointed. Plans continued into the following year, but by March 1976, it transpired that, as Danny Newman put it, 'Our composer's Muse deserted him'.[22] Penderecki failed to deliver the score in time for the Bicentennial, and the production was postponed for at least a year. Six months later, Sam was offered another opera. He cabled Penderecki: HAVE BEEN OFFERED STAGE NEW TIPPETT OPERA COVENT GARDEN SUMMER 1977 STOP UNLESS I HEAR FROM YOU AND LYRIC BY END OF WEEK REASONS WHY NOT I SHALL ACCEPT REGARDS SAM WANAMAKER.[23] He received no reply, and accepted the offer from Covent Garden.

Tippett's new opera was *The Ice Break*. Covent Garden had first offered the production to Peter Hall. In 1970, as director of productions at Covent Garden, he had staged the premiere of Tippett's *The Knot Garden*, but he was preoccupied with moving the National Theatre from the Old Vic into its new building on the South Bank. The next choice, since the score was influenced by American jazz and spirituals, was Harold Prince, American director of musicals and operas. When he turned it down, Tippett hoped Sam could be persuaded.

The Ice Break, Tippett's fourth opera, was dedicated to the conductor, Colin Davis, successor to George Solti as musical director at Covent Garden. It was very different from anything he had written before, and different from anything Sam had directed, an intense sixty-five-minute piece in three short conflict-filled acts. In the first act, set in an airport lounge in America, Lev, a Russian dissident (John Shirley-Quirke), arrives to join his wife Nadia (Heather Harper), and their son Yuri (Tom McDonnell, who had sung Andrei in *War and Peace*). Yuri's white girlfriend, Gayle (Josephine Barstow) and her black friend Hannah (Beverly Vaughn, fresh from a debut in *Porgy and Bess*) greet the arrival of Olympion, a black athlete, (Clyde Walker, from Opera/South in Jackson, Mississippi). The second act involves a mob riot between black and white gangs, in which

Olympion and Gayle die, and Yuri is wounded and hospitalized. In the third act, Nadia, on the brink of death, asks Hannah to look after Lev; in hospital, Yuri, encased in plaster, has the cast cut away, and reconciles with his father. Before that, comes an interlude with 'a psychodelic messenger' (James Bowman, countertenor). The title refers to the breaking up of frozen rivers at springtime, and begs the question whether people can 'break' from the stereotypes they represent.

As usual, Sam was eager to explore the various 'worlds' of the opera. He felt particularly close to the Russian theme, because 'Aunt Bassya', together with three of her children and their families, had been given permission to emigrate, like Lev, and had left the Soviet Union only months before. He visited Cedars Sinai Hospital, where his brother worked, spending half a day in the operating theatre. He sensed 'a strange futuristic feeling',[24] which he wanted to bring to the final scene. He suggested a few changes to Tippett's libretto, when the idiom was not quite American. He noted two archetypal sounds in the opera which Tippett himself identified: 'one relating to the frightening but exhilarating sound of the ice breaking on the great northern rivers in the spring; the other related to the exciting or terrifying sound of the slogan-shouting crowds, which can lift you on your shoulders in triumph, or stamp you to death'.[25]

The designer was Ralph Koltai, one of whose productions had been Wagner's *Tannhäuser*, which had followed *War and Peace* as the second production in Sydney Opera House. He was known for his daring, often abstract, sets. Sam's preparatory notes included images of icebreaks, airports and hospitals, sketches for laser effects and holographs. Koltai designed a two-tiered stage, with girders, and elaborate perspex screens which slid back and forth as the action moved between private and public events. Walter Raine, from the Dance Theatre of Harlem, the first black choreographer to work at Covent Garden, arranged ritualistic dances for the mob scene.

The Ice Break opened in July 1977. Some critics were impressed with the opera and the production: 'It is a work that haunts the ear, the mind and the imagination (Peter Heyworth)'. Desmond Shawe Taylor (*Sunday Times*) thought that Koltai's designs 'served very well for Sam Wanamaker's vivid and gripping production, which in its turn loyally seconded the poet-composer's strange idiosyncratic disturbing vision of a world in turmoil.' Peter Stadlen (*Sunday Telegraph*) wrote: 'Sam Wanamaker's splendid production mirrored the work's oscillations between inner and outer events.'[26] But others found the set, the costumes and the choreography busy and distracting, or objected to the ritualistic staging.

Sam himself felt that the set, though 'marvellous for the piece … made it very difficult for the actors [who] had to do certain things physically that made it difficult for them to sing,'[27] but he made it as easy for them as possible. Heather Harper, who played Nadia, told him: 'I really enjoyed working with you very much, as I think you must already know; – in my experience, it is so rare to find a good opera director who understands singers and their "special" problems'.[28] And William Mann (*The Times*) admired the characterizations: Heather Harper's 'fearful, regretful refugee mother', John Shirley-Quirke's 'shambling but spiritually strong ex-convict', Josephine Barstow's 'wildly enthusiastic teenager' and Tom McDonnell's 'tensely glowering Yuri.'[29]

Overall the opera was not considered a great success. Commenting on it some years later, Sam said that the production team had tried to 'make a statement through the set, and we went too far,' but he observed that if its 'failure' had been the result of the staging, 'then you would think that the music would have attracted other productions elsewhere, and it has not.'[30]

Later that year, Penderecki at last finished writing *Paradise Lost* and plans were made to stage it the following year. But Sam found himself in the same position as when, nine years earlier, he had made his presentation at the Lincoln Center for the *Iliad,* his first collaboration with Josef Svoboda. The production costs he presented to Chicago Lyric Opera were unacceptable. Carol Fox hoped he would find a way of trimming them, as the donor who had agreed to sponsor the opera had died, leaving her with no possibility of an increased sum, but eventually she sent him a 150-word cable, full of regret, saying that she had been forced to engage another production team:

> … My fondest hope was that you could have found some way to contain your ideas and moderate your concept of the opera … We love your talent and what you represent in the theatre and we know you would have made *Paradise Lost* a great success.[31]

No record survives of the proposed budget for either the *Iliad* or *Paradise Lost,* nor any evidence that Sam discussed the situation with Svoboda. The Czech word 'Svoboda' means 'freedom'; perhaps it was the designer who did not want to be constrained. The decision brought an end to Sam's dreams of an epic theatre production that would combine spectacular scenery, live actors, giant screens of moving images and magnificent music.

Paradise Lost was mounted a year later in Chicago, directed by Igel Perry, more experienced as a choreographer than as a director. It was a co-production with Teatro Alla Scala in Milan, where Penderecki conducted. It was still expensive and not the great success Danny Newman and Carol Fox had hoped for. Still eager to have Sam come to Lyric Opera, they asked him to stage and compère a Gala the following year, to celebrate the company's twenty-fifth anniversary. Newman admired Sam's ability to pull such an event together:

> ... he really did see all moves ahead on the dramatic chessboard, and could bring perfect order and clarity to what otherwise could easily have become ... chaotic and amorphous.[32]

Dozens of opera stars were there. Tito Gobbi reminisced and introduced veteran singers such as Elisabeth Schwarzkopf, the music included Luciano Pavarotti and Mirella Freni singing a duet from *La Bohème*, and Penderecki conducting an excerpt from *Paradise Lost*. Sam gave a running commentary on the company's history.

If Sam had made himself more obviously available, he might well have made a bigger name for himself as an opera director. Since his original apprehension that not reading music would put him at a disadvantage, he had grown more confident in the genre. His four productions, together with the work on *Paradise Lost*, had given him the opportunity to create work on a larger scale than any of the plays he had mounted, except what he had attempted with *Macbeth* at the Goodman. Opera chimed with his concept of theatre as 'an amalgam of all the arts – with a purpose', as he had described it in 1961. Although this was something like '*Gesamtkunstwerk*', as conceived by Richard Wagner, Sam was not a Wagnerian. He once told a colleague that he was off to see *Tannhaüser* 'because one day someone will ask me to direct Wagner so I'd better start liking it!'[33] but he had come a long way from the boy who was turned off opera altogether by the bad production of *Die Walküre*.

Sam's 'bread and butter' continued to come from film and television work. Although he was offered no more feature films to direct, he was still in demand as a film actor. In 1976, he was in *Billy Jack Goes to Washington*, the fourth of Tom Laughlin's films that featured his controversial half-Navajo hero. In the same year, he was in *Voyage of the Damned*, the star-filled film based on fact, about the SS St Louis, which carried hundreds of Jewish refugees from Nazi Germany in 1939, but found no port would let them disembark. He also played a small role in *Death on the Nile*, a follow-up to the successful *Murder on the Orient Express*, in which Albert Finney had played Hercule Poirot. Peter Ustinov played the Belgian detective this time. It was filmed in Egypt, with another stellar cast including Bette Davis,

Angela Lansbury, Mia Farrow, Maggie Smith, David Niven and Harry Andrews. Most of it was filmed in great heat on the steamer, *Karnak*.

The most prestigious acting work Sam did in the late 1970s was in the four-part NBC mini-series, *Holocaust*, playing Moses Weiss, brother of Dr Josef Weiss, patriarch of the family who formed the subject of the story. At first, he wondered about the value of raking up such a grim part of European history, but then decided that the story needed to be told to the next generation. It turned out to be a less gruesome view of the horrific events than might have been expected, the prisoners at Buchenwald concentration camp looking remarkably well-fed, wearing blue-striped pyjamas that looked fresh from the laundry. When it was shown in Britain, one critic detected 'the deathly hand of Tinsel City'.

The American director Joseph Papp agreed with those who condemned it, but wrote in the *New York Times:* 'I cannot dismiss its impact on the general public. The enormity of the time and attention given to *Holocaust*, while broadcasting it in prime time, instead of the garbage that dominates this period, is no unimportant achievement.'[34] Despite negative criticism from some, *Holocaust* was nominated for fifteen Emmy Awards, including a nomination for Sam, for Outstanding Continuing Performance by a Supporting Actor in a Drama Series. He lost to David Warner for his performance in the same series. (Rosemary Harris lost to Meryl Streep as Leading Actress, Fritz Weaver lost to Michael Moriarty as Leading Actor, and there were awards for Outstanding Limited Series, for Writing, Costume Design, Editing and Directing.)

More acting work followed, still in America. At the beginning of 1980, Sam was in Los Angeles, having just finished playing Goldie Hawn's father in *Private Benjamin*, and about to start work on *The Competition*, in which he played Andrew Erskine, a character based on Leonard Bernstein. Charlotte was in Africa, where Abby and her second husband were living. Abby had just discovered she was pregnant. This was welcome news, but Charlotte nevertheless wrote to Sam in a despairing mood, having expected a phone-call from him before she left London, and knowing he would be with 'JS'.

Sam found it perfectly possible to love both the women in his life. 'I love you for what you are to me – and for yourself,' he had written to Charlotte earlier, 'and another part of me has other feelings for her.'[35] Abby had been shocked when a friend in Los Angeles wrote to ask if Sam and Charlotte were divorced, as Sterling had been introduced as 'Mrs Jan Wanamaker' at a fundraising event for a public television service. When Abby challenged Sam about this, he showed her letter to his mistress, who wrote her an eight-page screed, explaining how she had tried to minimize the effect of the mistake, and describing how difficult the situation was for all involved. Just as Charlotte had to accept that Sam was not going to end the affair, she had to accept that he would never break up his marriage.

Sam was not forgotten in the British television industry. Also in 1980, the BBC commissioned *Winston Churchill: The Wilderness Years,* an eight-part series about the years 1929 to 1939, when Churchill was out of office. It had a strong cast, with Robert Hardy as Churchill. Sam played Bernard Baruch, a powerful and successful Jewish businessman who turned to politics, advising Woodrow Wilson, and later, Franklin D. Roosevelt. Churchill and he had corresponded during World War I, and they became close friends as soon as they met. The character appeared in the opening episode of the series, offering help and hospitality to Churchill on a lecture tour around America. The climax of the episode was the Wall Street crash, when Churchill lost large sums he had invested, partly on Baruch's advice. It was a short but showy role, and must have reminded Sam of the days when the crash brought his own family to near destitution in Chicago.

He was also pursuing another project of his own. Through his brother, who had been in the same year at Tuley High School, he met Saul Bellow and obtained an option on his latest novel, *Humboldt's Gift.* Published in 1975, it is about the relationship between an older poet, Von Humboldt Fleisher, a version of Bellow's friend Delmore Schwartz, who ends up on the skids – Sam hoped to interest Walter Matthau – and a younger writer, Charles Citrine, partly based on Bellow, who has had some success, winning a Pulitzer prize and having a Broadway play produced, but is now broke – perhaps a role for Richard Dreyfuss. (Bellow himself won the Pulitzer prize for the book, and the following year was awarded the Nobel Prize for Literature.) The screenplay would be by Barry Levinson, who had scripted some television variety shows, and a couple of comedies for Mel Brooks. Sam himself would direct. The scope of the book is vast, and it is difficult to see how it could be contained in under two hours. But the Chicago background that Sam shared with Bellow appealed to him, as well as one of its main themes, the difficulty in creating and selling high art:

> There's the most extraordinary unheard-of poetry buried in America, but none of the conventional means known to culture can bring it out.[36]

The 'gift' of the title is a strange film treatment that Humboldt bequeaths to Citrine, about a man who takes his mistress on an idyllic trip, and then repeats it with his wife, a plot with resonances in Sam's own life. There are other parallels. Humboldt's widow invites Citrine to Alméria in Spain, where Sam had filmed *Catlow* and parts of *Sinbad*; she wants him to appear in a film that is full of 'sieges and things', reminiscent of *Taras Bulba*. Sam kept the project simmering for several years, but it never came off.

By the spring of 1981, he was back in Los Angeles, working on the pilot for a television series, *Our Family Business*. It was described as 'a mafia style *Dallas*', that Texan saga being then at the height of its popularity. Sam relished playing a villain, the head of an Italian clan, just released from prison after a tax evasion rap (a plot somewhat reminiscent of *The Criminal*, the film Joe Losey had directed him in, over twenty years earlier). He was so charmed by the role that he seriously thought he would enjoy playing it continuously if the series was taken up, even if that meant buying a property in LA. But the pilot, though well received, was not taken up. By the time it was aired, Sam had another short but major engagement. For the second time he was to direct a Verdi opera, *Aida* for San Francisco Opera, with Luciano Pavarotti – at the height of his fame among opera-lovers, if not yet among football fans – performing the role of Radamès for the first time.

Once more Sam studied the libretto, listened to the music and explored the world of the story. The General Director in San Francisco was Kurt Herbert Adler, an Austrian who had worked with Max Reinhardt and Otto Preminger. His first engagement in America had been in 1938, as assistant chorus director for the Chicago City Opera, when he prompted for performances of *Die Meistersinger*. He was as unimpressed by the standard of productions there as Sam had been in his youth, moved on to San Francisco, and worked his way up from chorus master, to Artistic Director, becoming General Director in 1953. A brooding bust of him, arms crossed and scowling like Beethoven, greeted Sam when he entered the Opera House, but one quoted remark of Adler's would have pleased him: 'Tradition is what you resort to when you don't have the time to do it right'.[37] Adler had seen Sam's *La Forza* production and was one of those who liked it. He was particularly interested in strengthening the dramatic elements of the operas he chose to mount.

This production was San Francisco Opera's contribution to the city-wide celebrations for the 800th anniversary of the birth of St Francis. It was Adler's last season. He engaged García Navarro as conductor, a Spaniard who had conducted his first opera only two years earlier; it was his American debut. The production was opulent in terms of set, costumes and choreography. There was a *corps de ballet*, a chorus augmented by music students, and a large number of supernumeraries for the final scene. The company had several weeks of rehearsal, unusual for opera. Sam thought that the story was actually more intimate and domestic than many productions made it; as well as co-ordinating such epic scenes as the Triumphal March, he worked hard on Radamès' relationship with Aida, sung by Margaret Price, and with Amneris, sung by a Polish mezzo-soprano, Stefania Toczyska.

During the rehearsals, Zoë heard, via Charlotte, that Sam was having problems. (She herself was having a great success starring in *Piaf!* on Broadway.) She wrote to him: '... by nature opera seems to bring larger headaches and bureaucracy than any other! Stamp your foot Daddy!'[38] And no doubt he did, whether at Adler, Navarro or the production staff, history does not relate, but it was not at Pavarotti, whom he found willing and amenable. Unlike Carlo Bergonzi, Pavarotti attended every rehearsal on time, but he found it difficult to respond to direction. 'Please, Luciano,' Sam pleaded, 'face the person you're singing at, so we can have connection in this particular duet.' But Pavarotti protested that his girth, already considerable, meant that he would not present his profile to the audience. 'He's not a natural actor in terms of movement,' Sam commented, 'He's a natural actor in terms of singing.'[39]

Tickets sold for as much as $500; the theatre was filled to capacity and 3000 Pavarotti fans watched on closed circuit television in a nearby auditorium. On the opening night Margaret Price sang, despite bronchitis. When she was too ill to sing at a later performance, Leontyne Price, experienced in the role, and in town to rehearse for *Il Trovatore,* came to the rescue. The critics admired the magnificent spectacle, and Sam's manipulation of 200 in the Triumphal March, but when the principals got themselves into 'stereotyped positions', they assumed that this was through lack of clear direction, rather than singers unable or unwilling to keep to what had been settled in rehearsal. One critic found Pavarotti's voice 'tarnished, steely and pressed, as if squeezed from a tube', but appreciated that Sam had 'maintained the intimacy that is the real essence of this opera.'[40] The opera was filmed and later broadcast on BBC2. The *Evening Standard* critic found it 'nothing less than magnificent'. Pavarotti and Margaret Price, he commented, 'are both a bit on the large side. Correction: they are a lot on the large side. But they sang magnificently.'[41]

There was a bonus for Sam in taking on this production. He met Gordon P. Getty, who was sponsoring the opera. Getty was the son of John Paul Getty by his fourth wife. John Paul had died five years earlier, and Gordon Getty was Trustee of his estate, and chiefly responsible for the Getty Museum in Los Angeles. Invited to dinner, Sam found Getty expounding on Shakespeare, and quoting accurately from the Sonnets. He was quick to seize the opportunity. Summoning all his charm and eloquence, he described the Globe project to Getty, and persuaded him to become involved. It was the precise moment when a serious amount of money was needed, and he was confident of his fundraising ability. 'There is no technique. If they believe your story they will respond.'[42]

12

Keeping the Flag Flying
1973–1981

S am's career, in the years described in the previous chapter, was as busy
as it had ever been, with artistic 'highs' such as *War and Peace*, screen
work that earned him good money and projects that did not come
off. His work took him to Spain, Australia, Jordan, Malta and Egypt. He
worked in New York, Washington, Los Angeles, Chicago, Houston and
London. Yet he put just as much, perhaps more time and effort into what
he called his 'brainchild', the Globe on Bankside, with all his work on the
project running alongside his professional life. His energy and powers of
concentration were prodigious.

When Sam returned from *War and Peace* in Australia in October 1973,
he was told the tale of the great rainstorm of August Bank Holiday which
had brought the second Bankside season to a disastrous end. Or rather, he
was given a version of it. First he had to take a look at the pathetic sight
of a collapsed theatre, with broken, sodden seats and ruined rain-soaked
costumes. He was told how the deluge that night was so heavy that the
actors could not hear each other. Bob Hoskins, playing Sextus Pompeius,
after an inaudible line from Dave King, who was Enobarbus, responded with
'What? I can't hear a bleedin word', to the merriment of the audience and
the 'corpsing' of his fellow-actor.[1] He was *not* told how an extra bar of lamps
had been hung at the top of the canopy, against all advice, compromising
its structure, and creating deep pockets out of which the rainwater did not
flow off as designed. At a crucial moment, the extra lighting bar broke free
and swung crackling in a live arc across the audience, while the scaffolding
serving as handrails on the audience stairways also became live.

According to one account, Bob Hoskins turned to the audience and said,
'Well, fuck this, let's all go and have a drink.'[2] He sat on the edge of the
stage and amused the audience with funny stories as they filed out into
the rainstorm. Someone turned the electricity off. Umbrellas were found
for a group of Russian visitors who did not want to spoil their Hepworth
suits. Tons of sodden canvas slowly descended onto the stage. Afterwards,
Vanessa Redgrave falsely remembered that Sam had been present, baling

out the flood water. But he, innocent of any liability for the damage, sat down soon after his return and put in an insurance claim for the useless canopy, seats and costumes.

Quite apart from the inauspicious end to the season, the Globe Playhouse Trust had accumulated a deficit of £60,738 (consisting of unpaid creditors £54,226, plus a loan Sam had made from his personal account). With the help of a company specializing in insolvency, Sam negotiated a low payment for most of the creditors, but that still left the Trust itself insolvent. In December, it ceased to trade. Undaunted, Sam set about changing the World Centre for Shakespeare Studies (WCSS), the educational arm of the organization, into a limited company with the same aims as the Globe Playhouse Trust, and registering it as a charity. In between his professional commitments, he continued to work towards his goal.

In Trinity Street, Sam was frustrated in his attempts to make the Surrey Dispensary a comfortable home. During the family's first year in residence, Trinity House, the charity that owned it, had put heavy restrictions on development. Charlotte continued to cook on a Baby Belling, and there was still only one comfortable room, which housed their collection of modern chairs. (Abby had started this collection by giving him a 'Barcelona', designed by Mies van der Rohe, and Charlotte a 'Wassily', designed by Marcel Breuer. Sam was particularly proud of his Charles Eames chair and footstool.) Not until the spring of 1974, was he able to have proper work done in the house, writing to his brother that he was finally getting electricians, plumbers and heating engineers in: 'We are encouraged, at least, that progress is at last being made to make the house liveable.'[3]

Over the next years, he continued to make alterations and improvements, enjoying his self-taught handyman skills. At 40 Bankside, he was diligent in keeping his office clean and tidy, despite its generally shabby appearance, regaling any volunteers or members of staff who happened to be around with a rendering of 'Life is just a bowl of cherries'.[4] He soon became a regular sight in the neighbourhood, greeted affably by some of the locals, as he walked the short distance between home and office, or at one time cycled, on a pale blue Moulton bicycle, arriving as early as 8.00 am to go through his post. He was always smartly dressed, often in suits he had worn for a film and bought at a knock-down price afterwards.

In pursuit of a permanent site for the Globe, Sam continued in discussions with Robert Buchanan-Michael of Town & Metropolitan Estates and with Southwark Council, hoping to reach an agreement. Early in 1974, a series of such meetings culminated in a statement of approval, in principle, for a redevelopment of Bankside, with the inclusion of a Globe reconstruction as planned by Sam and the Globe Playhouse Trust. Later, draft Heads of Agreement were drawn up for Chestergrove (Roger Wingate's company) and Bankside Globe Developments (Sam's company) to sell the Bear Gardens/Rose Alley properties to Town & Metropolitan for £78,000, on the understanding that Buchanan-Michaelson would contribute part of the site he had assembled, and the sum of £200,000, towards the construction of the Globe. An alternative scheme was for the Globe Playhouse Trust to buy Bear Gardens/Rose Alley for £20,000, then sell it to Town and Metropolitan, realising a profit of £58,000 which would have paid off the creditors – but for the Trust to find £20,000 was a chimera.

At around this time, Sam received a letter from a Mrs Theresa Lewis, Secretary of the North Southwark Community Development Group. This group had been formed in 1972, with an urban-aid grant. Its mission was 'to secure redevelopment which will primarily benefit, through low cost housing, industrial jobs, open space, shopping facilities, the traditional working-class community of North Southwark, and working people in other parts of Southwark.'[5] If you counted the Globe as a kind of 'open space', Sam could feel entirely sympathetic to its aims and objectives, and he applied to join on behalf of the Globe project. His application was rejected. In her letter Mrs Lewis stated:

> At our last Group meeting it was felt that these Aims and Objectives are at variance with those of you and your organisation. I hope you will respect this decision ...[6]

He did not worry unnecessarily over a group that, at the time, had little political clout. What was more concerning was that, following the oil crisis of 1973, and a stock market crash, property prices dropped, and the future of development companies like Town & Metropolitan Estates began to look bleak. While Sam was unsympathetic to its aim, to build offices that would bring in a quick profit, he had accepted the fact that a deal with such a company was the most feasible way to acquire land for the Globe.

His idea of a star-filled American tour to promote the idea of the Globe on Bankside had not materialized, but he was still eager to get some interest going there. He wooed many of the academics who had been at the World Shakespeare Congress in Vancouver in 1971. During 1974, on one of his trips to discuss *Paradise Lost,* he approached Lee A. Freeman, an old friend in Chicago, who was a supporters of the Lyric Opera. Freeman was a lawyer and helped Sam draw up the constitution for the 'World

Centre for Shakespeare Studies (US) Inc'. Professor Samuel Schoenbaum, from Northwestern University in Evanston, agreed to be its President, with Professor Michael Allan, from UCLA as its Executive Director. Two more academics joined, and a friend from Tuley High School, Morris Rotman, who ran a public relations company. He also recruited his friend Eddie Kook, and Jo Mielziner. These were to be the Directors, Mielziner bearing no grudge that he had been dropped as the designer for the *Iliad*. Sam drew up a list of over forty-five names who would form an 'Advisory Committee'.

In a correspondence relating to the stationery for the new organization, Samuel Schoenbaum advised Sam to design 'a simple letterhead rather than a Homeric catalogue of heroes,' but as with the Globe Playhouse Trust, Sam liked to see evidence of a large cohort supporting his venture. And as usual, he tended to jump the gun; he had suggested an additional name to Schoenbaum, who added in a PS '… if you think his presence … would help the cause, by all means add him on. But I see that you have already done so.'[7] The main achievement of this nascent organization was to sponsor a panel discussion on 'A Theatre for Shakespeare', at a conference held at Northwestern University. Schoenbaum contributed, as did J. L. Styan, an English theatre academic also teaching there, who later headed the American academics supporting Sam, and Walter Hodges. In 1976, Professor Schoenbaum moved on to the University of Maryland, and the academic activities dwindled, while Lee Freeman remained as nominal chairman of the company. Encouragement came at the next World Shakespeare Congress, held in Washington DC that year, which endorsed the Vancouver motion in support of a Globe.

According to his own later account, Sam had considered winding up the insolvent Globe Playhouse Trust and closing down the Bear Gardens Museum, but, given his usual optimism, this may have been a ploy, designed to elicit a further statement of support from Southwark Council. The Leader, the Chairman of the Planning and Development Committee and the Director of Development all encouraged him to keep the project going, and to wait for a turnaround in the economy. Meanwhile, he continued to proselytise, mount events and promote activities which would keep the idea of a Bankside Globe in the public eye.

Whenever he was available, Sam accepted engagements to give talks about the Globe to local groups and schools. He narrated, and helped to compile, a BBC radio programme for schools, about building the Globe. It included clips of Richard Hosley and Ronald (Ronnie) Watkins. Ronnie and his wife Bunty were good friends of Sam and Charlotte, and strong supporters of the Globe project. He was a schoolteacher, retired from over thirty years teaching at Harrow School, where he had staged twenty-one Shakespeare plays in something approaching Elizabethan conditions. Under his influence, Sam gave greater prominence to the educational value the completed Globe would have.

The Museum stayed open throughout 1974. One of the exhibitions was 'Shakespeare's England', with paintings from fifty schools, which the Minister of Education, Margaret Thatcher, came to open. A particularly enjoyable one was 'Harry Harris, Southwark lighterman', inspired by *Under Oars, Reminiscences of a Thames Lighterman, 1894–1909,* which brought some of the descendants of Harry Harris together for the opening. One, called 'A Very Rude and Nasty Pleasure' was on the history of fighting dogs, and on bull-and bear-baiting'. The summer school was held at the Museum this time, to save hiring the Chapter House. The Arts Council supported the publication of a third *Poems for Shakespeare.*

Sam tried to persuade a few 'fringe' companies to perform on the rostra saved from the previous season's catastrophe, surrounded by John Bratby's paintings. The best contribution was that of the veteran actor, Esmond Knight, who had devised a one-man show about Agincourt, called *The Archer's Tale,* which he had taken around the country and played on television. He performed it in what had been the Bankside cinema, after Sam and an assistant had cleaned out an old derelict stable behind it, to use as a dressing-room, pooh-poohing any risk, when they found they were stirring up clouds of asbestos. Just to show that he had not totally forgotten his political convictions, that summer Sam also put together a comic script of the Watergate tapes, based on newspaper reports, rehearsing in his office with four other actors, playing Richard Nixon himself, and performing it as a public reading at the Royal Court Theatre.

Early in 1975, while a band of loyal, underpaid staff and volunteers worked busily to keep activities going, Sam was absorbed in planning the designs for *Paradise Lost,* that was supposed to make a suitably grand contribution to Bicentennial celebrations in America. At one moment, he would be wondering if they could squeeze enough cash to pay the postage for a local mail-out, at another, checking if he approved the latest sketches for Svoboda's giant screens which would cost thousands of dollars. He did not seem to find the contrast absurd, giving equal attention to either task. It was the same with the split in his personal life. For anyone working in the Bankside office, there came a moment when they learnt that there was another woman in his life besides Charlotte. It usually came as a surprise, and perhaps as a disappointment, because he was so obviously devoted to Charlotte, a warm, lively and popular presence around the office. He never referred to his double life, but sometimes it could not be ignored.

One day, according to one of those same loyal, underpaid members of staff, Charlotte arrived at 40 Bankside loaded down with two plastic carrier bags of shopping. Sam was out on an errand, so she took them upstairs to Sam's office to wait for him. At the very moment he returned, there was an almighty screech. Sam bounded up the stairs and into the office, shutting the door behind him, but they could all hear the tirade that issued forth from Charlotte. No one ever knew what she had seen on his desk. After a few moments, the office door was wrenched open and Charlotte emerged, clutching her two bags, which she hurled down the stairs, so that they burst open, spreading groceries, tins and broken bottles all over the floor. She left the building, and the girls working downstairs salvaged as much as they could for Sam to take home. He said not a word about the scene, and nor did Charlotte.

In April the WCSS contribution to the Shakespeare Birthday Celebrations was a jazz concert. In June of that year, Colin Mabberley mounted his last exhibition at Bear Gardens, 'Plantagenet England'. Sam had asked him to continue without payment, and seemed surprised that he did not accept. There was no summer school. But while Sam went off to film *Sinbad*, there was a new Bankside Globe season in a new theatre space.

Sam had been approached by a civil engineer, who offered to provide a structure he had designed and built called Sumaspace, and install it on the Greenmore Wharf site at a cost of £20,000. It was elliptical in shape, consisting of reinforced fibreglass cement panels on an aluminium frame, covered with fireproof PVC. The original offer included the cost of stage and seating, and Sam was assured that the building would last until the permanent Globe was built (whenever that was), and it would then have a resale value. This Bankside Globe was not as elegant as the canopied tent theatre, but at least it was waterproof. The Arts Council contributed £3500 under its Housing the Arts scheme. The GLC offered some financial support, but its officers then proved difficult when it came to licensing the building for public performance. On the day of the first performance, two members of staff worked frantically to complete a long list of requirements that the officers presented, with the threat that if they were not fulfilled, the theatre could not open. The licence finally arrived during that evening's performance.

The short season consisted of a production of *Pericles* from Oxford University Dramatic Society (OUDS), Charles Marowitz's iconoclastic version of *Hamlet* (which included trampolines), starring Anthony Haygarth, and *This Wooden 'O'*, devised and directed by Douglas Cleverdon, best known as a radio producer. The critical response to these offerings varied. The new performance space was unattractive, and there was little to draw an audience to what was still an out-of-the-way part of London. Sam returned to find the season had been an expensive disaster. He was not amused to find a sign saying 'Messrs Boone and Crockett, The Alamo' on one of the office doors. The costs associated with constructing the theatre were much greater than expected, the Sumaspace company ran up debts, and some of its creditors appealed to the WCSS for payment.

By the end of 1975, Town & Metropolitan Estates had foundered. Robert Buchanan-Michaelson disappeared from the scene, and Sam was back to square one as far as plans for a permanent Globe. But he was still determined there should be some local events the following year. Shakespeare Birthday celebrations included another jazz concert in the Cathedral, and a devised show, 'Shakespeare in America', for a performance in Sumaspace. The fifth volume of *Poems for Shakespeare* was published, while unsold copies of the earlier editions piled up in the Museum. Another summer school was planned, but this had to be cancelled when it was seen not to be financially viable. Payment was returned to those who had enrolled, and no subsequent schools took place. A small company was put together to mount a Greater London Touring Programme, presenting Shakespeare scenes.

There were a number of one-man shows in Sumaspace during that hot summer, including a dance performance, and a play based on Lope de Vega's *Fuente Ovejuna*, ambitiously billed as 'The Greatest Show on Earth'. These were low-budget, often sparsely attended events. They raised the question whether they did more harm than good in promoting the idea of the Globe, just when Sam's 'rival', George Murcell, was mounting his first season at St George's Elizabethan Playhouse in Tufnell Park, with full-scale productions of *Twelfth Night*, *Romeo and Juliet* and *King Richard III*. But Sam was determined that the residents of Southwark should begin to identify the performance space as *their* theatre, and he hoped that an ever wider audience would be drawn to the venue.

In 1977, Sam thought, for a while, that he had found the perfect way to keep the Globe alive on Bankside while he waited for the economic upturn. Lew Grade, head of ATV, was co-producing (with an Italian company), a six-part series about Shakespeare's life, written by John Mortimer. The sets included a partial reconstruction of the Globe and its surroundings. The playhouse was designed along the lines of current thinking about the shape of the original, with a rectangular stage, supported by two pillars, and a gallery above; it included a part of the yard, from where some scenes were filmed. Why should this set not be moved to Bankside in time for Queen Elizabeth II's Silver Jubilee celebrations? With lots of 'Jacobethan' events taking place on and around it? He began negotiating with the Council to use their site, Greenmore Wharf, plus adjoining properties at 47/48 Bankside and Park St, as well as the site at 40 Bankside, which was now owned by Derno Estates, a property company that was part of the Freshwater group, as Town and Metropolitan had been.

How was the set to be transported from Elstree Studios? At one point Sam hoped to get the armed services to bring it in on lorries, a manoeuvre which would be worthy of publicity in itself. But the Chief Executive and Town Clerk of the Council, wrote that he saw no hope of getting the set onto Greenmore Wharf in time for the Jubilee. First, the planning permission for Sam to use the site was about to expire, so there would be a question of applying again, or else removing the set once the permission expired. Second, he felt the effort and co-ordination for what was a still a temporary project was too great. He recommended that 'we concentrate our effort on seeking a permanent solution'.[8] These were wise words, but Sam found it difficult to accept such advice. His inclination was always, 'the show must go on', even if the 'show' turned out to be a financial and/ or artistic failure.

A few years later, when giving an account of the events of this time, Sam wrote:

> In 1977 the summer festival theatre season on Bankside was recommenced on the Globe's 40 Bankside site with planning permission from the Council to put up a stronger and fully enclosed temporary theatre structure. The structure was in fact erected in 1978 and remained in use until 1982.[9]

His memory was not usually faulty. This wrongly-dated reference to a summer festival and his claim that Sumaspace remained 'in use' – rather than being what it became, a redundant eyesore on the site – was perhaps a deliberate attempt to claim that Globe events on Bankside were continuous. In fact, that year was something of a non-event. The Globe Playhouse Trust was removed from the Company register, and the WCSS ceased to trade, while keeping a nominal existence, its AGM attended by Sam and two remaining directors over tea at the Waldorf Hotel in the Aldwych.[10] The

North Southwark Community Development Group submitted a plan to develop the land on Bankside for residential accommodation. But a new phase of life *was* about to open up for Shakespearean activities in the area.

During the summer of 1976, when he was not away filming, and at the same time that he was in discussion with ATV about the Shakespeare set, Sam had a meeting with Alec Davison, who ran the Cockpit Arts Workshop in Marylebone, an educational theatre centre belonging to the Inner London Education Authority. Earlier that year, Davison had had built, and installed, a full-size replica of the Cockpit Plaiehowse in Drury Lane. (This was a Jacobean indoor theatre which theatre manager Christopher Beeston had converted from its original use for cockfights and opened in 1617.) Walter Hodges had researched and designed the reconstruction, and it had been used for Theatre-in-Education events. Davison was looking for somewhere it might be permanently housed. The Bear Gardens building, home of the Museum, was too small to accommodate it. Next door was a building owned by Derno Estates (the same company that now owned 40 Bankside). Sam began negotiating for a licence to use this building, 58 Park Street. In 1978 (while he was being lauded for his performance in *Holocaust*), a new company was formed, the Bear Gardens Museum and Arts Centre (BGM & AC).

The directors of the new company included Alec Davison himself, three lecturers from Rose Bruford College of Speech and Drama in Sidcup, two members of staff from the Curtain Theatre (another ILEA centre), and a drama lecturer from Goldsmiths College.[11] Later, the Principal of Webber Douglas Academy of Dramatic Art, joined, together with a qualified architect, and a young lawyer, who acted as Company Secretary. While they did not match the 'Homeric catalogue of heroes' Sam usually liked to recruit, they had the necessary expertise and manpower – especially when Rose Bruford students were brought in to help get the new enterprise going. Sam was Vice-Chairman.

The first task was to instal the Cockpit playhouse into the first floor of 58 Park St. It had to be rotated 90% from what had originally been planned, giving it a shallow auditorium with a small balcony above. The ILEA Curtain Theatre lent several models, adding to Sam's sparse permanent collection, which still included the Frost Fair. By the beginning of 1979, BGM & AC was offering a programme of 'fringe' events in the playhouse, alongside workshop sessions for ILEA schoolchildren, all unthreatened by wind or rain. Watching the classes coming regularly into the building reminded Sam of the children's theatre and film activities at Liverpool.

As he listened to their activities, led by knowledgeable drama teachers, he became even more convinced of the importance of education in his plans for the Globe.

As the end of the decade approached, Sam turned his attention back to that little area where a third Globe at last looked like becoming a real possibility. Derno Estates, owner of the 40 Bankside site, was in discussion with Southwark Council to acquire its adjoining Greenmore Wharf site, together with smaller adjoining properties, in order to build offices. As a 'community benefit', they would allocate the northern riverside part of the site, the very land that had housed the tent seasons and Sumaspace, for the Globe to be built. Sam remained unsympathetic to the idea of offices, having hoped there would be housing around the Globe. But this was the way he could acquire a prime site, only a few hundred metres from the original playhouse.

Although no agreement had yet been signed, the scheme was sufficiently definite for Theo Crosby, who had remained on the sidelines until there was the real prospect of a site, to start designing the Globe complex. He needed the academics to tell him what the playhouse actually looked like, and how it was built. That year, 1979, Sam was somewhat put out when a project to create a third Globe at Wayne State University, Detroit, was launched. Many academics participated in a symposium there, including those he felt should be focusing only on the Bankside Globe – Samuel Schoenbaum, Glynne Wickham, Walter Hodges and Richard Hosley.[12] Another scholar who attended was John Orrell, from the University of Alberta in Canada. He was familiar with the work of Richard Southern and impressed with that of Richard Hosley, who had analysed all the available evidence and come up with a plan that represented the best of current thinking. At the conference, Orrell presented a paper on the Wenceslaus Hollar engraving, *A Long View of London from Bankside*, 1647, on which some of Hosley's calculations had been based. Schoenbaum was sufficiently impressed with Orrell's scholarship to put him in contact with Sam, who set up a meeting in London, which went well. John Orrell then met Theo Crosby, agreed to act as his principal historic advisor, and began a close collaboration and friendship.

In 1980, Sam moved ahead on other fronts. The Globe Playhouse Trust no longer existed, and the WCSS was inactive. Ever resourceful, Sam had set up an Action Committee, an interim organization which could take responsibility for the next steps. It included Theo Crosby, Sir Hugh Casson, Neville Labovitch, a business man turned impresario, who had been a driving force in the Queen's Silver Jubilee celebrations, Melvyn Bragg, writer and television presenter, Guy Munthe, grandson of Axel Munthe, who lived at nearby 49 Bankside (the house opposite St Paul's Cathedral, wrongly identified as Christopher Wren's) and Barry Shaw, already Company Secretary for the Bear Gardens company. The Committee took legal advice and set about devising the structure for a new company. It commissioned Crosby to start work on the designs. (Since there was no money to pay him as yet, it was fortunate that Pentagram, the design company in which he was a founding partner, had a policy that each partner would work on one project *pro bono*.) The next step must be to revitalize the American side, from where Sam was sure the money to build the Globe would be forthcoming. There was much to be done. After years of marking time, he could at last start to put the pieces – and the budget – in place for the greatest 'production' he had ever mounted. He ended the year 1980 in buoyant mood.

Charlotte was not so happy. Jan Sterling had now set up house in London, perhaps recognizing that Sam's preoccupation with the Globe was going to keep him there for much of the time. She was leasing a mews house in Kinnerton Street, Belgravia, where she kept a low profile, but she was also Sam's close companion when he was in Los Angeles. She boldly referred to him in an American press interview as her 'fellah'. In London, while arranging discreet visits to his mistress, Sam continued to live a full family life with Charlotte. Their daughters, ever protective of their mother, had made sure that Sam was with her to celebrate their Ruby Wedding in May 1980. But a few months after that Charlotte was furious to discover that Sam was contributing substantially to the bills at Kinnerton Street, and that the property was leased in his name. Still, when, that November, Abby was in London for the birth of her son, it was an occasion for family celebration. Charlotte still hoped that Sam would come to see that the close partnership they had developed over many years was enough for him. It was not, but it was the main purpose of her life, and so she rarely thought of leaving him.

One of the people Charlotte confided in was Doris Perry. In the spring of 1981, Doris was diagnosed with cancer, and Sam's response showed his wholehearted commitment to the 'family' side of his life, however necessary he found his liaison with Jan Sterling. Doris wrote gratefully to him about 'that particular Sunday when you both burst in … you were both so bright and lovely, talking about everything except me and armed with gifts of champagne and salmon and love'.[13] They followed this up with a birthday party at the Surrey Dispensary for Jack and Doris, and their family and friends. Their daughter Vivien wrote a note of heartfelt thanks:

> The idea conceived by you both grew not only from a deep friendship and closeness to Mum and Dad, but also from a sharp understanding of the situation and a willingness to give the help and support that only true friends can give. You made them cross the first major hurdle, and they are now steeplechasing down the course, crossing hurdles at regular intervals … your house radiated a bonhomie which my friends could not comprehend … they have never experienced such a party of love and hospitality.[14]

During that spring, the Globe project took up much of Sam's time and attention. He was busy organizing a Gala Benefit to take place in New York to celebrate Shakespeare's birthday. The actor Ian McKellen agreed to give a performance of *Acting Shakespeare*, the one-man show he had devised, in aid of the Globe. The Shubert Organization offered the use of the Broadhurst Theatre. Through such contacts as Arnold Weissberger, who had a large address book, Sam gathered a galaxy of influential people to attend, including Her Serene Highness Princess Grace of Monaco, who was the chief guest and patron of the occasion. Friends and associates from Chicago were listed as Board members, including Saul Bellow and Studs Terkel. Producers Roger Stevens and Alexander Cohen were 'Eastern Region Associates'. Tickets were $250. The British Council sponsored a reception at Sardi's (the theatrical restaurant where there was still a cartoon of Sam). His friend Merle Debuskey acted as press agent. Sam only just managed to squeeze time from filming *Our Family Business* in Los Angeles to be there. It was a prestigious start.

Over ten years earlier, he had assured Alexander Cohen that financing the project was the least of the problems. Now that it was really going to happen, he would need a strong American organization to spearhead a fundraising campaign. At the same time, the operation in England must be put on a firm footing.

Amongst the people who received an invitation to the Gala was Jerome (Jerry) Link, a friend of Jack Perry. They had met in the 1970s. At that point, Perry was still not allowed to enter America, so they met in Montreal, but relations between China and America were beginning to thaw. Link was head of the Celanese Corporation; on a trip to Britain, he had been put in touch with Perry at his company, London Export, as someone who could give him advice about opening up business with China. They soon became close friends. Still not wishing to play an active part in Sam's Globe scheme, Perry was nevertheless happy to recommend his friend as a potential supporter. Link had recently spent time in South America, become disillusioned with the politics there, and was in the mood for some philanthropic project. After the Gala, Sam and he lunched together at Sardi's, and Sam's usual flow of eloquence persuaded him to get involved. Lee Freeman had set up the legal framework of the WCSS (US) Inc in Chicago. Now Link helped to re-form it as the Shakespeare Globe Centre (NA) Inc, structured to offer tax advantages to donors, with a head office in New York, regional offices in Chicago and Los Angeles, and hopefully some interest from Canada.

In August, Sam was briefly back in England before going to San Francisco to direct *Aida*. There was an unexpected setback. He went to Stratford-upon-Avon to attend the Third World Shakespeare Congress. He, and many of the academics present, assumed that the motion to support the Globe would be passed again without discussion, as it had, five years earlier, at the Second Congress in Washington DC. But the Chairman, Kenneth Muir, perhaps irritated that approval was taken for granted, refused to allow that, at which point, participants reported afterwards, there was much tearing of hair on Sam's part, and general disarray, and the motion was neither discussed nor passed. Andrew Gurr, a recognized authority on Elizabethan/Jacobean theatre, author of *The Shakespearean Stage: 1574–1642*, had given the plenary lecture at the Congress, but left before the fracas. John Orrell was deputed to invite him to head an Academic Committee in support of the Globe project. He agreed, and immediately shot off letters to two hundred Shakespeare scholars, asking them to sign a statement in support of the rebuilding. Ironically, Professor Muir was one of the first people to sign, and almost everyone else signed too. All was sweetness and light again in the groves of Shakespearean academe.

A meeting at Theo Crosby's office followed, where Andrew Gurr met Sam properly for the first time. Eight years earlier, the subject of the conference Sam had organized at the Festival Hall had been: 'The Third Globe – Ancient or Modern'. During the intervening years, when negotiating with Southwark Council and Town and Metropolitan Estates, he had sometimes hedged his bets, proposing *either* a modern theatre building *or* a historical reconstruction. As he listened to Andy Gurr and John Orrell, he became more and more convinced that they should plump for a design as close to the original first Globe as possible, whatever technical and legal problems that threw up. Andrew Gurr was relieved when, after a half hour discussion on whether the playhouse should have a plastic roof, Sam 'held up a finger and said "No compromise"'.[15]

From then on, the triumvirate of Theo Crosby, John Orrell and Andy Gurr worked harmoniously together towards the design of the Globe centre. The idea was for the complex to include a second, indoor playhouse (based on designs said to be by Jacobean architect/designer, Inigo Jones), as well as a Museum of the Elizabethan Stage, and a pub/restaurant. There would also be a number of flats, following Sam's first scheme, when he had envisaged houses surrounding the playhouse. Crosby began drawing up plans. His own inspiration was the Italian cities he had visited during the war, where ancient and modern buildings jostled each other. In his plan for the Globe centre, the other buildings besides the two playhouses, such as the restaurant and flats, would have a different vernacular from late Elizabethan architecture. Gurr began to organize what became a series of Pentagram seminars, in which a number of academics and theatre people met at Crosby's office and argued out all the design elements, both practical and academic. (One interested party coined the phrase: 'Always err on the side of Gurr, but never quarrel with Orrell.'[16]) Orrell's crucial contribution at this time was to reorient the playhouse as originally conceived. He had conducted a number of experiments with light, and come to the conclusion that Shakespeare's actors performed in afternoon shade, not sunlight. The stage should face north.

Theo Crosby made a new contact that was to prove crucial. Through Pentagram he was working on the refurbishment of Unilever House, the London headquarters of the Anglo-Dutch conglomerate. The building stood on a corner to the north-west of Blackfriars Bridge. From the eighth-floor office of the Chairman, Sir David Orr, you could look down the river and glimpse the derelict site on which the Globe was to be built. Crosby pointed this out, and arranged for Sam and Sir David to meet. Sam conjured up a vivid picture of what the Globe would look like, and how important it would be, as a theatrical and educational centre. Sir David, a Dubliner by birth, had joined Unilever in 1955, worked his way up the company, become chairman in 1974, and was now about to retire. Listening to Sam, he was hooked, just as Crosby himself had been, over ten years earlier. He agreed to become Chairman of the newly-formed Shakespeare Globe Trust. This was the charitable arm of the organization, which would collect the money. At the same time WCSS Ltd was transformed into a trading company, the International Shakespeare Globe Centre (ISGC), which would spend it.

For twelve years, Sam's work time had been split between film and television commitments, opera productions, tentative film projects, alongside all his efforts to keep the Globe idea alive on Bankside, while pursuing every avenue that might lead to a permanent centre. Voluminous correspondence filled his office, which was now at the top of 58 Park St, Derno having demolished the office building at 40 Bankside. Now there was yet another dimension to his work, as he set about wooing potential donors, schmoozing with rich industrialists, cajoling wealthy individuals. Very soon, in the early stages of raising money in America, questions were raised about how the Globe centre would actually operate. He quickly sketched out a five-page outline of proposals in block capitals, with his usual black marker pen.

The playhouse would be a full-scale outdoor exhibit of Elizabethan theatre. School groups, tourists and the general public would be led on a guided tour by 'docents' (the usual American word for gallery or museum guides). They would visit the dressing-rooms and see costumes, make-up, jewellery and stage props. They would see the stage-machinery and the musicians' gallery, with a display of period instruments. They would watch a short excerpt from a Shakespeare play. During May, June, July and August a leading professional company would mount a season of four plays by Shakespeare or one of his contemporaries, one of which would be 'in the style and manner of the seventeenth century'. For May and June, he envisaged morning performances for schools and an afternoon performance for the general public. For July and August, an early evening performance would replace the one in the morning. The plan sounded plausible, which was all that it needed to be at this point.

He asked – and answered – the question 'Will there be a conflict with other theatres?' by saying that the Globe would <u>complement</u> and <u>support</u> the National (by that time well-established on its South Bank site) and the Royal Shakespeare Company (about to move to the Barbican Theatre as its London home) by promoting and developing new audiences for Shakespeare. He asked – and tried to answer – the question of how the Globe could be historically accurate and at the same time meet modern building regulations. The architectural team would later deal thoroughly with these matters; for now it was convincing enough that he could say they were being thought about. He included the somewhat outlandish suggestion that the Globe would be built with removable parts, so that it could be historically accurate at times, and conform to regulations at other times. (It is doubtful if Theo Crosby ever considered that proposal.) He asked – and tried to answer – the question 'Under what agency will the theatre be operated?' His answer was complicated by the fact that there were already three charities involved: The Shakespeare Globe Trust and the Bear Gardens Museum and Arts Centre in London, and the American organization, as well as the International Shakespeare Globe Centre, the trading company in London.

The most powerful statement in Sam's draft was his definition of the Globe as 'an historic theatre structure which uses no scenery, no modern stage machinery or devices, no stage lighting to create mood and atmosphere, and depends, as it did in Shakespeare's day on the words and the actor's talent.'[17] This concept of theatrical performance was far removed from the operas he had mounted, or his 1964 production of *Macbeth*, or his collaborations with Josef Svoboda. He was conjuring up a form of theatre that he had not aspired to in his own work. Perhaps he doubted if he would ever have had the skill to hold an audience purely through the delivery of Shakespeare's lines, or to help other actors to achieve that. But the *idea* of such a theatre excited him more and more.

13

Alarums and Excursions
1982–1986

A
t last, the Globe was on its way, but there was still the need to earn a living. In the summer of 1982, Sam played the genial father of the heroine in *I Was a Mail Order Bride*, a romantic comedy made for television, which received lukewarm praise for having some 'fluffy charm'. In contrast, he then fitted in a short but challenging assignment at Tanglewood, in the Berkshires, mounting a performance of Stravinsky's *Oedipus Rex* with the Boston Symphony Orchestra, as the second half of a Stravinsky programme. The performance had originally been scheduled for April, to be directed by Peter Sellars, a young American well-known for his avant-garde productions of opera and drama, with Vanessa Redgrave narrating. Her appearance was cancelled, because of her support for the PLO, and her departure prompted Sellars to withdraw. Sam agreed to take over as director and narrator of the opera/oratorio.

Sam felt some guilt that he did not refuse the assignment as a gesture of support for Redgrave. He had long ceased to take up a public position on world affairs, at first because of genuine apprehension about the 'blacklist', then concern about his British residence and American citizenship, later from a continuing fear that his employability might be compromised, and, once he started on the Globe project, from a wish to keep on the right side of whichever British political party might lend their support. But he respected anyone who, as he had done in his youth, spoke up for what they believed, and he was no Zionist. His public silence did not stop Charlotte and him from sharing their private views, which were firmly against the policies of Margaret Thatcher and Ronald Reagan, who was in his first year of Presidency. 'A frightening reversal ... back to the good old days,' Charlotte wrote in response to a letter from Sam, 'when America was "Great and Powerful". How naive and childish to believe that he (or anyone) could bring them back again ... Isolationist – reactionary ... Macho impotence of the Thatcher, Milton Friedman disastrous economy. God help the world.'[1]

Oedipus Rex was Sam's only foray into Greek drama, except for his much larger, thwarted *Iliad* project. Perhaps that attracted him to the project, plus the fact that the great Jessye Norman was to sing Jocasta. First performed in Paris in 1927, the work has a libretto by Jean Cocteau, with the musical roles rendered into Latin, while the narrator speaks in the language of the audience. The Boston Symphony Orchestra gave its American premiere in 1928. There was a Sadler's Wells production in 1960, directed by Michel St Denis, and a film version conducted by Leonard Bernstein in 1973, either of which Sam might have seen. However familiar he was with the piece, it was quite an undertaking to prepare and direct it for just one performance, at a time when he was becoming increasingly absorbed in furthering the Globe project. By the time he arrived, Jessye Norman had withdrawn for health reasons. Sam went for simplicity, with a raked stage built behind the orchestra, and entrances through stone monoliths. The movement of the men's chorus 'accentuated the action without distracting from it', and Sam was 'a powerful narrator, delivering the English text with admirable sonorousness and directness'.[2]

After the performance, Sam returned to California for a meeting of the Directors of the newly reconstituted Shakespeare Globe Center (NA) Inc. It took place at the Beverley Wilshire Hotel in Hollywood in September 1982. The new Board made as impressive list as any Sam had gathered together before. One of his 'coups' was that, through his contact with Buckingham Palace, he had met Dr Armand Hammer – head of Occidental Oil, and a well-known philanthropist – and worked his magic on him. Dr Hammer agreed to Chair the new Board of Directors, Gordon Getty agreed to be Vice-Chairman. There were several philanthropists already attracted by his plans,[3] as well as Jerry Link. 'Star' names included Richard Burton, Douglas Fairbanks Jr, Cary Grant, Bob Hope, Charlton Heston and Leonard Nimoy. Lee Freeman and Maurice Rotman, Sam's friends from Chicago, and a couple of academics, remained from the original charity formed eight years earlier, Sam was 'President'. Prince Philip attended, put his seal of approval on the project, and let it be known that he would be Patron. (His own idea for fundraising was that a royalty of one penny be raised on every performance of a Shakespeare play throughout the world, but the idea was never taken up.)

Twelve years earlier, Sam's plan to have John Gielgud and Richard Burton tour the various American Globes had not got off the ground. Now, he saw that, to raise significant sums of money, the best idea was to mount prestigious evenings hosted by wealthy philanthropists interested in the arts. Princess Grace, perhaps eager to keep in touch with American audiences, agreed to make some appearances at a ten-city tour across the country. Sam thought of devising a programme for her, drawing on material in all the *Poems for Shakespeare* that had been commissioned and published since 1972. Her untimely death in a car accident, less than two weeks after the Board meeting, put paid to that scheme, but Sam persuaded her children, Princess Caroline and Prince Albert, to replace her at a number of events. He gathered a group of first-rate performers together, and compiled and staged a sort of modern 'court masque', called 'Brush Up Your Shakespeare'.

There were dinners and performances in Washington DC, Chicago, Denver, Dallas, San Francisco and Houston. Perhaps the most glamorous was at Helmsley Palace in New York, in March 1983, hosted by Liona and Harry Helmsley. She was known as 'Queen of Mean', and the couple would later be prosecuted for tax avoidance, when she famously averred 'We don't pay taxes, only the little people do'. According to the Globe's Executive Director in New York, Sam was rather taken with her.[4] (Perhaps he regretted not having had more of a chance to get into the skin of the mafia type in *Our Family Business*.) The performers at Helmsley Palace included Douglas Fairbanks Jr, Millicent Martin, Lisa Harrow, Michael York, Nicol Williamson, John Dankworth and Cleo Laine, whose recording of 'Shakespeare and all that Jazz' had made Sam an instant fan.

Sam had told Gordon Getty that he would never ask him directly for money. But back in London, he set about an event to soften him. A prolific composer, Getty had recently written a song cycle, *The White Election*, based on poems by Emily Dickinson. In April 1983, Sam arranged for Eilene Hannan, who had sung Natasha in *War and Peace*, and was now making an international career, to perform the cycle in a recital at the American Embassy in Grosvenor Square. Getty later promised to donate £1m, as soon as £9m had been raised from other sources.

In May, Sam's father died, just after his eighty-eighth birthday. He had had a pacemaker fitted a year or so earlier, but became increasingly frail. Aunt Bassya was now living in Los Angeles with her daughter and son-in-law, who acted as carers. Maurice left the house at North Croft Avenue to Bill and Sam. Having long hankered after having his own property in Los Angeles, Sam bought his brother out. Now he had a proper base, and he provided Abby with a home there, when she and her husband returned from working abroad, with their baby son. He established a small office in a room off the garage at North Croft, where his West Coast secretary and he could work on Globe business.

Within a short time, Sam had five 'Founding Sharers' who committed themselves to contributing $10,000 per annum for five years, besides Gordon Getty's promise..[5] This would be held in escrow, until needed for the building. There were other donors, whom he named as 'Founding Members'[6] It was time to bring them all to England to witness the laying of a Foundation Stone. There was one problem. Southwark Council had not yet cleared their part of the site, so that Derno could move in. Therefore, the Globe could not be seen to be occupying any of it. Never mind. Instead of the laying of a Foundation Stone, Sam announced that there would be a 'Dedication Ceremony', just outside the site.

Twenty-eight American donors duly arrived in July and were given five days of treats. Using all his best contacts, Sam negotiated a lunch at the House of Lords, hosted by Earl and Lady Bessborough, dinner at Sutton Court (previously owned by J. Paul Getty, recently refurbished by Hugh Casson), a Thames river trip, a reception at Winfield House, hosted by the American Ambassador, a garden party, a visit to Althorp House, home of Lord Spencer, Princess Diana's father, tea with sculptor Henry Moore and a reception at St James's Palace, hosted by Lady Rupert Nevill.

The Dedication Ceremony itself was attended by the Mayor of Southwark and Simon Hughes, newly appointed Liberal MP for Bermondsey and Southwark, together with King Constantine of Greece. The group gathered on the riverside. In his speech, Sam said that Shakespeare's time was the period of the greatest drama in the world, His Majesty made a slight deprecatory gesture, and Sam allowed that perhaps there *was* competition from Ancient Greece. Charlotte pulled a string that unloosed a flight of white balloons, which rose up and floated into the ether, turning all eyes away from the stark fence before them. The occasion was marred when Sam got into fisticuffs with some protesters from the North Southwark Community Development Group, but few of the American visitors observed the incident. They were then whisked off to a reception at Buckingham Palace, followed by dinner at the Savoy Hotel, hosted by Dr Hammer. They returned home satisfied that the Globe was on its way.

Soon after these events, Sam went through something of a crisis with regard to his position, and threatened to resign as Executive Vice-Chairman of the Shakespeare Globe Trust. This was the title he had given himself and it enabled him to take the lead in all operational matters in England. There were now three organizations dedicated to bringing the Globe into existence: the American company, operating in three different regions, the

Shakespeare Globe Trust and the International Shakespeare Globe Centre. The word 'world' had been superseded by 'international'; Sam wanted to create Globe Centres in other countries than Britain and North America, and to that end, he had already established an International Council. Andrew Gurr headed an Academic Committee. Each of these entities sported a long list of directors, or members, or associates, or sponsors.

Despite the number of people supporting him, everyone looked to Sam as the mover and shaker in all aspects of the project. When he was in London, he worked out of a small office at the top of 58 Park Street, with minimal administrative support. Soon after the Dedication events he was off to Los Angeles for another film. Yet, although there was so much to do, and a living to earn, he wanted to have his finger in every pie. The Executive Director who ran the New York office, found that when the American Board made an action plan, Sam then popped in and overrode their instructions whenever he thought fit.

So far Sam had never defined what role he would play once the Globe was actually running. He did not make any claim to be its future Artistic Director. After his apprentice days at the Cleveland Globe, the sum of his Shakespearean experience was that he had played Iago, directed *Macbeth* and played the lead, and devised 'Brush Up Your Shakespeare'. He was over sixty years old, but bursting with energy. Some of his frustration was born out of a wish to be free again to take on a variety of exciting projects. Sir David Orr wrote reassuringly: 'We know we cannot expect your continued involvement in the administration.' He agreed with the Executive Committee, that 'the job could best be done by a suitably qualified girl or lady,'[7] someone, presumably, who would know her place!

An underlying reason for Sam's outburst was that relations with the people running Bear Gardens were deteriorating. The company that formed Bear Gardens Museum and Arts Centre was licensed by his company, Bankside Developments, to occupy 1 and 2 Bear Gardens. In addition he had an agreement with Derno – unsigned – to occupy 58 Park Street, where the Cockpit Theatre stood. He envisaged that eventually the Museum and its activities would move into the Globe. His main gripe was the state of the building, which he considered to be BGM & AC's responsibility. He complained that flowers planted in the forecourt at Bear Gardens had been left unwatered and had died, that toilet holders were missing, paper towel dispensers not replaced, burnt-out bulbs left hanging, curtains in need of mending.

From the point of view of the ILEA (Inner London Education Authority), housework and maintenance were not the responsibility of their two members of staff, who were seconded to the ILEA Curtain Theatre in Shoreditch to lead workshops at Bear Gardens during the school term, and to promote appropriate events in the Cockpit Playhouse. Despite his trades union background, Sam was not one to take much notice of job descriptions. He had planted the flowers himself. (One friend of Sam's, dropping into the Museum unexpectedly, came across Jan Sterling watering them.) Years before, he had filched a sapling from a Southwark park, so that cherry blossom graced the forecourt every spring. In the years of the tent theatre seasons, he had swept the gravel outside if he saw it needed levelling. For him, a dead light bulb was something you did something about as soon as you saw it.

The ILEA Drama Inspector could not accept the terms on which Sam wished to grant a new licence. By the end of 1983, the Bear Gardens Company was wound up. The Cockpit Playhouse remained, but its lighting equipment, several playhouse models and a number of photographs on display were returned to Shoreditch. Once again, the Museum was closed, its remaining exhibits gathering dust until a new manager could be funded and appointed. Appropriately, one of the films Sam acted in that year was called *Irreconcilable Differences*. He played a Hollywood film producer, one of whose lines was, 'Thirty-five years I worked on this project.'[8] Sam had been working on his for a mere fourteen years.

1984 began well. There was a new administrator in place in Park Street, and a new museum manager who would also run education events. In celebration of Shakespeare's Birthday, BBC1 broadcast a documentary about the Globe. Derek Jacobi presented the programme, which followed some of the history up to the Dedication Ceremony, covering the struggle to find a site, arguments over the design, and the fundraising tour, with clips from the Helmsley Palace performance of 'Brush Up Your Shakespeare'. It was meant to be a prologue to fundraising in Britain.

But the following month, the Labour councillors on the Planning Committee of Southwark Council decided, summarily, to reject the 1982 agreement with Derno, without giving that company or the Globe an opportunity to object. In July Derno and the Globe were informed that 'a political decision' had been made, with no further explanation given. In October, there was a closed meeting of Labour Councillors, who voted, with one lone dissenting voice, in favour of voiding the agreement. In November, the whole Planning Committee put the rubber stamp on it.

The background to this alarming decision was that in May 1982, a month after a second version of the agreement had been signed, a local election had brought in a Labour Council of a very different colour from the one Sam had been negotiating with for so many years. The new Leader and the new Chairman of the Planning Committee were both staunch members of the North Southwark Community Development Group, entirely opposed to office development, and convinced that the Globe project was an elitist scheme, run by a rich American who was in it for the money. They were determined that the site should be for housing. (The previous Council had decided the site was unsuitable for residential use, being too near the river, which threatened the foundations of buildings on its bank.) By 1984, the Leader was Tony Ritchie, who famously declared 'Shakespeare is a lot of tosh'. The verse that Derek Jacobi had spoken in the BBC programme was ominous, ending:

> But opposition's hard –
> 'This land', the people cry, 'is steeped enough in culture,
> Tis homes we need – not art!'[9]

Spokesmen for the Council claimed, ingenuously, that they were unable to rehouse the dustcarts that sat on their part of the site. Councillor Ronald Watts, Leader at the time the original agreement was hammered out, had earmarked a site in a railway arch owned by British Rail, but spokesmen for this Council claimed that it was 'inappropriate use in a residential area'. Derno and the Globe both suggested other sites. In the autumn, the *Evening Standard*, which was following the story, reported that the Planning Committee had rejected a fifth suggested site. The most immediate problem for Sam was to convince the American Board, and all the generous donors, that this was just a local difficulty that would soon be overcome. But when Jerry Link, by then Chair of its Executive Committee, heard the news, he took the decision to freeze the fundraising drive, holding the view that it was unethical to continue while the Bankside site was unavailable.

This period was made more heartbreakingly difficult for Sam when Charlotte suffered a brain aneurism She was operated on, apparently with success, but then the wound split open, her speech became incoherent, and he lost, for a time, her unstinting support and encouragement.

Meanwhile, the whole Globe project was in jeopardy. Ironically, Sam's career was going well at the time. After several years playing supporting roles in feature films, and in films made for television, he had the leading part in an American television series, as Simon Berrenger, owner of an eponymous department story in Manhattan. (He often had to explain that the famous Wanamaker Department Store in Philadelphia had nothing to do with his own family.) Berrenger was described as 'an empire builder, an ego crusher.' Following the formula of the popular *Dallas* and *Dynasty* series, the plot lines focused on family relationships, including dramas in the lives of his two sons and his daughter, as well as hardheaded business practices. It had a luxurious setting, with glamorous gowns for the ladies, and suited the upbeat confidence of the Reagan years in America.

Before *Berrengers* was aired, Sam had two more jobs. He flew to Yugoslavia to film *The Aviator*, which starred Christopher Reeves and Rosanna Arquette. 'I like to visit places I have never been,' he told an interviewer. He said he was looking forward to his next two projects[10] – the adaptation of *Humboldt's Gift*, and another book on which he had taken an option, Moris Farhi's *The Last of Days*, a complicated thriller about an Islamist terrorist plot.

In November, Sam gave a distinguished performance as E. I. Lonoff, a reclusive elderly writer, in an adaptation of Philip Roth's 1979 novel, *The Ghost Writer*. It was produced by Adrian Malone and Michael Gill, the team behind the iconic *Civilisations* series, for BBC2 and a Boston station, and was subsequently shown on PBS. Lonoff is the idol of the hero, Nathan Zuckerman, a budding writer bearing a close resemblance to Roth himself. The theme had some parallels with *Humboldt's Gift*. Claire Bloom, the English actress living with Roth, played Lonoff's wife. Tristram Powell, son of the novelist Anthony Powell, adapted it, with some input from Roth, and directed it, bringing out its strange mixture of truth and fantasy. The London *Times* critic wrote that 'only Sam Wanamaker I thought successfully bridged the gap between written and filmed medium' and the *Daily Telegraph* critic wrote that he 'effectively played the cool and dainty attentiveness of Lonoff.'[11] The *New York Times* critic wrote that Sam played Lonoff 'with shrewd insight' although he was physically wrong, since the character was described as having 'jowls, a belly and the white-fringed bald cranium'.[12]

As 1984 drew to a close, the situation in Southwark was critical. The Globe Trustees took legal advice from Frere Cholmeley, a well-established firm of London solicitors. They advised that the Globe had some grounds for suing Southwark Council for voiding the agreement, but that Derno's case was much stronger as a principal signatory to the agreement. They advised working in alliance with Derno against the Council, despite the fact that the company had themselves been dilatory in pursuing the agreement, having gone cold on it, as property prices dropped. At the end of the year, Derno issued a writ suing the Council for £12m, and the Globe sued for the restoration of the 125 year lease of the site on a peppercorn rent and for costs. The Globe also sought an order against Derno, requiring them to honour the original agreement.

On the advice of Tom McNally, originally a Labour MP, by then a member of the SDP, Sam set about a public relations campaign, to raise local support for the Globe, in the hope of refuting the Council's view that Southwark did not want Shakespeare. Tony Ritchie's view that 'Shakespeare is a lot of tosh', was provocative enough to do some good. A local businessman took it upon himself to address the tenants' associations in Bermondsey and Southwark, and collected many signatures for a petition in support of the Globe. It turned out that, quite apart from whether they had any enthusiasm for Shakespeare (and many of them did), the majority of the local people approached thought that jobs, which the Globe might provide, was more important than housing.

It was reminiscent of the local support Sam had gathered, in vain, to keep the New Shakespeare Theatre open. He wrote to members of the Labour Party he had known in Liverpool, and persuaded several to write to Southwark Councillors describing his work there as evidence that his aim was, as it had been then, to create a centre which would welcome and engage local people, and especially the children. There were a number of willing young people around the Bear Gardens Museum, involved in workshop sessions in the Cockpit Playhouse. They were commandeered to walk the streets, collecting more names for the petition, and delivering leaflets advertising a public meeting to take place at the South Bank Polytechnic (now the University of the South Bank) in March 1985.

The day before the meeting, a Southwark Councillor phoned the office in Bear Gardens and offered to be one of the platform speakers. She was Ann Ward, Deputy Leader before the 1982 election; she had been the one dissenting Labour voice when the decision to void the agreement was made, and was passionate in her indignation. The next day, the hall was full, and enthusiasm for the Globe was high. The most supportive actors present were Richard Griffiths and Jeremy Child. Speakers were able to boast how well established were the Globe's activities on Bankside, with an almost unbroken six-year record of providing events, workshops and lectures for schools and colleges at Bear Gardens. Those opposing the Globe were shouted down. The immediate outcome was the formation of a campaigning group, the Friends of the Southwark Globe, who set about making their presence felt in the local community.

The problems besetting the Globe were mirrored throughout Britain. The miners' strike, when Arthur Scargill, President of the National Union of Miners, squared up against Prime Minister Margaret Thatcher, had ended in March 1985, just before the Globe's public meeting. At that time, many Labour Councils were trying to force the Conservative Government to withdraw its powers restricting local government spending. Southwark, under Tony Ritchie's leadership, was one that refused to set a rate. From the last week of April to the end of May, every Council meeting was long and stormy. Tenants' groups invaded the chamber on one occasion, and the Mayor had to put a stop to the meeting. Another meeting was adjourned when Ritchie himself was taken ill. Finally, at a meeting on 30 May, the Council set a rate at the maximum level allowed, even though the budget was then £9m short of its spending commitments.

Ann Ward, swiftly becoming the heroine of the Globe project, hosted a breakfast meeting for Sam and some of his inner circle. After one of these Council sessions which had lasted into the early hours, she regaled the company with what was almost literally a 'blow by blow' account, until Sam broke in: 'Well, as we say in my family, what has this to do with the Jews?',[13] and the discussion turned to the issues confronting the Globe.

If the Council was short of money, so was the Globe. The office and small staff in 58 Park Street were financed by a reasonable percentage for administration costs taken from funds raised, supplemented with small extra tranches that arrived from time to time. Theo Crosby, for example, telephoned the office one day to say that he had got access to £10,000 to build a display of posters about Shakespearean theatre for the Museum, depleted by the departure of the ILEA models. He never said where it came from. From time to time, Sam appealed to Mrs Henny Gestetner, whom he had known as far back as 1956, when she had been on a Gala Committee for the Royal Court Theatre. She was the widow of Sigmund Gestetner, manager of the Gestetner Company, and generous to Jewish and Zionist causes. Although Shakespeare did not come into her usual range of beneficiaries, Sam was persuasive. His greatest triumph was when she agreed to fund a much-needed loo for the Park Street office. It was duly installed in a spare corner at the top of the building. It turned out to be rather too small for the actor Richard Griffiths; his considerable girth meant that he had to go in and out sideways. The Trustees and Directors rarely came to Park Street themselves, preferring to hold meetings in their own more comfortable offices.

Sam's career continued unabated throughout 1985. *Berrengers* was shown in a prime Saturday evening slot on NBC. He became the subject of more publicity than he had enjoyed recently, but this included some interest in his private life. In April, a so-called 'close friend' was the source for an article in the *National Enquirer* about his affair with Jan Sterling, informing readers that it had been 'on again, off again'[14] ever since they first met.

But Sam felt particularly close to friends and family in England at this time, as Doris Perry died in May, and he was in London during her last few weeks. Charlotte and he had been close to Jack and Doris for over thirty years. Jack wrote to Sam : '... you gave me and our whole family the blessing of your presence, your words and your emotions to render to Doris the tributes we felt in our hearts.' He described what the friendship meant to him: 'Sam, you brought a new dimension into our lives, not just the show biz bit, but the capacity to link meaningfully the realities of life and its artistic expression. You widened our horizons and deepened our understanding of the culture that surrounds us.'[15] Charlotte was left without the friend she had confided in most.

Berrengers was not given a second series, but other television films followed. Sam was in *Heartsounds,* with James Garner and Mary Tyler Moore, *Deceptions,* a two-part mini-series in which Stefanie Powers played twin sisters who swapped lives and *Embassy,* a thriller set – and filmed – in Rome, in which Sam, as Special Guest Star, played the American Ambassador. Opportunities to direct were fewer, although Ted Downes asked him to direct and narrate a performance of *Oedipus Rex* in Manchester. He had made no films or television dramas that measured up to his visions of what could be achieved, though he was still exploring projects of his own that might, or might not come to fruition. Increasingly, the Globe project replaced the lofty schemes like *Iliad* and *Paradise Lost* he had worked on in the 1960s and 70s. He envisaged a Globe centre buzzing with activities, day and evening, like the New Shakespeare in the 1950s. But the reality was further away than ever.

Sir David Orr was a calm but determined Chairman. He combined the meetings of the Trustees (the charity) and the Board of Directors of ISGC (the trading company) so as to go forward with one purpose. There seemed little hope that the Council would change their minds, but it was worth a try. With Sir Peter Parker, another staunch Trustee, he set up a meeting with Tony Ritchie, Council Leader, but they reported back with an account of a stubborn, pig-headed response. For Sam, the situation was complicated by the fact that his daughter Jessica was a Labour member of Southwark Council.

One scheme the Trustees and Directors considered was to renovate and expand the Bear Gardens Museum as a 'stepping stone' strategy, which, as Sir David put it 'will maintain the interest of our supporters and demonstrate to the local community our commitment to the project'.[16] The Trustees now included Evelyn de Rothschild, chairman of Rothschild Continuation Holdings AG, part of the banking group, and he thought that might be a commercial proposition. But as the year 1985 ended, without any hope of an out-of-court settlement, the main concern was whether or not to go ahead with suing Southwark Council. The last role that Sam undertook that year was playing a forceful lawyer in a courtroom scene in *Judgement in Berlin*, a film adaptation of Herbert J. Stern's book, starring Martin Sheen and Sean Penn. Perhaps he would be in a real-life courtroom before long.

In the early months of 1986, Sam made the decision to give up the Surrey Dispensary, despite the effort they had put into making it handsome, habitable and hospitable, and find a smaller, more convenient place that would be easier for Charlotte to run. He settled on Bentinck Close, a block of 1930s mansion flats in St John's Wood overlooking Regent's Park. They would return to their old haunts north of the river.

By March, the Trustees and Directors had to consider the grim facts as set out by the partners at Frere Cholmeley. They put the chances of winning at 50:50. The firm had agreed to waive their own fees, but Queen's Counsel had to be paid. Stephen Perry, son of Jack, and a member of the Executive Committee, was deputed to send a personal telex to Jerry Link in New York, asking if some of the money in escrow could be released. All those who had contributed gave their consent, and he released $100,000 towards legal costs. But if the case was lost, there would be the Council's costs to be covered and each Trustee or Director would carry personal liability. Sir David rallied the troops and told them: 'If we believe in this project, we have no choice',[17] and they agreed to go forward to the court action. The decision was the clearest evidence Sam could have had that he now had colleagues who shared his own courage and will.

The office staff were cut down to two full-time, one part-time. The matter was now *sub judice*, so there could be no further public statements or events. All involved went into a kind of *purdah*, waiting for Monday 16 June, when the case of the co-plaintiffs, Derno and the Globe, v Southwark

Council, together with the Globe's supplementary request for an order against Derno, were scheduled to be heard in the Royal Courts of Justice.

In May, Southwark Council was up for election. Ann Ward stood down, and no longer had any political responsibility. As a private citizen, with a track record as a press photographer, she took her camera down to Greenmore Wharf, to see what really went on with those dustcarts for which, the Council claimed, they had been unable to find a suitable alternative site. She arrived there around 6.30 am. The only sound was that of birds. Just after seven, the first man arrived and the rest trickled in, up to fifteen men in all, some on foot, a few on bicycles, two in a car. They put their dustcarts together, had a cup of tea and left the site. All was silent, apart from the birdsong, until mid-afternoon, when they returned, dumped their carts and left the site. It was reminiscent of a Beckett play. She handed her report and photographs to the Globe's lawyers, and also made them available to a *Sunday Times* journalist.

For the second time in his life, Sam drafted a long Affidavit. He traced the history of the project back to his visit to the World Fair in Chicago in 1934, when he had first seen a reconstruction of the Globe, and to Bankside in 1949, when he first sought out the site of the first Globe and located it in a rundown redundant riverside area.[18] He picked through files going back to 1969, both as evidence, and as a sort of farewell, in the event that the case was lost, and the project really at an end.

The case was heard in Court 36, Chancery Division, before Judge Harman. Although it was well understood by the lawyers that Derno had the stronger legal case against Southwark Council, the Globe's QC, Gavin Lightman, persuaded Derno's QC that he should open the proceedings, since the Globe case had more 'merit'. Sam had directed and acted in countless courtroom dramas, but this was the first time he had taken part in one in real life. Despite the suspense under which he was living, the first couple of days were therapeutic, as he listened to Lightman laying out in painstaking detail the Globe's dealings with Southwark. It soon became clear that Judge Harman was not impressed with Southwark's claim that they could not find a suitable site to rehouse the dustcarts. He began to make references to the Leader of the Council as the *gauleiter*, and at one point asked that a Council document not be read out 'to avoid party political guff being spewed about the court.'[19] His attitude worried the lawyers, because his hostility was so blatant.

But over the weekend, the picture began to look better. On Saturday, Ann Ward heard that the Labour group at the Council had called a special meeting. The claim that the dustcarts could not be rehoused was clearly weak. And it transpired that a report from the Deputy Town Clerk, advising the Labour group, as early as 1982, that they would be in breach of the law if they reneged on the original agreement, had not been shared with the Planning Committee. The next day, the *Sunday Times* carried an article entitled 'If Shakespeare moves in 'ere, I'm moving out',[20] with photographs of the rubbish collectors and their famous dustcarts. That afternoon the Globe's lawyer received a telephone from the Council's lawyer at his home, requesting that they ask the judge to adjourn the hearing on Monday. Judge Harman gave them until lunchtime to decide if a settlement was feasible. It was, and the lawyers spent Tuesday working out the details, including a lease for the Globe site for 125 years at a peppercorn rent, plus costs, while Derno received £9m compensation. The Globe's order against Derno was not needed. Unfortunately, the Council leaked the news to the press, and Judge Harman said huffily 'Why am I the last to know?'[21] before congratulating all parties for coming to a speedy and sensible conclusion.

Sam had tried to insist that the Derno property at 58 Park Street be assigned to the Globe. But Sir David said 'No,' so firmly that he was reduced to mere grumbling. It was assigned to Southwark Council with the proviso that the Globe could use it until they moved onto the main site. Sam grudgingly admitted that, yes, he was pleased the Globe site had been won back. Then he called a press conference on the site and was photographed waving a bottle of champagne and a bunch of sweet williams in one hand, and a copy of the agreement in the other. Later, he had himself photographed with the roadsweepers, against whom, of course, he had no grudge.

It had taken four years to ensure possession of the site, and while the pockets of the Trustees and Directors were saved, the Globe received nothing in compensation for those wasted years.

14

'An American Chicago-born and All These Other Events and Notions.'

(Saul Bellow)

1986–1993

Relieved at the successful outcome of the Court case, Sam set off for his next professional project. He was to direct *Tosca* at San Diego Opera, leaving Charlotte to settle into their new home. This was a simpler task than the move to Southwark, fourteen years earlier. He downsized, sending a large number of papers to Boston University, where a Sam Wanamaker Collection was already established. He was putting past schemes and achievements behind him.

The invitation to direct the opera had come from Ian Campbell, an Australian tenor, who had had a small role in Sam's *War and Peace*, and had taken over as Chief Executive of San Diego Opera three years earlier. 'It would give me a great deal of personal pleasure, Sam,' Campbell wrote, 'to have you work with [us] ... and it might be something we could look at on an ongoing basis if you want to keep your hand in.'[1] But it was not as exciting a project as the other operas Sam had directed, as the company had little money to spend, and would be using existing sets and costumes. He agreed on the understanding that if an 'important movie' came up, someone else could take over. In the event, he did manage to add more supernumeraries, and made a few visual changes, though not as many as he would have liked, and he did not feel that it was really *his* production. He worked to get the singers to perform in a 'credible human and emotional way',[2] likening the opera to the popular drama series *Dynasty* and *Dallas* in its focus on jealousy, love, lust, hate and violence. But he was not tempted to take on another production in San Diego. It turned out to be the last opera he directed, as he focused more and more on screen-acting that was lucrative, but did not require so much time and preparation. His main purpose, more than ever, was to promote the Globe.

Acting was now something of a relaxation, in comparison with the vicissitudes around the Globe. With no significant decision-making involved, he could simply learn his lines, hit his marks and draw on his long experience to project himself into the character and situation of whatever supporting role he was playing. He was in *Baby Boom*, starring Diane Keaton, much of which was filmed in New York. (He insisted on having his Jaguar shipped over.) The film was such a success that he was back the following year playing the same character in an eight-episode television series. He was in *The Two Mrs Grenvilles*, starring Ann-Margret, and Claudette Colbert in her last screen role. He was in *Superman IV*, most of which was filmed in England.

Progress on Bankside was painfully slow. Dr Armand Hammer had withdrawn his support. Other American donors found it difficult to understand the ramifications of local politics in Southwark. Planning permission to build the Globe had expired, and while the newly elected Council was more sympathetic to the project, there were still bureaucratic hoops to be jumped through. After a brief period of euphoria, it became clear there was, as yet, no possibility of drawing up a contract with a building company. Trustees and Directors, staff and supporters were back to the difficult task of making it look as if the project was going forward, when it fact it had once again stalled. The situation was not helped when 'Travellers' moved onto the site – though Sam enjoyed chatting to them as much as he had enjoyed talking to the roadsweepers.

One difference, however, was that there was now an official group of supporters, the 'Friends of the Southwark Globe', its committee consisting of a team of active, morale-boosting, local people. The organization quickly developed its own momentum, with garden parties, jumble sales, Twelfth Night celebrations and other fundraising activities. Members staffed the Museum at the weekends. They gave talks about the Globe to interested groups, not just in London, but further afield, building up national awareness of the project. Sam encouraged the activities of his various committees, too, who met at regular intervals to discuss how the Globe would operate, *when* it was completed. There was a Museum Committee, an Academic and Educational Committee, an Audio Visual Committee (he envisaged a sound and vision library of Shakespeare performances), as well as the design seminars at Theo Crosby's base at Pentagram, and an Advisory Council that also met there, over delicious lunches, and drew some of the plans together. Positive thinking, that was the idea. 'Anything a man can imagine is possible' was the key line in Sam's first film, *My Girl Tisa*. Such thoughts were infectious.

Another group was the Artistic Directorate, consisting of a number of actors and directors who met every three months or so to discuss how the theatre seasons should be run. The membership was fluid, since Sam enrolled any willing theatre person he thought likely to be useful. While many started off eager to support Sam, their careers often made them drift away. Stalwart members sometimes attended meetings when only two or three thrust their way through the stiff, narrow door at 58 Park St and gathered in the ever-shabbier Bear Gardens building, its Museum entrance guarded by a great big ragged bear.[3] There was a sense that they were whistling in the dark, simply propping up Sam's faith in his dream. One lady actor who attended a few meetings suggested 'What we need is a philosophy!' After she left, Sam said 'I don't want a philosophy, I just want money.'[4]

Faithful American supporters continued to spread the word. Those in the Mid-West Region, based in Chicago, dreamed up themed events that were enjoyable, kept the project in the public eye, and raised some cash: a *Hamlet* dinner, an *Othello* dinner, a benefit for a touring production of *Macbeth*, an annual Shakespeare Globe horse race and 'The Bard meets the Car' (centring on Jaguar cars, which must have tickled Sam.) Los Angeles and New York mounted their own events. But there were no big donors coming forward.

Showman that he was, Sam wanted something to happen on the site, even in its derelict state. Just as he had created a Dedication Ceremony in 1983, in July 1987, he devised a Groundbreaking Ceremony, when Prince Philip donated an oak post from a tree in Windsor Great Park, and ambassadors from twenty-three countries were each approached to donate one. These were solemnly placed in holes around the Globe site, the spaces between marking where each bay of the polygonal playhouse would stand. It was a splendid *coup de théâtre*, aptly illustrating the internationalism that Sam wanted to encourage; but afterwards the posts were all removed, so that excavation of the site could really begin.

Never wanting to do anything by halves, Sam made sure that the oak-post ceremony was one of a number of events, creating an International Shakespeare Week. Unfortunately, the Week turned out to be a financial failure, eating up even more of the ISGC's slender resources. One event was a Shakespeare Gala Concert at the Royal Festival Hall, which Ted Downes conducted. A committee was put together who put much effort into organizing it, and finding sponsorship. They were disconcerted when they discovered that the main items on the programme were by Harrison Birtwhistle, Sir Peter Maxwell-Davies and Gordon Getty, who composed a piece about Falstaff, 'Plump Jack', especially for the occasion. These pieces were not exactly crowd-pullers. In the end, eleven tickets were sold, and great effort had to be made to paper the concert-hall.

Nevertheless, at the end of that year, with the help of bank loans, the ISGC was in a position to appoint a building company, Lovells, with Buro Happold as engineers. A specialist firm was brought in to help build a diaphragm wall, to keep the site dry. Only then could foundations be laid, and then a piazza, raising the playhouse itself higher than ground level.

For Shakespeare's Birthday in 1988, over 400 children from different countries processed into Southwark Cathedral carrying candles, wishing Shakespeare 'Happy Birthday' in their own language, while, on the Globe site, Judi Dench, newly made a Dame, donned a yellow helmet and operated the crane to dig the first hole on the site. The crane's claw, full of dirt, swung perilously near Sam's head, threatening to deposit the lot on top of him.

Although he did not again mount such events as 'Brush Up Your Shakespeare', Sam worked hard to re-awaken enthusiasm in America, and to raise funds from other countries. His aim was that 50% of the funds would come from Britain, 35% from other English-speaking countries and 15% from the rest of world. After the Birthday event, Charlotte and he visited Tokyo, where Panasonic had funded the construction of its own roofed Globe theatre. They found plenty of enthusiasm for the London Globe, and then moved on to Beijing, Shanghai and Hong Kong, hoping to awaken Chinese interest. But still, no major donors appeared.

In London, fundraising events included a benefit performance of the restored version of Orson Welles' film of *Othello*, and a Shakespeare Moot at Middle Temple Hall, suggested by writer Jeffrey Archer, during which Lord Alexander of Weedon, Counsel for the Earl of Oxford, and Sidney Kentridge, QC, Counsel for Shakspere [sic], put forward their claims of authorship. (Judgment was made in favour of the man from Stratford-upon-Avon.) In the autumn, the Friends, helped by other volunteers, took part in the Lord Mayor's Show. Events such as these, raised the profile of the project, created good will and brought in a trickle of income.

Early in 1989, a completely new factor entered the complicated Globe story. Imry Merchant Developers had acquired a property on Park Street almost opposite the plaque marking the first Globe. They proposed to demolish the existing seven-storey building, replacing it with ten storeys, and they agreed a short period for an archaeological investigation, before the site was bulldozed and the new building begun. A team from the Museum of London moved in just before Christmas 1988. In February 1989, they uncovered part of a wall built of chalk and brick. It was the first sighting of the remains of the Rose Playhouse, the first Bankside theatre, built in 1587 by Philip Henslowe, manager of the acting company known as the Lord Admiral's Men. It should have been a glorious moment for those supporting the reconstruction of the Globe – the first substantial evidence of an Elizabethan theatre.

Scholars and archaeologists walked the site, discovering parts of the foundation of a fourteen-sided polygon, with the stage facing south, not north, as John Orrell had postulated the orientation of the Globe. Actors came to drink in the experience of standing where their predecessors had declaimed the words of Shakespeare and his contemporaries, four hundred years earlier. The period of excavation was extended to May. Soon, a campaign to save the playhouse was started. Sam offered help. He proposed a Globe/Rose partnership. He put up banners reading: 'Save the Rose: Build the Globe'. He suggested that visitors could access it via a tunnel from the Bear Gardens Museum. He provided a room there for the committee to meet.

Most of the actors who were threatening to stand in the path of bulldozers showed little interest in the project to build a living theatre for Shakespeare a few hundred metres to the west. One day, walking past the wooden hoarding surrounding the Globe site, Sam saw that someone had scrawled along it: 'Shakespeare's Rose versus Wanamaker's Globe.' 'I suppose that's fame of a sort,' he remarked to his companion, 'and at least I get equal billing.'[5] On the day before demolition would begin – with wheelbarrows rather than bulldozers – rallying speeches were made about preserving England's theatrical heritage, but the American who had already devoted twenty years to the idea of a living monument to Shakespeare, was largely ignored.

Imry Merchant eventually changed their original design, which would have meant driving pilings through what was now known to be the stage of the Rose. The remains were mothballed, the office block went up above them. Relations between the Globe and the Rose remained frosty, and the media enjoyed stirring up rivalry. At one point, Sam insisted in a press interview that, 'there isn't a shred of evidence that Shakespeare acted or wrote for the Rose', and his loyal group of academics had to correct him. In the same article, he claimed 'I don't get really angry, I get passionate',[6] and admitted that he sometimes rubbed people up the wrong way. The 'Rose' committee continued to use a room at Bear Gardens for their meetings, but did not include Sam in their discussions. Perhaps they were apprehensive he would dominate their project. Yet it was obvious the two organizations should have worked in tandem.

The archaeological story was not yet over. Lord Hanson, an industrialist who headed Hanson plc, had added to his property portfolio the site of

the Courage Brewery in Park Street, where the first Globe was thought
to have stood. He allowed, and indeed financed, the Museum of London
to undertake a dig on the site. In October 1989, they uncovered a layer of
hazelnuts, such as had been found covering the 'floor' of the Rose. It was
proof enough that this was indeed the site of the Globe. The difficulty was
that much of the rest of the site was covered by Southwark Bridge Road, and
by Anchor Terrace, a block of houses built in 1834 that, in the eyes of the
Georgian Society, deserved conservation in its own right. English Heritage
became involved and there were lengthy negotiations. Sam hoped that
the importance of excavating the Globe would win out over the Georgian
Society. In the end, it was agreed that the Museum could conduct a scan of
the site, and then dig four 'test pits'.

One advantage of discovering the site of the original Globe, apart from
its historical significance, was that the negotiations and the excavation
itself provided a cover story for a pause in construction work on Sam's
Globe, when the real reason was lack of money. By the spring of 1990,
the diaphragm wall had been completed and there was a great hole in the
ground where the Globe would stand, but after that, work ceased until there
were sufficient funds to start the next phase.

At this frustrating point of stasis, came public recognition of Sam's
achievements. On 23 April 1990, Prince Philip, in his capacity as President
of the Royal Society of Arts, presented Sam with the Benjamin Franklin
Medal, an annual award given to those who forwarded Anglo/American
understanding. 'In every other case,' said His Royal Highness, speaking to
the guests assembled at Windsor Castle, 'the Benjamin Franklin Award
has been given for a completed achievement. This time, we make it in
anticipation of completion.'[7] Accepting the Award, Sam pointed out that
Franklin and he had certain things in common: both Americans, both
associated with communications, both living for long periods in London,
both given encouragement and support by the Earls of Bessborough, and
both honoured by the Royal Society of Arts, Manufacture and Commerce.
He acknowledged, among other donors who were present, Samuel Scripps,
American patron of the arts, the first Founder donor, and Gordon Getty,
whose pledge of £1m might encourage others.

The next day, there was a gathering on the forlorn Globe site, and a
magnificent 20' x 30' banner displaying Shakespeare's head was unfurled
over it. It was the work of Gordon Schwontkowski, a young man from
Chicago, who had laboured over it for many weeks, laying it out in a school
gymnasium, and then persuaded his employers, United Parcel Services, to

air-freight it free of charge. On the same day, Stan Shakespeare, who had been Sam's barber in the 1960s, and was a fervent supporter of the Globe project, hosted a party for 'Friends of Shakespeare', for all the people that he had managed to trace whose name was Shakespeare.

A few weeks later, Sam and Charlotte were in Chicago themselves, where he received an Honorary Directorate from Roosevelt University. Prompted by the Midwest Region of the Globe Centre, the Mayor of Chicago, Richard M. Daley, proclaimed that 19 May was SAM WANAMAKER DAY IN CHICAGO, and the Governor of Illinois, James R. Thompson, sent his greetings. There was a festive evening at the Casino Club, and the next day Sam received his award at the magnificent Auditorium Theater, where his brother and he had once been ushers, and where he had made his first appearance onstage as a spear-carrier in the Ballets Russes de Monte Carlo production of *The Firebird*.

In his acceptance speech, Sam told his audience of graduands and their families about his youth in the city, and of his wish to be independent of his parents. He said that his involvement in the project to rebuild the Globe had its origins in the insecurities of a theatrical profession and 'the sharp memory of deprivation and struggle for survival in my family'; he had wanted something permanent where 'I and others would be our own masters, be in control of our destinies'. He spoke of how the project had stretched his field of vision and also brought him hundreds of new friends all over the world, 'and particularly here in Chicago'.[8]

In truth, Sam was nearer than he had ever been to establishing that, 'something permanent', which had been his aim for the New Shakespeare in Liverpool, and which he had spoken of fourteen years earlier, before the first tent season. 'I have the need', he had said, 'to make a home and more than just the narrow thing of doing plays, making it part of the community, with activities from morning to night.'[9] Progress on building was frustratingly slow, but there was a growing community inspired by the idea of the Globe. The 'Friends of the Southwark Globe' had been in existence for five years. They had recently changed their name to 'Friends of Shakespeare's Globe', since, although they cherished their local identity, their reach was spreading wider. When Sam was not wooing rich potential donors, he was just as eager to talk to people who would come to the Globe when it was built, and who were eager to have a stake in its future, however small. Stars such as Cary Grant, Anthony Hopkins, and later Robert de Niro, were walked round the muddy site, and expected to share Sam's vision of how glorious it would look in the future. He enjoyed giving talks to schools. Those at one school in particular, Giggleswick, in the Yorkshire Dales, were sufficiently enthused that a group took on the leadership of the recently-founded Young Friends of the Globe, and set about building a network of schools interested in the project. One link Sam made through the main Friends' group was the Stamford Shakespeare Festival in Lincolnshire, which he visited with Charlotte. They later staged a Gala in aid of the Globe. The network of supporters was growing.

With his Appeals Committee, Sam had priced some of the individual parts of the building. The Friends decided to raise the £50,000 required for the First Gallery. Two enterprising volunteers organized a Gala evening at Middle Temple Hall, for which all proceeds would go to the Musicians' Gallery, also priced at £50,000. The most imaginative scheme these two dreamed up was Globelink, designed to fund the 'Heavens' above the stage, priced at £125,000; every school that raised £200 towards it buried a specially made time capsule in the centre of the site, to be opened in fifty years' time. The motto of the scheme was '... our children's children/ Shall see this and bless heaven.'[10] These projects kept enthusiasm high, but they did not contribute to the main building fund.

In his speech at Roosevelt University, Sam had made reference to the years when he had 'faced the same fate as his liberal-minded friends', who were being frozen out of jobs 'because of their commitment to achieve real democracy in America.' There were particular reasons why he remembered the blacklist years that spring. He was in the middle of filming *Guilty By Suspicion*, which concerned that very subject. The film was based on *Season of Fear*, a 1956 novel by Abraham Polonsky, himself a blacklisted film director and writer, who, subpoenaed in 1951, had refused to testify to HUAC. The film was produced by Irving Winkler, who had many successful films to his credit, including *They Shoot Horses Don't They?* (1969), *Raging Bull* (1980) and *Goodfellas* (1990). Polonsky was to write the screenplay, and Bertrand Tavernier was to direct, but both withdrew when Winkler turned the main character, played by Robert de Niro, into a political innocent, instead of a committed Communist. Winkler took over the screenplay and the direction. Sam played the studio lawyer who urges De Niro's character to take the easy way out. In March 1991, when the film was shown at the Cannes Festival, he spoke about his own support for the Hollywood Ten. He said that making the film had unearthed painful memories. 'It was a period of intimidation and fear when we all constantly wondered what would happen to our lives.' He felt, he said, that he was 'one of the lucky ones, in the sense that I was able to get away to England and work'.[11] At the same time that Sam was working on the film, Zoë was at the National Theatre in London, playing Elizabeth Proctor in *The Crucible*, Miller's play evoking those 'witchhunt' years, which Sam had wanted to direct.

The coincidence of the film and this revival prompted Sam to more retrospection. He sketched out the synopsis of what he called 'Variations on a theme by Irwin Winkler', making himself, as 'hero/victim', the subject of a treatment that would cover his life up to his return to Chicago at the end of 1960. He objectified the 'moral dilemma' that he would have faced if he had not stayed in England, and if a subpoena had successfully been served on him to appear before HUAC. The 'hero/victim' would have had to choose between being 'a FINK, a SQUEALER, an informer, a JUDAS' or to refuse to name names which meant 'the destruction of his burgeoning and successful career, with all its ramifications for his family'. 'Our victim,' Sam's version continues, 'decides not to confront the dilemma ... At least he will be free to pursue his work and career and provide for his expanding family.'[12] He wondered, in discussion with Zoë, if his decision had been cowardly – but it had protected her sisters and her while they were growing up.

Such retrospection did not distract Sam from the Globe, which occupied most of his waking hours. At any opportunity, he would talk to interviewers, potential donors, always hopeful that his eloquence would open the coffers. In his London office, he treated everyone who came through the door with equal enthusiasm, and his optimism was infectious. At the end of a day when only one visitor had ventured into the Bear Gardens Museum, the takings were just £1. 'Only one person today,' he told the volunteer at the desk, '– in years to come, thousands!'[13] Somehow, he also found time to deal with general requests, setting aside an hour, for example, to give advice to a young man who wanted to start in the film industry.

He continued to take on film work, so as to have money coming into his account. In October 1990, Douglas Fairbanks Jr, faithful friend and supporter, wrote an admiring letter.

Dear Sam

Dear most remarkable Sam –

How the hell do you do it? Dashing and flying across oceans and continents, memorising lines for movies (and/or plays, and/or speeches) retain your energy and looks (<u>looks</u> like a damned juvenile – <u>almost</u>) ... How do you do it? And do it so well?

In any case, the last blow-out at Steuben[14] here in the Big Rotten Apple was about as glamorous as they come – the quality of attendance was a fine tribute to you. I grow increasingly proud of my association with the Shakespeare Globe enterprise and of being

Your friend Doug (F)[15]

Since 1986, Sam had appeared in four American television dramas. He had directed an episode of *Columbo*, which turned out to be the last directing job he accepted, since preparation took much longer than studying a part. He had turned down the part of Joe Keller in Miller's *All My Sons* which he was asked to do on BBC radio. He had played opposite Angela Lansbury in the television mini-series of Rosamund Pilcher's *The Shell Seekers*. He had taken Charlotte to Yugoslavia when he played the American Ambassador in *Cognac*, originally known as *Tajna manastirske rakije* (*Secret Ingredient*), directed by a Serbian director, Slobodan Šijan. Now he was off again a few weeks after Fairbanks' letter, to film a small part as an affectionate grandfather in *Always Remember I Love You*, a tear-jerker about adoption. Jet lag never seemed to bother him, and he insisted on travelling in Economy class, to save money.

Early in 1991, the bleakness of the financial situation at the Globe had to be faced. Sam had written to Trustee Sir Evelyn Rothschild: 'We need approximately £100,000 to ensure our ability to operate in the next six months, and we need to raise £3.2m by March 1991, to start up construction again.'[16] There was a particular problem in that Terresearch, the company that had built the diaphragm wall, were demanding payment. Fortunately, an anonymous donor was found to buy out the debt, in order for Phase II to begin, which involved building the piazza on which the Globe playhouse was to stand. Sam wrote to Michael Perry, Chairman of ISGC: 'If the Trustees decide not to go ahead, the deal with Terresearch will be off, as the "White Knight" will not pay over the monies to pay the debt.'[17] The 'White Knight' was Sam himself.

A new scheme was launched, the 1000 Club. The idea was to persuade 1000 people to commit to donating £250 each for the next four years. Prince Philip agreed to host a reception at Buckingham Palace to encourage members to join this exclusive group. That would help towards the £100,000, but the £3.2m was not forthcoming. At this point, Theo Crosby, who had been working on the project almost as long as Sam, put his thinking cap on and came up with the idea of Direct Build. Since there were not sufficient funds to sign a new contract with Lovells to complete Phase II, why should the Globe not take over as contractors, employing builders and craftsmen directly, undertaking the work in tranches, as and when funds were available?

By this time, despite the painfully slow progress, the momentum behind the project had grown sufficiently for the Trustees and the ISGC to be able to call on a fair amount of good will. By the end of April, Sam was able to report that the banks had agreed to extend the maturity of their loan for three years or possibly longer, that they supported the 'Direct Build' and agreed with the proposal to start construction again in July. There were already promises of materials, service and staff secondments, and these would come under the direct management of the Globe's architects, engineers and quantity surveyors, who would give their services free for a year. Lovells were willing to second one of their senior site managers. Theo Crosby prepared a feasibility plan which depended on finding £300,000 for the following twelve months, one-tenth of the original target. In order to achieve even that sum, Sam had to ask the Friends to lend the £50,000 they had raised towards their own goal, the First Gallery.

At last they were on their way again, encouraged by yet more new appeals. There was the flagstone appeal; for a few hundred pounds, every donor would have their own name, or someone else's, inscribed on the flags that would pave the piazza. Less wealthy supporters could 'buy' a brick and receive a certificate. (One volunteer found himself signing a certificate for 'The New Hampshire State Prison Education Facility'.)[18] In New Zealand, an imaginative scheme had already come to fruition to create hangings for the Globe stage. Under the auspices of the Wellington Shakespeare Society, 500 embroiderers each worked on a section of the design. Two narrow panels, designed for the central door at the back of the stage, carried the figures of Atlas and Hercules, the logos of Shakespeare's company, while two wider panels for each side of the *frons scenae* depicted Venus and Adonis, in honour of Shakespeare's most famous poem.[19]

Early in 1991, Sam gave a talk at the Folger Library in Washington DC, for the Association of Shakespeare Festivals and Theatres. In describing the Globe project he reiterated: 'There will be no roof, no artificial lighting, no air conditioning and no heating, no amplified voices, nor artificial sound or music.'[20] His confidence in the kind of performances this would lead to had been strengthened by hearing from Patrick Spottiswoode, formerly the Museum Manager, now carrying the title Director of Globe Education, about a theatre company in Germany, whose work, he reported, was as close to the way Shakespeare's company worked as any he had seen. Germany had had a strong Shakespeare tradition ever since English companies had visited in the seventeenth century. Norbert Kentrup, a German actor, had become interested in this approach to Shakespeare after reading Robert Weimann's

Shakespeare und die Tradition des Volkstheaters.[21] He had founded the Bremer Shakespeare Company in 1983, a small group working on Shakespeare and other plays in an empty space, without a set, sharing the same light as the audience.

That summer of 1991, they were playing in a replica of the Globe in the city of Neuss. Sam was persuaded to visit Neuss, and see the little 500-seater Globe, built of wood and steel. He watched the Bremer Company playing *The Taming of the Shrew* there. He soon met Norbert Kentrup and his wife Dagmar Papula, and they struck up an immediate rapport. Kentrup's English was minimal, but Sam helped out with Yiddish, which was close enough to German for them all to understand each other.

Soon after he returned from Germany, there was another production that showed Sam what performances at the Globe might be like. The actor Mark Rylance, who ran the Phoebus Cart company (and had brought a production of *Othello* to the Cockpit in Bear Gardens, six years earlier), was touring sacred sites in England with an open-air production of *The Tempest*. He brought it to the Globe site, and performed on the bare concrete of the Globe foundation floor, some of the audience sitting on blankets, others standing around the actors. Sam later evoked the magic of one performance: 'It was midnight of the summer solstice, under a clear London sky. Lit by moonlight and general floodlight.'[22] Performances ran until mid-July, but Sam was off and away to attend events in Chicago, and to Hollywood, for yet another film (a comedy, *Pure Luck*) and a Gala event for the Globe.

By this time, he had made improvements to North Croft, and added a swimming pool, to make it a more inviting place for Charlotte, when she could be persuaded to join him. A satisfying project, compared with the major building scheme which occupied his mind 90% of the time. The previous year, while he was filming *Guilty by Suspicion*, Sam and Charlotte had celebrated their Golden Wedding in Los Angeles. He had become adept at managing his double life, even taking Jan Sterling on one of his overseas trips promoting the Globe, while always sending reassuring messages to Charlotte.

Back in London, the design team turned their attention to the oak bays that would form the polygonal frame of the Globe playhouse. The limited excavation on the original site had convinced John Orrell and Andrew Gurr that it had twenty sides, not the twenty-four that had previously been surmised. Theo Crosby had accordingly adjusted his design. With his usual forwardness, Sam approached the Private Secretary and Treasurer to the Prince and Princess of Wales, to ask if His Royal Highness would donate some oak trees from Highgrove. He specified that the beams needed to be 17" in quarter girth, with a minimum length of 12", 'and of course straight'.[23] A brief reply informed him that the oaks at Highgrove did not measure up to those specifications.

Sam had been trying to woo the Prince of Wales for some time, even though Prince Philip was the official patron of the Globe Trust. In April 1991, Sam had heard Prince Charles give the twenty-eight Annual Shakespeare Lecture in Stratford-upon-Avon, when he had talked about the centrality of Shakespeare to British culture, and suggested that it should be part of every child's curriculum. He said that he had first learnt to enjoy Shakespeare by hearing Cole Porter's brilliant lyrics, 'Brush Up Your Shakespeare'. 'That Shakespeare can be fun,' he went on, 'seems to me to be something which each generation has to discover anew for itself.'[24] Sam was quick to write a fan letter: 'You touched a strong responsive chord in the hearts and minds of the British people with your concern for the education of their children.' He went on: 'By your address you have immensely helped the cause and objectives of Shakespeare and of the Globe project', and came to his real point at the end: 'I hope there will be an opportunity to give you a presentation on the details and aspirations of the project.'[25] Prince Charles replied courteously:

> Dear Mr Wanamaker
>
> I was enormously touched by your kind and encouraging letter after my Stratford speech and I can't thank you enough for taking the trouble to write as you did. If I may have helped the cause of your project in some small way, then I couldn't be more thrilled. I do wish you all possible success and good fortune, however hard the going may be ...
>
> Yours sincerely
>
> Charles[26]

The Prince never did find time to arrange for a presentation about the Globe. The following year, Sam was a little peeved when His Royal Highness sent him an invitation to attend a function of the British Friends of the Gdansk Theatre Foundation of which he was patron, and whose aim was to build a modern Shakespeare theatre inspired by the architecture of the Fortune Playhouse in London. Sam replied that attending would be incompatible with raising funds for his own Globe.

Even with Self-Build, as the new scheme was generally termed, managing the finances of the project was like walking on a tightrope. In October, Lord

Alexander of Weedon, who had joined the Trust after taking part in the Shakespeare Moot, wrote warningly to Sir David Orr to point out that if the Trust or the ISGC took on commitments which it could not meet, it was in danger of being guilty of 'wrongful trading' under the insolvency act of 1986. In November, Sir David set out the situation. Running costs could be met for the next twelve months, and the Trust had 40% of the likely cost of completing Phase II. The banks had agreed to change the Loan Agreement to 'no fixed date' for repayment. Pentagram confirmed they would not call in the debt for all the architectural work. Lovells and Buro Happold agreed to do the same. From then on, every Board meeting had to end with a resolution that the Trust and the ISGC could meet their current financial obligations.

Late in the year, Sam was in Boston, trying to raise funds from Credit Suisse. 'What I need is something to be built that will show what it's going to look like when constructed.' He wanted *someone* to fund the first two oak bays that would form the frame of the polygonal structure (£50,000 each). Jerry Link stepped forward – he would donate the cost of one oak bay. Nancy Knowles, one of the Mid West donors, offered the cost of another. Sam also persuaded Jacqueline Mars, heiress to the chocolate company, at which point, Nancy Knowles generously stepped aside. (Later, her donation would fund the Lecture Theatre.)

The search for suitable oak was meeting with some success. Sam took Jon Greenfield, Theo Crosby's assistant architect, to visit a man in Sussex who had offered to build one of the bays, using his own timber. Jon Greenfield took Sam to meet the carpenter he himself had in mind. Peter McCurdy had workshops in Berkshire, his base for the specialism he had developed, restoring Elizabethan timber-frame houses. He had made a full study of materials and techniques, and his obvious knowledge, skills, enthusiasm and experience was impressive. Off they went to York, to look at Barley Hall, a fourteenth century hospice which McCurdy was restoring for the York Archaeological Trust. It was enough to convince Sam and Jon Greenfield that he was the man to follow in the footsteps of Peter Street, the Elizabethan carpenter who had build the original Globe. He was commissioned to build two experimental oak frames, which were duly set up on the Globe foundations in June 1992. With the New Zealand hangings already completed, Sam now at last had tangible evidence that the project was properly on its way.

Soon he was off again, this time to Rome, then on to Hungary, Mexico, Germany and America, as usual juggling film commitments with fundraising, including the Shakespeare Globe race at Arlington Park, Chicago, which had become an annual event. The visit to Germany was to see another production of the Bremer Company in Neuss. This time they were performing *Die Lustige Weiben von Windsor* (*The Merry Wives of Windsor*), with an all-male cast, Norbert Kentrup giving a large performance – in every sense of the word – as Falstaff. Sam made up his mind. This production must play at the Globe.

The autumn of 1992 was as busy as ever. Sam acted in two television films which were little more than potboilers. In contrast, he took part in an event in Chicago which was a reminder of the big part that music had played in his career. The Globe Centre there mounted 'a magical evening of MUSIC, POETRY AND CELEBRATION' in the Orchestra Hall. The concert marked the opening of the Chicago Sinfonietta season, and included Sibelius's Incidental Music to *The Tempest*, with Sam narrating selections from the Shakespeare text.

A couple of days before the concert, Sam was interviewed by a music journalist and broadcaster, about his experience of directing opera. Sam spoke with his usual eloquence about his approach, starting with the libretto, moving on to the music, bringing out the human situations, never asking the singers to do anything that interfered with their vocal delivery. By the end, he could not help reverting to the obsessional topic of the Globe. When the interviewer asked, just before Charlotte arrived to take him away, if he had ever directed a Shakespeare opera, he was quick to respond, 'I have not, and it's one of the things I'm looking forward to.'[27] The idea that there would still be a challenging professional life ahead, *after* the Globe was built, appealed to him.

In October, Sam was back in Europe, recording a television programme in Bremen, giving a talk at Queen Mary and Westfield College, keeping the Prince of Wales up to date, just in case he felt like lending his support. Money was creeping in to build the piazza. He had arranged for the family to celebrate Christmas together in Los Angeles. And there, he shared with them at last some news he had been holding to himself for nearly four years. They knew he had had bowel cancer some years before, concealing it so as not affect his employment opportunities. It had been successfully treated, but early in 1989, he had developed prostate cancer. He had been told then that it was terminal, that he had perhaps four years left. This time, he had kept the news even from the family, and gone on with his busy, not to say hectic life, as if there was nothing wrong.

On 28 December, now that he had told them the truth, Sam laid out his financial situation for his 'beloved children'. He had set up a trust, which was on file with a lawyer cousin, Alan Watenmaker. There were three properties: the North Croft house, owned by the family trust, the lease on Bentinck Close, his share of Bear Gardens/Rose Alley. He had a company, Sam Wanamaker Productions Inc, which he had set up in order to establish a pension. There were his various sources of income, his bank accounts, his cars, at that time a Mazda and a Jaguar, both owned by the company. He noted the loan he had made to the Globe to pay off the Terresearch debt. Charlotte and he had made their wills some years earlier. He explained that they would each inherit one third after their mother's death. His executors were to be Jessica and his investment advisor.

Returning to London early in 1993, Sam continued to behave as if there was nothing wrong, though people close to him were aware that he was ill. His then Personal Assistant, who had first met him many years before, in New York, noticed the effort that it took for him to make preparations for his next fundraising trip. In February, he was off to Malaysia, Taiwan and Japan, sending optimistic messages back to London.

His left arm became swollen and painful, as he developed lymphedema. He began to wear a sling, claiming to be suffering from 'frozen shoulder'. He was cast in a bigger role than he had played recently, in *Wild Justice,* a spy film based on a best-selling Wilbur Smith novel, starring Roy Scheider as a CIA agent; Sam played his control, Kingston Parker. When it was shot (including a scene filmed at Tower Bridge, from where he could look upriver to the Globe site), he moved slowly, spoke carefully and deliberately, and kept his arm as still as possible. Yet his acting was as effective as ever.

Meanwhile, two more oak bays were under construction, and plans were made for them to be in place on the piazza on 23 April, when there would be a grand opening, and the Bremer Shakespeare Company would perform. In one way the order of building was entirely wrong. Theo Crosby was eager to get on with laying foundations for the rest of the site, where the restaurant, the indoor theatre, the offices and the flats would go. (The museum was to be in the undercroft beneath the piazza.) But for Sam, knowing that he had limited time left, and also that the event might convince journalists, supporters, funders and the general public that the Globe was finally in business, it was the right order.

On Tuesday 20 April, there was a press conference on the site, with Sam shouting to be heard over the sound of scaffolding being raised for a temporary stage and seating. Richard Griffiths and Jeremy Child expressed their enthusiasm for the kind of theatre the Globe would offer, when it opened the following year. Norbert Kentrup described his involvement in the project. The next day, *The Times* leader warned against the Globe becoming a 'Falstaffland theme-park', and Benedict Nightingale, theatre critic, wrote an article, doubting if it would ever be built, and if so if it would 'add enough to the nation's cultural life to justify its hard-won existence.'[28] His pessimism nearly caused Sir John Gielgud to back out of his scheduled appearance. But the actor Keith Baxter, a great ally of Sam's, who was organizing part of the event, persuaded him to keep his promise to be there.

On Friday 23 April, rain poured down. There was a procession to the site from Southwark Cathedral. Some of the Globelink time capsules were buried. On a rudimentary stage, Gielgud proclaimed James Mabb's lines in the introduction to the First Folio:

WEE wondred, Shake-speare, that thou went'st so soone

From the Worlds-Stage, to the Graves-Tyring-roome.

Wee thought thee dead, but this thy printed worth,

Tels thy Spectators, that thou went'st but forth

To enter with applause. An Actors Art,

Can dye, and live, to acte a second part.

That's but an Exit of Mortalitie;

This, a Re-entrance to a Plaudite.

An array of actors, including Derek Jacobi, Simon Callow, Janet Suzman, Felicity Kendal, Timothy West, Prunella Scales and Peter McEnery, each declaimed a line from the First Chorus from *King Henry V*, over the noise of the occasional helicopter. The five actors from Bremen played their ribald, cut-down version of *Die Lustige Weiben*, a lively reminder that the Globe was to be an international project. Sam and Charlotte and many invited guests sat under a marquee – royalty represented this time by Princess Michael of Kent. 'Groundlings' stood or squatted. Later, the Young Friends of the Globe performed their own forty-five-minute play, *Will Shakespeare Save Us?* By the end of the day, the sun was shining.

In May, Sam was interviewed about his appearance in *Wild Justice*. His real life performance was as convincing as ever. After explaining that he had always been fascinated by spy thrillers in books and films, he told the journalist that he continued to juggle three careers: acting in television and film, directing, and building the Globe. He said that he had no intention of slowing down. 'Age is not important. If you have all your marbles and your strength, there should be no stopping of activity.'[29] Yet a few weeks later, after a dinner party given by the Managing Director of Leeds Castle in Kent, who was on the ISGC Board, Sam finally told his brother Bill, over from Los Angeles, about his terminal illness. Bill reacted with anger as well as grief and sympathy, indignant that, as a doctor, he had not known much earlier, when treatment might have been effective.

A few days later, the Queen's Birthday Honours were announced: Sam was to be awarded an Honorary CBE, for his 'contribution to international relations between Britain and the United States.' As so often, the powers that be had chosen to recognize his achievements rather late in the day. He was asked where he would like to receive the award and said 'I'll have the award in London, where I did all the work, and I'll have the party in America, where I might get some more money'.[30] Prince Philip and Princess Michael of Kent sent congratulatory telegrams.

In August, Sam was in Los Angeles. Back in England, he wrote a request that his remains should be cremated. 'I further request', he wrote, 'if at all possible, that following my cremation, my remains be kept at or near the location of Shakespeare's Globe, in London, England, which edifice I hold dear to my heart.'[31]

Towards the end of September, progress on the Globe advanced further, with two more oak bays being unveiled. These were donated by Glaxo, through the offices of John Hignett, who was one of its executives. He was now Chairman of ISGC, and Michael Perry was Chairman of the Trustees. Sir David Orr had retired just after the Shakespeare Birthday celebrations, having played his crucial part in the project. Sam looked frail, his hair thinner, his arm in the familiar sling.

He was still out and about through much of the autumn, including a short trip to Germany. There was a warm occasion organized by the Wanamaker and Perry families, to heal what had become a rift between Sam and Jack. It worked, and the two men reminisced happily about their first meeting in New York forty years earlier. He still visited the site. Walking over it with two companions, he stumbled, and remarked how great it would be for the project if he died there and then. He had told his brother Bill, amongst others, 'When I'm gone, this will all be finished much faster'. The desk diary that marked his engagements began to show cancellations, and on 11 November, it bore the words 'Bravo Sam!' perhaps marking his last visit to the shabby office that had been the base for all his efforts for the Globe.

Soon after that, the family closed round him at Bentinck Close. He persuaded Zoë to drive him to Kinnerton St for one last visit to Jan Sterling. He sent out Christmas cards early. On Michael Perry's he wrote: 'Mike – you will make it happen. Sorry I won't be there with you to share the celebrations, but I've been celebrating already.'[32] He sent a message for the newsletter that went out to all the Globe supporters: 'You have dreamed this dream with me until now, but you must finish it.'[33]

The last few weeks were painful and difficult. Painkillers no longer helped. Morphine that was supposed to put him out for several hours had only a brief effect on this man of so much energy. He wished to have help to die.

On the evening of 18 December, BBC Radio 3 broadcast a programme Sam had recorded some months before. It was called *The Sandbar, A Poem for Voices*, its title taken from Alfred Tennyson's 'Crossing the Bar'. It consists of monologues spoken by three different characters as each stands on the beach and looks towards a sandbar on the Atlantic coast of Georgia, USA. Sam, the third to speak, plays a man dying of cancer. 'How much time have I got?' he asks. He wants to end his life: 'When it gets too much I'm going to grab a handful of barbiturates and a bottle of Scotch … Doctors won't let you go quietly.' He looks at the starlight glittering on the sandbar 'glowing white like gull rings … Life after death may be a mirage.'[34]

Ever the actor, he was playing his own end; he died earlier on the day of the broadcast. Hundreds were shocked when they heard the news, as he had acted so well, with such vigour, and for so long, the part of a healthy man with plans for the future.

Afterword

In 2017, Shakespeare's Globe celebrated twenty years since its festive opening. For one event, in that summer of 1997, Queen Elizabeth I (the actor Jane Lapotaire, President of the Friends) arrived on horseback, and Queen Elizabeth II and Prince Philip, Duke of Edinburgh, arrived by boat. When the audience had taken their places in the playhouse that afternoon, drumbeats reverberated through the 'wooden O', Zoë Wanamaker entered from the tiring house, struck a staff on the stage floor and spoke the first Chorus from *King Henry V,* introducing an entertainment of 'Triumphes and Mirth'.

Writing in 1993, Benedict Nightingale had expressed serious doubt that Sam's vision for the Globe and for Bankside would ever be fulfilled. But Sam's long-term view and his optimism have proved truer than Nightingale's pessimism. The reality then, as Nightingale saw it, was that 'the most dominant neighbouring buildings are a bank sorting office and a vast disused power station which will surely take years to redevelop'. He listed some of the things Sam was looking forward to: 'a radiantly regenerated Bankside with flats, restaurants and a stop on the Jubilee Line, and on the Globe site a second theatre, a Shakespeare Museum ... a substantial audio/visual library. Eventually he wants a footbridge across the river linking St Paul's steps with his theatre. He even talks of one day constructing a small opera house to which Glyndebourne could transfer productions.'

Bankside is indeed 'radiantly regenerated'. Today, you can walk west from London Bridge, stop off at the vibrant food stalls in Borough Market to the south of Southwark Cathedral, visit the reconstruction of Sir Francis Drake's *Golden Hinde,* berthed at St Mary Overie Dock, admire the remains of the Great Hall of Winchester Palace, set in a 'medieval' garden, dominated by its magnificent rose window, continue along the cobbled street to the Clink Prison Museum, emerge from under Southwark Bridge to the riverside pub, The Anchor, and on past several restaurants towards the Globe. Or you can walk east from Blackfriars Bridge, a few hundred metres from Southwark Station on the Jubilee Line, joining a throng of people bound either for a specific destination or simply strolling along enjoying the atmosphere, flats to the right, the river to the left, the walkway full of buskers and street entertainers, till you come to the Millennium Bridge, envisaged by both Sam and Theo Crosby, its north end at St Paul's steps, and at its southern end, the towering edifice that was once Bankside Power Station and is now Tate Modern. A few metres further on, is Shakespeare's Globe, sited, like the Goodman Theatre as Sam knew it, next to a major art gallery.

When I walk into the Globe playhouse my first thought is still: 'We did it!' My second thought is 'I love it!' – having had some apprehension that it might not, after all, fulfil my expectations. My third thought is: 'It's a success!' Sam's most ambitious scheme has turned out to be his greatest legacy, carried forward by thousands of people he never knew. It has a beautiful candle-lit indoor theatre, named for Sam, which has indeed housed a number of operas, as well as plays and concerts. It has an exhibition, rather than a museum, while the next development project includes the research library he envisaged. Sam's ashes, as he had hoped, are buried beneath the stage, mingled with Charlotte's.

The whole building is as busy, day and evening, as Sam could ever have wished. Theatregoers mingle with schoolchildren, students, scholars, and visitors taking a guided tour. There are those who have come to eat and drink, or to attend a special event. In due course, the Globe acquired from Southwark Council the old leaky, rat-ridden building at Park Street, and it has been converted into a thriving education centre, with a spacious rooftop rehearsal room. His original development plan for Bankside included a children's theatre. How appropriate that the Unicorn Theatre now stands close to London Bridge. The company, founded by Caryl Jenner, had performed for Sam in Liverpool.

Soon, Shakespeare's Globe will have been in existence for longer than the many years Sam worked to bring it about. It's unlikely he would ever have been satisfied with what has been achieved; his mind was always on to the next thing. But the fact remains that through the dedication, talent and hard work of many who have come after him, it is an artistic, academic, educational and popular success, locally, nationally and internationally. Its work is exciting and innovatory. With no regular subsidy, the company balances its books, and raises funds for current and future projects before embarking on them, a prudent approach which Sam always found difficult to follow.

In his obituary for Sam, Michael Billington (*The Guardian*) wrote of him as 'a hard-headed romantic.' Perhaps that describes his private as well as his public character. There were five important women in his life: his wife, his mistress and his three very different daughters, all of whom he loved and needed; he was not prepared to turn his back on any of them.

Billington summed up Sam's career: 'Although the Globe will be his lasting monument, one should also not forget that he brought the Method to Britain, directed many landmark American plays and was a versatile all-rounder, at home in theatres, studios and opera houses all over the world.'[1]

The shape of Sam's life was directed by the politics of his time. His war experience had little bearing on his subsequent career, but the 'blacklist' of the 1940s and 50s drastically affected him. After coming to England, he was never again politically active. As a resident alien in Britain, with American citizenship, he was often seen as something of an outsider, a streetwise Chicago Jew, while Americans found he had acquired a patina of Britishness.

Until the Globe looked possible, his proudest achievement was in Liverpool, creating a centre that was an integral part of its community. The desire for permanence was fed by the fact that he had chosen a profession that rarely offered it. His artistic ideas were not settled, but in flux. He began with a respect for the work of the Group Theatre. It was no longer active when he began his career, but he worked with several of its members. He was interested, then, in plays that gave an illusion of reality and said something about the world. By the time he reached England in the 1950s, he had honed his skills as a director, drawing on Stanislavsky and the best of the Actors Studio teachers. His impact on the British theatre was considerable, achieving a level of believability and consistency from his cast that was unusual at the time.

Gradually, through his eclecticism and wide reading, he extended his idea of theatre. Sean O'Casey's *Purple Dust* was the first of his productions that went beyond realism, using music, dance and an exuberant and fantastic front cloth. A few years later came his conversion to the work of Bertolt Brecht. The richness of his work in Liverpool convinced the conductor John Pritchard that he could bring something to the world of opera. He devised a method of working with singers that was new to many, encouraging them to explore their characters' thoughts and feelings, so that the music was an outcome of the drama, not separate from it. At the same time, he was careful never to place a singer in a situation which hindered their musical performance.

In the 1960s and 70s, he developed a larger sense of what theatre could be, collaborating with Josef Svoboda, and envisaging a kind of total theatre, where music, language, film, lighting and scenic design combined to create an epic experience. Neither project with Svoboda came to fruition. His production of *Macbeth* was unwieldy. The most successful of his opera productions were *King Priam* and *War and Peace*, though some rated his controversial production of *La Forza del Destino* as equally impressive. While his fiery temperament sometimes led to ructions in rehearsal, he succeeded in coordinating all the elements of a production, however complicated.

As a film director, Sam achieved less than he aspired to. He was in a Catch 22 situation: without a proven track record, he made little headway pushing his own projects, but the four feature films he did direct gave him limited opportunity to show his potential. Perhaps if *Kyle* had been completed, or one of the projects he promoted had come off successfully, such as the Great Train Robbery, with Burton and Taylor, he would have established a stronger foothold in the film world. As a television director, he was a safe pair of hands, but refused to commit himself to long-term projects.

Sam began and ended his career as an actor, starting in his schooldays, developing through the training he received at the Goodman Theatre, then honing his craft on radio.

In the theatre, he rose quickly to become a leading actor in New York and in England. He was proudest of his performance as Iago. He contributed significantly to the American theatre in the 1940s and 60s, both in principal and supporting roles. In the 1950s, his acting in England was a wake-up call. Young actors aspired to achieve the level of truth and immediacy which characterized his performances. He remained suspicious of the emotional self-indulgence of Lee Strasberg's work and felt liberated when his encounter with Bertolt Brecht returned him to a confidence in the energy, instinct and enjoyment which had led him to acting in the first place. But in the mid 1960s, he turned away from the live theatre, so audiences after that saw only his screen performances.

Of his film performances he was proudest of his role as Geremio in *Christ in Concrete*. By the end of his career he had embodied many hundreds of characters on radio, television and film, ranging from Mike Carter, the smooth gangster in Losey's *The Criminal*, to the absurd Ukrainian warrior Filipenko in *Taras Bulba*, and the courageous Jacob Weiss in *Holocaust*. Directors knew that in signing Sam for a part, they could be confident of a thoroughly prepared, skilfully delivered performance. He continued acting right up to the last year of his life, with the TV mini-series, *Wild Justice*, aired after his death, and the strangely personal role in *The Sandbar, A Poem for Voices*. But once the Globe project became his chief priority, he seemed to take his acting skill for granted. He no longer made any particular effort to advance his acting career, except to make sure that enough roles came his way, that he could make a living.

I am amongst the last generation who saw Sam Wanamaker in the theatre, and his charismatic stage presence remains vivid in my memory, playing the would-be rainmaker who, until the very end, has failed to bring about what he promised:

(*Suddenly* STARBUCK *stands on the threshold – with a look of glory on his face.*)

STARBUCK: Rain, folks – it's gonna rain! Lizzie – for the first time in my life – rain! … (STARBUCK *rushes to the door and turns to* LIZZIE *long enough to say:*) So long – beautiful! (*And he races out.*)[2]

Abbreviations

British Film Institute	BFI
Goodman Theatre Archives	GTA
Howard Gotlieb Archival Research Center Sam Wanamaker Collection	HGARC
New York Public Library of Performing Arts: Special Collection	NYPL
Shakespeare's Globe, Library & Archive	SGA
Royal Opera House, London	ROH
The National Archives	TNA
Theatre and Performance Collection, V& A	V & A
Charlotte Holland Wanamaker	CHW
Sam Wanamaker	SW

Endnotes

Foreword

1. English theatre director best known for directing the plays of T S Eliot, and also the English Mystery Plays
2. Copy in personal papers
3. Cable and letter in personal papers

Chapter 1

1. Pcyga, Dominic A, *Chicago: A Biography*, 2007, p152
2. Zangwill, Israel, quoted in Cutler, Irving, *The Jews of Chicago, From Shtetl to Suburb*, 1996, p40
3. quoted in Day, Barry, *The Wooden O*, 1995, p45
4. SW, Affidavit drafted for the American Embassy in London, 1957, p13, copy in personal papers
5. Wanamaker, William, *The Depression, Bootlegging and the Boy*, private paper, 2002
6. ibid
7. SW, text of speech to graduating class at Roosevelt University, Chicago, 20 May, 1990, SGA SGT/SW/2/4
8. ibid
9. ibid
10. Fisher, Caroline, quoted archivesjsonline.com
11. SW, interview in Consedino, Gene, *Two Planks and a Passion*, written and directed as part of MFA, Columbia College, Chicago, January 1994
12. Dunning, John, *On the Air: the Encyclopedia of Old Time Radio, 1998*, #404

Chapter 2

1. Two from Chicago who later made it to Hollywood were Owen Jordan and Lou Gilbert
2. Kazan, Elia, *Elia Kazan: A Life*, 1988, p191
3. Atkinson, Brooke, press review, NYPL
4. Programmes for *Café Crown*, NYPL
5. Terrace, Vincent, *Radio Programs, 1924–1984: A Catalogue of Over 1800 Shows, 1999*, #1202

6   Carpenter, Clifford, 'Remembering Sam and Charlotte', unpublished ms, 2000, personal papers
7   SW, Affidavit, 1957, pp 16 and 18
8   ibid, p19
9   ibid, p17
10 Dunning, # 726
11 SW, Affidavit, 1957, p19
12 ibid
13 Dail, Krystyna, *Stage for Action: US Social Activist Theatre in the 1940s*, 2016, p49
14 SW, 'The Brecht Revolution', draft for article published in *Harper's Bazaar*, September, 1956, HGARC Box 30
15 Dail, p53
16 SW to Bill Sweets, 31 March, 1944, HGARC Box 31
17 SW, undated press cutting, 1947, supplied to author by Cliff Carpenter
18 Recounted by William Wanamaker to author, June 2002
19 Evans, Maurice, *All this and Evans Too*, 1987, p174
20 SW to Shani Wallace, 1 and 4 March, 1958, HGARC Box 14
21 SW to Oliver Crawford, 13 November, 1945, HGARC Box 31
22 Press reviews, HGARC Box 24
23 SW, 'The Brecht Revolution'
24 Souvenir programme for *Joan of Lorraine*, NYPL
25 Pia Lindstrom in *Ingrid Bergman in Her Own Words*, documentary film by Stig Björkman
26 Maxwell Anderson to Ingrid Bergman, April 23 1945, *Dramatist in America: Letters of Maxwell Anderson 1912–1958*, p134
27 Sheehy, Helen, *Margo: The Life and Theatre of Margo Jones*, 1989, p116
28 ibid
29 Ibid, p119
30 ibid, p120, based on interview with SW, 1987
31 Press reviews, NYPL
32 McCrary, Tex and Falkenburg, Jinx, *New York Herald Tribune*, 14 August 1950
33 Ager, Shana, undated press cutting, supplied to author by Cliff Carpenter, *Success story; Sam Wanamaker has hit the Broadway jackpot as Bergman's leading man.* She later worked on *Life*, and the TV show *60 Minutes*.

Chapter 3

1   SW, undated interview by George Freedley (internal evidence dates it February 1949), supplied to author by Cliff Carpenter,
2   John Houseman, quoted in Caute, David, *Joseph Losey: A Revenge on Life*, 1994, p168
3   SW 'Variations on theme by Irvin Winkler', unpublished ms, HGARC Box 30
4   Doherty, Thomas, *Show Trial: Hollywood, HUAC and the Birth of the Blacklist*, 2018, p194

5   quoted in Dick, Bernard F, *Radical Innocence: A Critical Study of the Hollywood Ten*, 1989/2009, p7

6   quoted in Prime, Rebecca, *Hollywood Exiles in Europe*, 2014, p31

7   quoted in Doherty, p262

8   Brooks Atkinson, *New York Times*, 10 December, 1947

9   Carpenter ms

10   SW, Freedley interview

11   GBS to Hardwicke, May 9, 1949, quoted in *A Victorian in Orbit: The Irreverent Memoirs of Sir Cedric Hardwicke*, as told to James Brough, 1961, p221

12   Brough/Hardwicke, p225

13   SW to Richard Aldrich, 21 April, 1952, HGARC Box 17

14   Sam Zolotow, undated cutting, supplied to the author by Cliff Carpenter

15   Brough/Hardwicke, p223

16   Brough/Hardwicke, p225

17   Richard Aldrich to SW, HGARC, 11 April, 1952 HGARC Box 17

18   Barnouw, *The Golden Web: A History of Broadcasting in the United States, Volume II – 1933 to 1953*, 1968, p266

19   SW interviewed by Robert Seidenberg, 'An Actor Relives a Tumultuous Past', *New York Times*, March 10, 1991.

20   SW interviewed by Vernon Riche, 'Curtain Cues', undated article supplied to author by Cliff Carpenter

21   Francis, Bob, *The Billboard*, 12 August, 1950

22   *The Sun*, Baltimore, 2 August, 1950

23   SW/Terese Hayden, HGARC Box 24

24   Jack Perry dated their first meeting at the time of Sam's performance in *Arms and the Man*. (SGA SGT/SW/6/29). This corresponds with Jerome Link's recollection to the author that Perry was keen to meet Howard Fast, with whom Sam was lunching the very next day. Jack Perry's grandson, Alastair Tallon, tells a different story, as he remembers Perry and SW reminiscing about seeing a production of *Finian's Rainbow*, which completed its New York run in October 1948.

25   SW interviewed by Pearl Sheffy Gene, undated, unidentified article, 1991, HGARC Box 30

26   Howard Fast to SW, 8 March, 1951, HGARC Box 8

27   Howard Fast to SW, 19 March, 1951, HGARC Box 8

28   *Thirty Years of Treason: Excerpts from Hearings before the House Committee on Un-American Activities, 1938–1968*, ed Eric Bentley, 1971, p307

Chapter 4

1   Charlotte Wanamaker to SW, 17 May, 1951, HGARC Box 31

2   *L'Écran Français*, 23–29 mai, 1951

3   Metropolitan Police, Special Branch, to MI5, 30 August, 1952, reporting the conditions under which SW was registered, serial number CX.212661

(registration certificate No.A.464382); CHW was registered under serial number CX.231040 (certificate No A.408223), TNA, KV-2-3106, Item 17A

4 Clifford Odets to SW, 25 July, 1951, HGARC Box 14

5 Prime, note to p51, quoting a letter received from Donald Ogden Stewart Jr in 2007

6 SW interviewed by Ron Ramdin, recorded in 1987, Globe Editions ,2007; article in *Chicago Tribune* 3 June, 1990

7 SW to Hannah Weinstein, undated, HGARC Box 4

8 quoted in Redgrave, Michael, *In My Mind's Eye,* 1983, p244/5

9 Michael Redgrave to SW, 14 February, 1952, HGARC Box 10

10 'Me' to SW (SW and CHW normally signed 'Me' when writing to each other), HGARC Box 10

11 Michael Redgrave to SW, undated, HGARC Box 17

12 SW interviewed for BBC Radio 4 'Down Your Way', 7 June, 1992, SGA SG/SW/6/29

13 SW to Bill Wanamaker, dictated 20 March, 1952, papers of Marc Wanamaker

14 The title would later cause confusion, as Odets had drafted a play called 'A Winter Journey', which he retitled *The Big Knife.*

15 Press cuttings, HGARC Box 29

16 Press cutting from *Picture Post*, V & A

17 Pearson, Kenneth, *Daily Dispatch*, 18 October, 1952, HGARC Box 29

18 Chattie Salaman to SW, 11 June, 1952, HGARC Box 17

19 SW to Michel St Denis, 23 June, 1952, HGARC Box 17

20 SW to Chattie Salaman, 13 June, 1952, HGARC Box 17

21 Press cutting HGARC Box 34

22 quoted Strachan, Alan, *Secret Dreams: A Biography of Michael Redgrave,* 2009, p280

23 Sherek, p 172

24 quoted Strachan, p279

25 Redgrave, p245

26 Michael Redgrave to SW, undated, HGARC Box 17

27 SW to Cliff Carpenter, 21 May, 1952, HGARC Box 17

28 Redgrave, pp245/6

29 Undated press cutting, HGARC Box 10

30 SW to 'Mum and Dad', 13 August, 1952, HGARC Box 17

31 Undated press cutting, HGARC Box 10

32 SW to 'Mum and Dad', 13 August, 1952, HGARC Box 17

33 SW to CHW, 13 August, 1952, HGARC Box 29

34 'Morty' to SW, undated, HGARC Box 17

35 SW to Lillian Hellman, 13 June, 1952, HGARC Box 17

36 Copy of letter provided by Metropolitan Police, Special Branch to MI5, TNA, KV-2-3106, Item 11A

37 Joan Littlewood to SW, 26 March, 1952, HGARC Box 8

38 Howard Goorney to Sam, 11 July, 1952, HGARC Box 8
39 Cecil Tennent to SW, 17 September, 1952, HGARC Box 17
40 SW to John Findlay, 21 April, 1952, HGARC Box 12
41 John Findlay to SW, 7 March,1952, HGARC Box 12
42 SW to Alec Guinness, 7 July, 1952, HGARC Box 8
43 Alec Guinness to SW, 12 July, 1952, HGARC Box 8
44 Harold Freeman, cable to SW, 14 November, 1952, HGARC Box 8
45 SW to Al Parker, 4 December, 1952, HGARC Box 8
46 Ronnie Waters to SW 29 January,1953, HGARC Box 8
47 Al Parker to SW 12 February, 1953 Box 8
48 S W Bindoff's criticisms contained in letter to SW, 8 December, 1952, HGARC Box 8
49 SW to Harold Freeman, 11 December, 1952, HGARC, Box 8
50 Findlater, Richard, *The Observer,* HGARC Box 12
51 Unattributed article, HGARC Box 34

Chapter 5

1 SW to Cliff Carpenter, 15 October, 1952, HGARC Box 17
2 O'Casey, Sean, *Purple Dust,* 1940, pp174/5
3 Daniel Angel to SW, 9 March, 1953, HGARC Box 12
4 O'Casey to SW, 5 April, 1953, HGARC Box 12
5 Peter Potter to SW, 6 May, 1953, HGARC Box 17
6 O'Casey to SW, 26 May, 1953, HGARC Box 12
7 Virginia Snyders and Lloyd Shirley to SW, August 1953, HGARC Box 17
8 Joan Littlewood to SW, 26 May, 1953, HGARC Box 17
9 O'Casey to SW, 10 June, 1953, HGARC Box 12
10 For b/w copy of the design, see Hoffnung, Annetta, *Hoffnung: his biography,* 1988, pp96/97
11 Metropolitan Police, Special Branch, report to MI5, TNA, KV-2-3106 Item 25a
12 Atkinson, Brooks, *New York Times,* 25 February, 1949
13 Cookman, Anthony, *The Tatler and Bystander,* V& A
14 Worsley, T C, HGARC Box 12
15 Shulman, Milton, *Evening Standard,* V & A
16 quoted in Croall, Jonathan, *Sybil Thorndike: A Star of Life,* 2008, p384
17 SW, 'TODAY's bulletin', HGARC Box 33
18 Sean O'Casey to CHW, 18 March, 1954, HGARC Box 31
19 Minute in MI5 file, TNA, KV-2-3106, Item 28a
20 SW to Arthur Miller, 20 May, 1954, HGARC Box 7
21 Minute in MI5 file, TNA, K-V-2-3106 28a
22 Metropolitan Police Special Branch report in M15 file, TNA, KV-2-3106, Item 33a

23 Worsley, T C, undated cutting, HGARC Box 9
24 Tynan, Kenneth, *The Observer*, 8 May, 1955
25 Henry Sherek to SW 10 April,1955, HGARC Box 8
26 Lewenstein p21
27 SW, 'The Brecht Revolution'
28 Lewis, Robert, *Slings and Arrows: Theatre in My Life*, 1997, p35
29 quoted in SW, 'The Brecht Revolution' as published in *Harper's Bazaar*, September 1956, HGARC Box 30
30 Marc Blitztein to SW, 8 November 1955, HGARC Box 11
31 SW to Blitzstein, 6 December, 1955, HGARC Box 11
32 Blitzstein to SW, 13 December, 1955, HGARC Box 11
33 Brecht, Bertolt to SW, 17 December, 1955, HGARC Box 11
34 quoted in Lewenstein, p24
35 Weber, Carl, to SW, undated, HGARC Box 11
36 Cardew, Anthony, press cutting, HGARC Box 11
37 SW to Blitzstein, 6 December ,1955, Box 11
38 Lewenstein, p22
39 This and subsequent reviews, HGARC Box 11
40 quoted Lewenstein, p 22
41 Lewenstein, p22
42 SW, 'The Brecht Revolution'
43 Nash, N Richard, *The Rainmaker*, 1954, p9
44 Ralph Alswang to SW, 27 December 1955, HGARC Box 6
45 SW to Dick (Richard) Nash, 25 April, 1956, HGARC Box 6
46 This and subsequent reviews, HGARC Box 6
47 Worsley, T C, *New Statesman*, HGARC Box 6
48 Terese Hayden interviewed by Casey Childs, August 4, 2014, primarystagesoffcenter.org
49 Noble, Peter, *Reflected Glory*, 1958, p173
50 Ben Barzman to Charlotte Wanamaker, 9 February, 1953, HGARC Box 17
51 Metropolitan Police Special Branch, report to MI5, TNA, K-V-2-3106 Item 35a

Chapter 6

1 SW, Affidavit 1957, p2
2 For a full account of the concert, see Hoffnung, pp137-142
3 ibid p136
4 Lisa Abarbinelli to SW, 19 September, 1956, HGARC Box 28
5 Lisa Abarbinelli to SW, 16 October 1956, HGARC Box 28
6 Artie Shaw, Friederick Guilda, Bobby Hackett, Phineas Newborn, Sidney Bechet, Lester Young
7 Rehearsal notes, *A Hatful of Rain*, HGARC Box 4

8   Press reviews, V & A
9   Denise Sée to SW, 17 April 1957, HGARC Box 31
10   SW, Affidavit 1957,p10
11   ibid p26
12   ibid p29
13   ibid p32
14   Vice-Consul Richard D Geppert to SW, 29 May 1957, HGARC Box 31
15   Denise Sée to SW, 5 July, 1957, HGARC Box 31
16   SW to Mickey Delmar, 3 July ,1957, HGARC Box 6
17   SW to Mickey Delmar, 17 July, 1957, HGARC Box 6
18   New Shakespeare Theatre press cuttings, HGARC Box 29
19   SW in Programme for *A View From the Bridge*, HGARC Box 34
20   SW to Kay Brown, 8 August 1957, HGARC Box 7
21   Metropolitan Police Special Branch, report on the New Shakespeare Club, 15 October 1957, in MI5 file, TNA, KV-2-3107 Item 51b
22   Cliff Carpenter to SW and CHW, 13 October, 1957, HGARC Box 13
23   New Shakespeare Theatre press cuttings, HGARC Box 29
24   Press quotes from New Shakespeare programme for *Tea and Sympathy*
25   SW to Arthur Miller, 14 November, 1957, HGARC Box 14
26   Arthur Miller to SW, 3 December, 1957, HGARC Box 14
27   'Tanfield's Diary', *Daily Mail,* 31 October, 1957, New Shakespeare Theatre press cuttings, HGARC Box 29
28   SW to Nonie Wallick, 11 November, 1957, HGARC Box 13
29   New Shakespeare Theatre press cuttings, Box 29
30   CID Special Branch report to The Chief Constable, Liverpool, 19 December,1957, in MI5 file, TNA, KV-2-3107 Item 55a
31   Director General to The Chief Constable, Liverpool, 1 January, 1958, in MI5 file TNA,KV-2-3107 Item 56a
32   SW in Programme for *Tea and Sympathy*, HGARC Box 34
33   SW to Wayland Young, 17 March 1958, HGARC Box 14
34   Maurice Stewart-interview transcript, Interviewer Kate Harris, 17 August 2006,Theatre Archive Project, http://sounds.bl.uk
35   SW in Programme for *A View From the Bridge*, HGARC Box 34

Chapter 7

1   SW to his 'folks' in LA, 11 February 1958, HGARC Box 14
2   *The Stage,* 13 February 1958
3   SW to Bill and Edith Wanamaker, 28 April 1958, HGARC Box 14
4   SW to Anna Deere Wiman, 6 March ,1958, HGARC Box 18
5   SW to Anna Deere Wiman, 31 March, 1958, HGARC Box 18
6   SW to Cliff Carpenter, 23 December 1957, HGARC Box 14
7   Trevor Entwhistle to SW, 6 March 1958, HGARC Box 18

8   Anna Deere Wiman to SW, 28 March, 1958, HGARC Box 18

9   SW to Anna Deere Wiman, 1 April, 1958, HGARC Box 18

10   SW to Lovat Fraser, 2 April, 1958, HGARC Box 19

11   *The Stage,* 15 May 1958

12   Cross, Beverley, *One More River,* 1958, p8

13   Programme for *One More River,* courtesy of Tom Baptiste

14   SW to Beresford Seligman, 21 May 1958, HGARC Box 14

15   Beverley Cross to SW, 23 May, 1958, HGARC Box 18

16   Some accounts wrongly state that this production was directed by Olivier and 'starred' Michael Caine

17   Charles Marowitz to SW, 1 April, 1958, HGARC Box 14

18   SW to Marowitz 11 April,1958, HGARC Box 14

19   SW to Bill and Edith Wanamaker, 28 April 1958, HGARC Box

20   SW to Joe Seigel, 12 June 1958, HGARC Box 14

21   Bergman to SW, 28 May, 1958, HGARC Box 14

22   SW to Bergman 30 May, 1958, HGARC Box 14

23   *Sunday Chronicle,* 23 February, 1958, HGARC Box 18

24   SW to Anna Deere Wiman 10 September, 1958, HGARC Box 18

25   George Cross to SW, 4 October, 1958, HGARC Box 19

26   Tony Richardson to SW, 22 October, 1958, HGARC Box 19

27   SW to Paul Robeson, 18 November 1958, HGARC Box 19

28   Jeffery, Sidney, *Liverpool Echo,* 27 October, 1959

29   Obituary for Toby Robertson, *Daily Telegraph,* 6 September, 2012

30   SW to Harold Hobson, 9 July 1958, HGARC Box 14

31   BBC Third Programme, 10 December, 1958, transcript HGARC Box 16

32   Brig Sir Norman Gwatkin, NCVO, DSO, Assistant Comptroller in Lord Chamberlains' office, 12 November,1958, HGARC Box 5

33   SW reported in *Daily Mail,* 8 January, 1958

34   Jack Perry to CHW 15 January ,1959, HGARC Box 33

35   *Manchester Guardian,* 16 January ,1959

36   *Sunday Times,* 18 January, 1959

37   SW to Harold Hobson, HGARC Box 11

38   Harold Hobson to SW, 18 January 1959, HGARC Box 11

39   Cotes, Peter, note to Obituary for Anna Deere Wiman, *The Stage,* 28 March, 1963

40   29 January, 1959, *Liverpool Daily Post*

41   Press release, 15 December 1958, HGARC Box 11

42   *The Times,* 19 January, 1959

43   Marriott, R B, 'New Shakespeare Theatre: Pioneer Experiment and Pattern for the Future', *The Stage,* 29 January, 1959

44   Cotes, *The Stage,* 28 March, 1963

45   See Alan Durband, en.wikipedia.org

Chapter 8

1   Glen Byam Shaw to SW, 10 February, 1959, HGARC Box 19
2   Martin Holmes to SW, 28 January, 1959, HGARC Box 19
3   SW/ Ramdin
4   Darlington, W A, *Daily Telegraph*, 8 April, 1959; this review and others, V &A
5   Bill Wanamaker to SW, 2 September, 1959, HGARC Box 28
6   SW/Ramdin
7   Glen Byam Shaw to SW, 26 November 1959, HGARC Box 19
8   Programme for *Lock Up Your Daughters*, Mermaid Theatre, May 1955 (courtesy of David Warren)
9   Press review and letters, HGARC Box 33
10 Michael Barry to SW, 1 December, 1959, HGARC Box 33
11 *I Wanna Mink* available at BFI
12 Eileen Atkins to SW, 25 August,1960, HGARC Box 28
13 quoted by Melanie Williams, *The Criminal*, screenonline.org.uk
14 Caute p239
15 Kenneth More to SW, April 1960, HGARC Box 25
16 SW, note on letter from Lucy Barry, 20 June, 1960, HGARC Box 11
17 SW to Maurice Wiggins, 17 August, 1960, HGARC, Box 11
18 'John Miller' to SW, 19 August,1960, HGARC Box 28
19 Arnold Weissberger to Al Parker, 14 September, 1960, HGARC Box 25
20 Milton Goldman to SW, 22 and 30 September, 1960, Box 25
21 SW, interview by Kenneth Herman, *L A Times*, October 10, 1986
22 Michael Tippett to SW, September 1960, HGARC Box 25
23 Milton Goldman to Al Parker, 20 October 1960, HGARC Box 25
24 SW to CHW, 2 February, 1961,HGARC Box 24
25 SW to Zoë Wanamaker, undated, HGARC Box 24
26 SW to CHW, undated, HGARC Box 24
27 Cassidy, Claudia, press cutting, GTA Production History Files Part 1, Box 15
28 John Reich to Kurt Hellmer, 7 February 1961, GTA PADF Box 4/F23
29 Newman, Danny, *Tales of a Theatrical Guru*, 2006, p66
30 SW interview, GTA PADF BOX 4/F23
31 SW to CHW, January 1961, HGARC Box 24
32 Press cutting, HGARC Box 24
33 Notes and cable, HGARC Box 24
34 Press reviews, HGARC Box 24
35 SW to CHW, 5 April, 1961, HGARC Box 31
36 SW to CHW, 25 May, 1961, HGARC Box 31
37 SW interview, press cutting, February 22, 1961, supplied to author by Cliff Carpenter
38 SW interview, press cutting, May 21, 1961, supplied to author by Cliff Carpenter

39 SW, interviewed for *Plays and Players*, 1961, SGA SAMWBOX Rc96\195
40 Campbell, Marion Gurney, and Athas, Daphne, *Ding Dong Bell*, typescript
41 SW to Charlotte, September 1961, HGARC Box 31
42 Brendan Gill, *New Yorker*, December 29, 1962

Chapter 9

1   Cairns, David, *The Spectator*, 15 June, 1962
2   Heyworth, Peter, *The Observer*, 10 June 1962, and following reviews, HGARC Box 25
3   Meeting of Opera Sub-Committee, Royal Opera House, 20 June, 1962, ROH
4   Press cuttings, HGARC Box 30
5   SW to Renato Guttoso, 19 July 1962, HGARC Box 25
6   Meeting of Opera Sub-Committee, Royal Opera House, 19 September, 1962, ROH
7   SW interviewed by Maureen Cleave, *Evening Standard*, 27 September, 1962, HGARC Box 25
8   SW interviewed in *Sunday Times*, 23 September, 1962, ROH
9   SW in *Opera News*, January 18, 1964, ROH
10 James Lockhart to SW, 4 October 1962, HGARC Box 9
11 Porter, Andrew, *Financial Times*, 29 September, 1962, ROH
12 SW interviewed by Bruce Duffie, *Actor/Director Sam Wanamaker*, September 1992, broadcast on WNIB, 19 December, 1993, www.bruceduffie.com
13 Hope-Wallace, Philip, *The Guardian*, 3 October 1962, ROH
14 Press reviews, ROH
15 Frank Granville Barker to SW, 6 October, 1962, HGARC Box 9
16 Humphrey Proctor-Gregg to SW, 16 November 1962, HGARC Box 9
17 Dominique Clauzet, Stuttgart, press cutting, HGARC Box 9
18 Brook, Peter, *Encore*, November/December 1962
19 SW to CHW, 23 March, 1963 HGARC Box 9
20 Martin Gabel to SW, undated, HGARC Box 9
21 SW to CHW, 2 December, 1963, HGARC Box 9
22 Van Heflin to SW, undated opening night note, HGARC Box 9
23 Cable from SW to CHW, 12 October 1963, HGARC Box 9
24 SW to CHW, 23 November, 1963, HGARC Box 31
25 SW to CHW, 2 December, 1963, HGARC Box 31
26 SW to CHW, 12 August, 1963, HGARC Box 31
27 Eyre, Richard, *Changing Stages* Episode 3, BBC Two, 1997
28 Arnold Weissberger to SW, 19 April, 1964, HGARC Box 24
29 Parnell, Michael, *Laughter from the Dark, A Life of Gwyn Thomas*, 1988, p192
30 SW to John Reich, 20 April 1964, GTA PADF 1964/5
31 John Reich to SW, 19 May 1964 GTA PADF 1964/5
32 John Reich to SW, 3 June 1964 GTA PADF 1964/5

33 SW, interview with Studs Terkel, 17 November, 1987, SGA SGT/SW/6/23

34 Press release, GTA PRODUCTIONS PT I Box 20

35 Lyon, Herb, *Chicago Tribune,* 27 November 1964, GTA PRODUCTIONS PT I Box 20

36 Programme for *Macbeth,* GTA PRODUCTIONS PT I Box 20

37 Memorandum, GTA PADF 1964/5

38 Press cuttings GTA PRODUCTIONS PT I Box 20

39 SW to Jan Sterling, 4 October 1964, HGARC Box 31

40 Wicking, Christopher and Vahimagi, Tise, *The American Vein; Directors and Directions in Television,* 1979, pp217/18

41 SW to CHW, 12 November, 1965, HGARC Box 31

42 CHW to SW 13 November, 1965, HGARC Box 31

43 SW to CHW 6 September 1965, HGARC Box 31

44 Jo Mielziner to SW, 25 March and 13 April, 1965, HGARC Box 20

45 Jo Mielziner to SW, 11 July 1967, HGARC Box 20

46 SW to CHW, 4 October 1967, HGARC Box 31

47 SW to CHW, 1 November 1967, HGARC Box 31

48 ibid

49 SW to Beverley Cross, 21 November 1967, quoted Wrigley, Amanda, 'The Anger of Achilles: A Prize-Winning Epic for Radio', in *Robert Graves and the Classical Tradition,* ed A.G.G.Gibson, 2015, p322

50 Undated press cutting, HGARC Box 30

51 Schuyler G Chapin, Lincoln Center, to SW 23 January 1968, HGARC Box 30

Chapter 10

1 Poster for *The File of the Golden Goose,* HGARC Box 30

2 Carol Wary to SW, 19 May 1992, SGA SGT/SW/1/8

3 Press reviews of *The Executioner,* HGARC Box 30

4 See *The Executioner,* Wikipedia

5 SW to Robert Graves, 20 June, 1969, HGARC Box 20

6 quoted Wrigley ed Gibson, p322

7 quoted in *The Globe, the Glory of the Banke,* Globe Playhouse Trust

8 Theo Crosby quoted Day, Barry, *This Wooden 'O',* 1996, p125

9 Juroe, Charles 'Jerry', *Bond, the Beatles and My Year with Marilyn: 50 years as a Movie Marketing Man,* 2018, p144

10 Memo to 20th Century Fox from William Kaplan, Executive Production Supervisor, HGARC Box 27

11 Tyrone Guthrie, SGA SGT/PPR/2/1

12 Lord Chandos to SW, 17 December, 1970, SGA SGT/SW/1

13 SW to Alexander Cohen, 3 October, 1970, SGA SGT/SW/1

14 SW to Richard Burton, 19 October, 1970, SGA SGT/SW/1

15 SW to Michael Langham, 4 January 1971, SGA SGT/SW/1

16 Tyrone Guthrie to SW, 14 June, 1971, SGA SGT/SW/1
17 Undated press cutting, BFI
18 Ronan O'Casey to Stephen MacDonald, 8 April, 1971, SGA SGT/SW/1
19 SW quoted Day p32
20 Report of World Shakespeare Congress, Day p23
21 SW to Peter Brook, 23 November, 1971, SGA SGT/SW/1
22 CHW quoted Day p60
23 Jerome Link to the author, December 2018
24 SW, note, HGARC Box 34.
25 Edited by Christopher Hampton, with contributions by C Day Lewis, Peter Redgrove, George Macbeth, W H Auden, Peter Porter, Stephen Spender, Norman MacCaig, Dannie Abse, Adrian Mitchell, Vernon Scannell, Robert Graves and R S Thomas.
26 Press release, SGA SGT/Comm/PPR/2/1
27 SW, interviewed by Ronald Hastings, *Plays and Players,* 3 June 1972
28 Spoken in the presence of the author
29 Press statement, 7 September,1972, SGA SGT/Comm/PPR/2/1
30 SW to Peter L Drew, World Trade Centre, St Katharine's by the Tower, 4 September, 1972, SGA SGT/SW/1
31 Report of Conference at Royal Festival Hall, 'The Third Globe-Ancient or Modern', SGA SGT/Comm/PPR/2/1
32 Report of Confence, October 1973, SGA SGT/Comm/PPR/2/1
33 SW to Robert Graves, 28 May, 1972, amongst others, quoted Wrigley ed Gibson, p322

Chapter 11

1 Oxenbould, Moffatt, *Timing is Everything, A Life Backstage at the Opera,* 2005, p218
2 ibid p219
3 *The Assessors' Report,* Timeline: 40 years of the Sydney Opera House', abc.net. au, 22 October 2013.
4 Arup, Ove and Zunz, G.J, *Structural Engineer,* Vol 47, March 1969
5 Ted Downes to SW, 22 August 1972, HGARC Box 28
6 SW to Tom Lingwood, 30 October 1972, HGARC Box 28
7 ibid
8 Tom Lingwood to SW, 25 May 1973, HGARC Box 28
9 SW to Tom Lingwood, 6 June 1973, HGARC Box 28
10 quoted by Verghis, Sharon,'For Sale: a first night etched into my memory', August 14, 2003, smh.com.au
11 Greenfield, Edward, *Manchester Guardian,* 29 September 1973, HGARC Box 28
12 SW in 'Larry Sitsky comments on the Sydney Opera House', clip 2, *Monster or Miracle? Sydney Opera House (1973)*, Australian Screen, asg.gov.au

13 Oxenbould, p237
14 ibid p238
15 Press reviews, HGARC Box 28
16 SW to Ande Anderson, 28 December 1973, HGARC Box 30
17 Press reviews, HGARC Box 30
18 *Sinbad and the Eye of the Tiger*, 1977
19 Ferrari, Maggie Southam, 'Sam's Song', unpublished memoir
20 Charles H Schneer, Producer, to Mr Peter Gruber at Burbank Studios, Columbia Pictures, HGARC Box 23
21 SW to Kenneth Maidment at Columbia, 4 August, 1975, HGARC Box 23
22 Newman, p63
23 SW, cable to Krzysztof Penderecki, 25 August 1975, HGARC Box 23
24 SW interviewed by David Fingleton, *Music and Musicians*, July 1977, HGARC Box 20
25 ibid
26 Press reviews HGARC Boxes 20, 29, 30
27 SW/Duffie
28 Heather Harper, note to SW, HGARC Box 29
29 Mann, William, *The Times*, HGARC Box 20
30 SW/Duffie. In 2015, Graham Vick mounted a production in Birmingham drawing on amateurs for the crowd scenes.
31 Carol Fox to SW, 30 November, 1977, transcribed from cable HGARC Box 25
32 Newman p65
33 SW to Graham Walne, email to the author, 6 January 2019
34 Press cutting, HGARC Box 30
35 SW to CHW 10 December 1978, HGARC Box 31
36 Bellow, Saul, *Humboldt's Gift*, 1975, p477
37 *Halifax Chronicle Herald*, March 29, 2007, quoted in Wikipedia: Kurt Herbert Adler
38 Zoë Wanamaker to SW, 29 September, 1981, SGA SGT/SW/1/3
39 SW/Duffie
40 Ulrich, Alan, *Examiner*, 19 November, 1981, HGARC Box 30
41 Grundy, Bill, *Evening Standard*, 14 January, 1982, HGARC Box 30
42 SW interviewed by Pauline Peters, undated, HGARC Box 34

Chapter 12

1 Ferrari, p11
2 Julian Glover, interviewed by Peter Jolly, 22 March 2014, SGA 4 April, 2014, SGA SGT/ED/LIB/OH/1/B/7
3 SW to Bill Wanamaker, 9 May 1974, SGA SGT/SW/2/3
4 Ferrari, p12
5 quoted Day p117

6   ibid

7   Samuel Schoenbaum to SW, 26 November 1974, SGA SGT/SW/2/3

8   S T Evans to SW, 13 January 1977, SGA SGT/Dev/Ev 42

9   SW, Affidavit, prepared for Frere Cholmeley, 9 June 1986, p26, SGA SGT/SW/2/14

10   Professor Roger Sharrock of King's College, London, and the author.

11   Dr Robert Cannon, Christopher Edwards and Anthony Hozier from Rose Bruford, David and Rosemary Linnell from the Curtain Theatre, and the author

12   This scheme was never carried out. Detroit will have to wait for the Container Globe, a mobile, modular reconstruction of the Globe, made out of ship containers, created by New Zealander, Angus Vail, a punk rock enthusiast, who hopes to find it a home there. (See perkineastman.com)

13   'Old Kate' (Doris Perry) to SW, 29 March, 1981,SGA SGT/SW/1/3

14   'Vivien' to SW, 29 March, 1981, SGA SGT/SW/1/3

15   Andrew Gurr, quoted Day p85

16   Rosemary Linnell in a doodle for the author

17   SAM WANAMAKER'S DRAFT PROPOSALS FOR USE AND OPERATION OF THE CENTER, July 1981, personal papers

Chapter 13

1   CHW to SW, 5 November, 1980, HGARC Box 31

2   Pincus, Andrew, *Berkshire Eagle,* 7 August, 1982

3   They included Samuel H Scripps, grandson of a newspaper publisher and a keen Shakespearean, and Marshall Wais, a steel magnate, originally from Chicago, by then living in San Francisco, where he supported the Opera Company

4   Edmée Firth, interviewed by Lyn Williams, 17 March 2018, SGA SGT/ED/LIB/OH/B/21

5   Anna Emery Hanson, Nancy W Knowles, Herbert Mendel, Samuel H Scripps, Marshall Wais

6   They included more donors from Chicago: Rhoda Pritzke, originally from England, and Gene Andersen, introduced to the project by Lee Freeman.

7   Sir David Orr to SW, 2 August, 1983, copy in personal papers

8   *Irreconcilable Differences,* 1984

9   Day p xiii

10   SW, 'Across the Ocean and Back', press interview, BFI

11   Hackett, Denis, *The Times,* and Day-Lewis, Sean, *Daily Telegraph,* 14 November, 1984, HGARC Box 30

12   O'Connor, John, *New York Times,* 17 January 1985

13   Personal memory of the author

14   Taylor, Richard, *National Enquirer,* 16 April, 1985

15   Jack Perry to SW, 22 May, 1985, HGARC Box 31

16 Sir David Orr to Trustees and Directors, 4 February 1986, personal papers
17 Alan Jenkins, interview with the author, 21 January, 2019
18 SW, Affidavit 1986, p2
19 Toomey, Christine, 'If Shakespeare moves in 'ere, I'm moving out', *Sunday Times,* 22 June 1986
20 ibid
21 Alan Jenkins interview

Chapter 14

1 Ian Campbell to SW, 18 July 1985, SGA SGT/SW/1/3
2 SW/Duffie
3 The bear was a gift from the National Theatre, left over from its 1978 production of David Mamet's *American Buffalo,* and growing ever more threadbare.
4 Keith Baxter, interviewed by Peter Jolly, 22 March 2014, SGA SGT/ED/LIB/OH/B/5
5 SW, quoted Day p200
6 SW, undated press cutting, BFI
7 Prince Philip, Duke of Edinburgh, 23 April, 1990, account in HGARC Box 30
8 SW, text of speech at Roosevelt University, 20 May, 1990, SGA SGT/SW/2/4
9 Interview by Ronald Hastings, *Plays and Players,* 3 June, 1972
10 Shakespeare, William, *King Henry VIII,* Act V Scene v
11 SW/Seidenberg
12 SW, 'Variations on a theme by Irwin Winkler' ms, HGARC Box 30
13 Stan Shakespeare, interviewed by Alan Williams , 17 December, 2018, SGA SGT/ED/LIB/OH/1/B/22
14 Steuben was a jewellery firm in New York which had hosted a Gala event in support of the Globe
15 Douglas Fairbanks Jr to SW, 6 October, 1990, SGA SGT/SW/2/11
16 SW to Sir Evelyn de Rothschild, 3 October, 1990, SGA SGT/SW/11
17 Memo from SW to Michael Perry, 19 February, 1991, SGA SGT/SW/2/12
18 Stan Shakespeare/Williams
19 The hangings were designed by Raymond Boyce, theatre designer, and the Project Manager was Dawn Sanders, founder of the Shakespeare Globe Centre, New Zealand.
20 SW, Speech to Association of Shakespeare Festivals and Theatres, 12 January 1991, SGA SGT/SW/2/4
21 Weimann, Robert, *Shakespeare und die Tradition des Volkstheaters:Soziologie, Dramaturgie, Gestaltung,*1967, published in English in 1978, as *Shakespeare and the Popular Tradition in Theater: Studies in the Social Dimension of Dramatic Form and Function.*
22 SW in 'Muse of Fire', address to Queen Mary and Westfield College, 17 March, 1992. SGA SGT/SW/2/4

23 SW to Major General Sir Christopher Airy, 21 March, 1991, SGA SGT/ SW/2/7
24 Copy of Prince Charles's speech in Stratford-upon-Avon, 22 April 1991, SGA SGT/SW/2/7
25 SW to HRH Prince Charles, 29 April, 1991, SGA SGT/SW/2/7
26 HRH Prince Charles to SW 23 May, 1991, HGARC Box 30
27 SW/Duffie
28 Leader, and article by Nightingale, Benedict, *The Times*, 21 April, 1993
29 Stanley, John, *San Francisco Chronicle*, May 23–29, HGARC Box 30
30 SW quoted Day, p282
31 Memorandum, HGARC Box 30
32 Michael Perry, speaking at 'A Service to Celebrate the life of Sam Wanamaker, CBE', Southwark Cathedral, 2 March, 1994
33 SW, The Globe Newsletter, The Newsletter of The International Shakespeare Globe Centre, Winter 1994
34 SW in *The Sandbar, A Poem for Voices*, Roberta Berke, BBC Radio 3, 18 December, 1993, British Library Sound and Moving Image Collection, H2510/1

Afterword

1 Billington, Michael, *The Guardian*, 20 December, 1993
2 Nash, Richard N, *The Rainmaker*, 1954, p98

Bibliography and Sources

Archives and digital sources:

BBC genome genome.ch.bbc.co.uk for copies of the *Radio Times*, providing a record of radio and television broadcasts.

Björkman, Stig, director, *Ingrid Bergman In Her Own Words*, documentary film, 2015

British Film Institute – collection of press cuttings on Sam Wanamaker

British Library Sound and Moving Image Collection – recording of *The Sandbar:A Poem for Voices*, by Roberta Berke

Carpenter, Cliff

   Friend of SW, who supplied me with a small collection of press cuttings, often undated.

Consedino, Gene, *Two Planks and a Passion*, DVD about Peninsula Players, including interview with SW, written and directed as part of MFA, Columbia College, Chicago, January 1994

Howard Gotlieb Archival Research Center, Boston University, Sam Wanamaker Collection. First deposits in 1968, with more material added in 1969 and 1986. Further deposits made after SW's death, in 2006, 2012 and 2014

Internet Broadway Database ibdb.com

Internet Movie Database imdb.com

New York Public Library for the Performing Arts

newspapers.com

Royal Opera House Archive

San Francisco Opera Archive archive.sfopera.com

The British Newspaper Archive britishnewspapersarchive.co.uk

The National Archives – MI5 files on Samuel and Charlotte Wanamaker

Shakespeare's Globe Library and Archive

   As well as material on the Globe, the archive holds some of Sam's personal papers, and a collection of audio material, including Globe Memories, an ongoing oral history project, and 'Sam Wanamaker talks about Paul Robeson', SW interviewed by Ron Ramdin in 1987, CD Globe Editions, 2007

Special Collections, Harold Washington Public Library, Chicago, for Goodman Theatre Archives

Theatre and Performance Collection, V & A

Theatre Archive Project, http://soundsbluk

Theatre Collection, University of Bristol (Mander and Mitchenson Collection)

Who Do You Think You Are? Zoë Wanamaker, BBC One, Series 6, Episode 4, 2009

www.abc.net.au : 'Timeline: 40 Years of the Sydney Opera House, 22 October 2013

www.aso.gov.au : 'Larry Sitsky comments on the Sydney Opera House', *Monster of Miracle? Sydney Opera House (1973)* Clip 2

www.bruceduffie.com: *Actor/Director Sam Wanamaker*, transcript of interview in Chicago, September 1992, broadcast on WNIB, 19 December, 1993,

www.goodmantheatre.org

www.istructe.org

   for article by Ove Arup and GJ Zunz, *The Structural Engineer*, Volume 47, March, 1969

www.otrcat.com Old Time Radio Catalogue

www.peninsulaplayers.com

www.primarystagesoffcenter.org

www.smh.com.au

   for 'For Sale: a first night etched into my memory', 14 August, 2003

Books and plays

Anderson, Maxwell, ed Shivers, Alfred S, *Dramatist in America: Letters of Maxwell Anderson, 1912–1958*, 1977

Anderson, Max, *Joan of Lorraine*, 1947

Anderson, Robert, *Tea and Sympathy*, 1953

Axelrod, George, *Will Success Spoil Rock Hunter?* 1955

Ayling, R, and Durkan, M J, *Sean O'Casey: A Bibliography*, 1978

Barnouw, Eric, *A History of Broadcasting in the United States, Volume II – 1933–1953*, 1968

Bellow, Saul, *The Adventures of Augie March*, 1953

_____, *Humboldt's Gift*, 1975

Bentley, Eric, ed, *Thirty Years of Treason: Exerpts from Hearings before the House Committee on Un-American Activities, 1938–1968*, 1972

Bigsby, Christopher, *Arthur Miller: 1962–2005*, 2011

Brough, James, *A Victorian in Orbit: The Irreverent Memoirs of Sir Cedrick Hardwicke, as told to James Brough*, 1961

Caine, Michael, *What's it all about?* 2010

Callow, Simon, *Orson Welles: Vol 1, The Road to Xanadu*, 1995

_____, *Orson Welles: Hello Americans*, 2006

_____, *Orson Welles: One Man Band*, 2015

Campbell, Marion Gurney, and Athas, Daphne, *Ding Dong Bell*, typescript

Carpenter, Clifford, 'Remembering Sam and Charlotte', unpublished ms, 2000

Caute, David, *Joseph Losey: A Revenge on Life*, 1994

Croall, Jonathan, *Sybil Thorndike: A Star of Life*, 2008

Cross, Beverley, *One More River*, 1958

Cutler, Ivor, *The Jews of Chicago: From Shtetl to Suburb*, 1987

Dail, Chrystyna, *Stage for Action:US Social Activist Theatre in the 1940s*, 2016

Day, Barry, *This Wooden 'O': Shakespeare's Globe Reborn*, 1996

Denker, Henry, *A Far Country*, 1962

Dick, Bernard F, *Radical Innocence: A Critical Study of the Hollywood Ten*, 1989/2009

Doherty, Thomas, *Show Trial: Hollywood, HUAC, and the Birth of the Blackllist*, 2018

Duberman, Martin Bauml, *Paul Robeson: A Biography*, 1989

Dunning, John, *On The Air: The Encyclopedia of Old Time Radio*, 1998

Endfield, Mo, *The Film Director's Wife*, 2016

Evans, Maurice, *All This and Evans Too*, 1987

Eyre, Richard, and Wright, Nicholas, *Changing Stages: A View of British Theatre in the Twentieth Century*, 2001

Fahi, Moris, *The Last Days*, 1983

Ferrari Maggie Southam, 'Sam's Song', unpublished memoir

Gazzo, Michael V, *A Hatful of Rain*, 1954

Gibson, A.G.G, ed *Robert Graves and the Classical Tradition*, 2015

Gordon, Mel, *Stanislavsky in America*, 2010

Gressieker, Hermann, trans George White, *Royal Gambit (Heinrich Der Achter und Seine Frauen)*, 1959

Gurr, Andrew, and Orrell, John, *Rebuilding Shakespeare's Globe*, 1989

Herrick, Mary, *The Chicago Schools, A Social and Political History*, 1971

Hoffnung, Annetta, *Hoffnung: his biography*, 1994

Horn, Barbara Lee, *Maxwell Anderson: A Research and Production Sourcebook*, 1996

Inge, William, *Bus Stop*, 1955

Jamiaque, Yves, adapted White, George, *A Murderer Among Us*, typescript, 1964

Juroe, Charles "Jerry", *Bond, the Beatles and My Year with Marilyn: 50 Years as a Movie Marketing Man*, 2018

Kazan, Elia, *A Life*, 1988

Kernitz, Harry, *Reclining Figure*, 1954

Lardner, Ring Jr, *I'll Hate Myself in the Morning: A Memoir*, 2000

Lewenstein, Oscar, *Kicking Against the Pricks*, 1994

Lewis, Robert, *Slings and Arrows: Theater in My Life*, 1984

Miller, Arthur, *A View From the Bridge*, 1956

Mulryne, J R, and Shewring, Margaret, eds, *Shakespeare's Globe Rebuilt*, 1997

Nash, N Richard, *The Rainmaker*, 1954

Newman, Danny, *Tales of a Theatrical Guru*, 2006

Noble, Peter, *Reflected Glory: An Autobiographical Sketch*, 1958

O'Casey, Sean, *Purple Dust*, 1940

Odets, Clifford, *Winter Journey*, 1955

_____, *The Big Knife*, 1949

Osborne, John, and Creighton, Anthony, *Epitaph for George Dillon*, 1958

Pacyga, Dominic A, *Chicago; A Biography*, 2007

Parnell, Michael, *Laughter from the Dark: A Life of Gwyn Thomas*, 1998

Perry, Jack, *From Brick Lane to Forbidden City*, private publication

Pfaff, Tim and others, *Kurt Herbert Adler and the San Francisco Opera: The Life and Career of Kurt Herbert Adler*, Regional Oral History Office, The Bancroft Library, University of California, 1994

Prescott, Paul, 'Sam Wanamaker', in *Poel, Granville Barker, Wanamaker: Great Shakespeareans Volume XV*, ed Cary Mazer, 2015

Prime, Rebecca, *Hollywood Exiles in Europe*, 2014

Redgrave, Michael, *In My Mind's Eye: An Autobiography*, 1983

Sheehy, Helen, *Margo: The Life and Theatre of Margo Jones*, 1989

Sherek, Henry, *Not in Front of the Children*, 1957

Shivers, Alfred S, *Maxwell Anderson*, 1976

Spoto, Donald, *Notorious: The Life of Ingrid Bergman*, 1997

Strachan, Alan, *Secret Dreams: A Biography of Michael Redgrave*, 2004

Terrace, Vincent, *Radio Programs 1924–1984: A Catalogue of over 1800 Shows*, 1999

Wanamaker, William, *The Depression, Bootlegging and the Boy*, private paper, 2002

Williams, Tennessee, *Cat on a Hot Tin Roof*, 1955

_____, *The Rose Tattoo*, 1951

Acknowledgments

My thanks go to Abby and Zoë Wanamaker for their encouragement and help. Either of them could have written their own memoir of their father. Instead they shared many memories generously with me.

At Shakespeare's Globe, archivists Victoria Lane and Mathilde Blum have gone out of their way to identify and supply relevant documents and audio material. I am hugely grateful to them, and to the many who have contributed to Globe Memories, the ongoing oral history project. I thank Neil Constable, Chief Executive, Mark Sullivan, Commercial Director, Anthony Hewitt, Director of Development, and members of their staff for their help, and especially Patrick Spottiswoode, Director of Globe Education, for encouraging the project from the start. I spent three weeks at the Howard Gotlieb Archival Research Center at Boston University, which holds the Sam Wanamaker Collection. I owe gratitude to the staff there, who were unfailingly helpful, especially Ryan Hendrickson and Sean D Noel. I thank Sarah Zimmerman and her staff in Special Collections at the Harold Washington Library Center in Chicago for their assistance with the Goodman Theatre Archives. Also Paris Hart and other staff at the Royal Opera House, and Barbara Rominski at San Francisco Opera. I thank my longstanding friend Penny Baker for help with research into Sam's New York career, at the New York Public Library of Performing Arts.

I am grateful to the many people who have delved into their archives, or their memories of Sam and often Charlotte: Gene Andersen, Audra Baakari Boyle, Tom Baptiste, Jonathan Broadbent, Alan Butland, the late Clifford Carpenter, the late Merle and Pearl Debuskey, Judy Digney, Charles Duff, Maggie Southam Ferrari, the late Madeleine Lee Gilford, Siri Fischer Hansen, Alan Jenkins, Aviva Kahn, Peter Kent, Norbert Kentrup, Jerome Link, Colin Mabberley, Blanche Marvin, Robert Mitchell (and for help with photographs), Stephen Perry, Alastair Tallon, Julia Thornton, Graham Walne, Marc Wanamaker, who supplied many photographs and family documents, the late William Wanamaker, Lyn Williams, Roger Wingate.

Acknowledgments

I have been supported throughout by the Biography Group. The enthusiasm and inspired guidance of its leader, Professor Jon Cook, University of East Anglia, have been critical to the enterprise, and its members have been unstinting in their thoughtful comments and support: Liza Coutts, Carrie Dunne, Monique Goodliffe, Lyn Innes, Ted Powell, Jo Rogers, Barbara Selby, Ann Vinden, David Warren and Hephzi Yohannan.

I thank my agent, Robert Dudley, for his active promotion of the project, and all at Oberon Books, especially James Illman, Margaret Byron and Cara Thompson, with particular gratitude to editor George Spender for all he has done before and after leaving the firm.

Apologies to my extended family and friends for paying them scant attention while I have been researching and writing.

Index

Index

Index

Index

Index

WWW.OBERONBOOKS.COM